the About.com guide to
JOB
SEARCHING

Tools and Tactics to Help You Get the Job You Want

Alison Doyle

Adams Media
Avon, Massachusetts

About **About**.com

About.com is a powerful network of 500 Guides—smart, passionate, accomplished people who are experts in their fields. About.com Guides live and work in more than twenty countries and celebrate their interests in thousands of topics. They have written books, appeared on national television programs, and won many awards in their fields. Guides are selected for their ability to provide the most interesting information for users, and for their passion for their subject and the Web. The selection process is rigorous—only 15 percent of those who apply actually become Guides. The following are some of the most important criteria by which they are chosen:

- High level of knowledge/passion for their topic
- Appropriate credentials
- Keen understanding of the Web experience
- Commitment to creating informative, actionable features

Each month more than 48 million people visit About.com. Whether you need home repair and decorating ideas, recipes, movie trailers, or car buying tips, About.com Guides can offer practical advice and solutions for everyday life. Wherever you land on About.com, you'll always find content that is relevant to your interests. If you're looking for "how to" advice on refinishing your deck, About.com will also show you the tools you need to get the job done. No matter where you are on About.com, or how you got there, you'll always find exactly what you're looking for!

About Your Guide

 ALISON DOYLE is a job search expert with twenty-five years of experience in human resources, career development, and job searching. Her career began in human resources, where she spent many years on the other side of the desk from the job seeker—recruiting, interviewing, hiring, and training. She has spent the last fifteen years in a career services office, and is currently Associate Director for Information Technology at Skidmore College, developing and managing information technology resources to assist students and alumni with their search for jobs and internships. Alison has been the Guide for the About Job Searching (job search.about.com) site since 1998. She has researched and written extensively for About.com, and elsewhere, about all facets of job searching. Topics include how to create compelling **resumes** and cover letters, how to research career options, how to successfully change careers, and how to find and apply for jobs, with a focus on using the Internet for job searching. Her articles have been published online, in newspapers, magazines, and in other print media.

Acknowledgments

I appreciate the support provided by Skidmore College's career services office, the staff and Guides at About.com, and the job seekers who visit my site. Your inspiration, advice, and words of wisdom are invaluable to me. I especially appreciate all of you who have taken the time to share your stories with me.

The support of my family, especially my husband, daughter, and mother, enabled me to write this book. I greatly appreciate it. This book is dedicated to the memory of my father, Richard Hadcock, who taught me the value of work and the importance of spending your working life in a career you love.

ABOUT.COM

CEO & President
Scott Meyer

COO
Andrew Pancer

SVP Content
Michael Daecher

VP Marketing
Lisa Abourezk

Director, About Operations
Chris Murphy

Senior Web Designer
Jason Napolitano

ADAMS MEDIA

Editorial

Publishing Director
Gary M. Krebs

Associate Managing Editor
Laura M. Daly

Development Editor
Katie McDonough

Marketing

Director of Marketing
Karen Cooper

Assistant Art Director
Frank Rivera

Production

Director of Manufacturing
Susan Beale

Associate Director of Production
Michelle Roy Kelly

Senior Book Designer
Colleen Cunningham

Published by Adams Media, an F+W Publications Company
57 Littlefield Street
Avon, MA 02322
www.adamsmedia.com

ISBN 10: 1-59869-097-3
ISBN 13: 978-1-59869-097-2

Printed in China.

J I H G F E D C B A

Library of Congress Cataloging-in-Publication Data
is available from the publisher.

This publication is designed to provide accurate and authoritative information with regard to the subject matter covered. It is sold with the understanding that the publisher is not engaged in rendering legal, accounting, or other professional advice. If legal advice or other expert assistance is required, the services of a competent professional person should be sought.

—From a *Declaration of Principles* jointly adopted by a Committee of the American Bar Association and a Committee of Publishers and Associations

Many of the designations used by manufacturers and sellers to distinguish their product are claimed as trademarks. Where those designations appear in this book and Adams Media was aware of a trademark claim, the designations have been printed with initial capital letters.

This book is available at quantity discounts for bulk purchases. For information, please call 1-800-872-5627.

How to Use This Book

Each About.com book is written by an About.com Guide—an expert with experiential knowledge of his or her subject. While the book can stand on its own as a helpful resource, it can also be coupled with the corresponding About.com site for even more tips, tools, and advice to help you learn even more about a particular subject. Each book will not only refer you back to About .com, but it will also direct you to other useful Internet locations and print resources.

All About.com books include a special section at the end of each chapter called Get Linked. Here you'll find a few links back to the About.com site for even more great information on the topics discussed in that chapter. Depending on the topic, these could be links to such resources as photos, sheet music, quizzes, recipes, or product reviews.

About.com books also include four types of sidebars:

- **Ask Your Guide:** Detailed information in a question-and-answer format
- **Tools You Need:** Advice about researching, purchasing, and using a variety of tools for your projects
- **Elsewhere on the Web:** References to other useful Internet locations
- **What's Hot:** All you need to know about the hottest trends and tips out there

Each About.com book will take you on a personal tour of a certain topic, give you reliable advice, and leave you with the knowledge you need to achieve your goals.

CONTENTS

CONTENTS . . . *continued*

Introduction from Your Guide

Are you in the market for a new job? Are you considering a career change? Depending on the type of position you are looking for, finding a job can seem like hard work. Having to get a job can even seem like a scary proposition, especially when you are searching for your first job or you have just lost your position. It doesn't have to be. If you take the time to plan your job search and to take it one step at a time, you will have that job of your dreams in no time. This book will step you through the process of making your job search manageable, will help you get your job search organized, and will help you get a job—the right job!

First things first: It's important to get all the tools you will need in place before you start. That includes a phone number where you can be reached during the day, an e-mail address that you check frequently, a computer or access to one, Internet access, and the office equipment you will need to conduct a professional job search.

Next, you will need to spend some time researching career and job options. What type of company do you want to work for? What industries are you interested in? What type of job sounds appealing? What is important to you? Do you want (or need) to make a lot of money? Or are you more interested in doing something you enjoy than the paycheck you will earn? Are you a student or a parent who needs flexibility? All those factors will enter into the equation of what type of job you are going to look for.

Your resume will need to be written, and you will need to learn how to write a cover letter that specifically targets the positions you are applying for—with no typographical or spelling errors. Focused job search correspondence is essential. It will get you interviews and will help you secure a job.

Where to look for jobs? There are almost too many online job sites that have job listings. Job seekers can narrow down their search and focus on sites with listings that match their skills and interests. They can also look at niche sites that list jobs in a particular industry or location. Networking is important too. It remains one of the most important job search tools available, and you can network both offline and online.

Your interviewing skills may need to be polished. It's important to prepare and practice so you can ace the interview and get that job offer. It's also important to spend time researching the company so you are prepared to answer questions and prepared to ask your own questions. Of course, you will follow up that interview with a thank-you note and an offer to provide references.

It's important, once you get the offer, to take the time to decide if it's a job you really want. Are the salary and benefits acceptable? Does it actually sound like a job you would enjoy doing? How about career paths and opportunities for the future? Will this job move you up the career ladder? Will it provide you with the security you need? Or will the job give you the adventure you crave or the chance to grow?

Job searching doesn't have to be overwhelming. If you take the time to be organized and efficient, it can be manageable, efficient, and fast. In fact, it can even be fun. The job search tips, techniques, timesavers, and tools that are covered in this book will help get your job search started, and help you keep it on track.

You will also find references to information on my About.com Job Searching site that will help with your job search. There are samples to review, checklists to download, and additional online information that will supplement the material in the book.

Most of us want to find that one special, perfect job. This book will help you do that, simply and clearly, and most importantly, quickly!

Shelton State Libraries
Shelton State Community College

Chapter 1

Choosing Career and Job Options

Getting Started

Sometimes we change jobs because we want to. In other cases, we don't have a choice about losing a job. I actually made my best career moves when I was pushed into job searching—one time by company restructuring, and another time by company bankruptcy. In both cases, it was a positive change that might not have happened otherwise. In either case, it's important to take the time to prepare to job search so that all the resources you need are in place before you start seeking employment.

It's important to have a good idea of the type of job that you are interested in, to have a resume written, to have references ready, and to have the proper equipment (phone, fax, computer, etc.) in place before you start looking for work. It can be stressful, and a waste of time, for both you and a prospective employer, to realize that you don't really want the job you were just offered. Or

even worse, to realize that you don't want the job after you already started it. Someone who once worked at the same company I did started a new job and knew the very first day that she didn't want to be there. She called and asked whether she could have her old job back. It was too late. We had already hired a replacement and she was stuck in a job that she didn't want to have while she job searched, again.

Most people change jobs many times throughout their working life. The Bureau of Labor Statistics reports that the younger baby boomers surveyed changed jobs 9.6 times before they turned thirty-six. Seventeen percent held over fifteen jobs during those same years. That's a lot of jobs, and this statistic is good to know, especially if you're a job changer. Unlike the past when it was normal to work for the same employer until you retired, it's much more common today to change jobs. There isn't the same expectation on the part of employers that you should stay or that the company should provide long-term employment for you. It's not your parents' workplace anymore, where most people worked for the same company for thirty years, then retired. There isn't the obligation, on either side. Employers don't feel like they need to protect their employees, and workers have few qualms about quitting.

In some industries, especially high-tech ones, you are expected to change jobs if you want your career to progress. It's the norm, not the exception. At some companies, especially smaller ones, there may not be enough options to move up the career ladder. In other cases, you may get tired, or bored, and want to try something different. All of these are good reasons for changing your job.

We all change as we age. The job that was perfect when you were in school may not be what you want to do now. There are some people who are thrilled to have a high-pressure job, even

▶ It's always important to be prepared to change jobs, because you never know when it might unexpectedly happen to you. If you have an up-to-date resume and insight in the job market as it relates to your employment goals, you will be able to start a job search right away. Always have a current resume that contains your latest employment information, as well as your skills and education, ready to send to a prospective employer.

if it means working sixty hours a week. They thrive on it. Others would prefer to work less and earn less. What we want from our job changes over time, as well.

Health insurance and other benefits become more important as we age. Flexibility is important to those job seekers who have a family or are planning on one. So, what we want from our work changes as we change. It's important to be aware of that. It's also worth taking the time to assess, every few years or so, what it is that we want from our work. There are few things worse than getting ready to retire and realizing that you really hated the job you worked at for all those years.

The jobs that are available change on a regular basis. Technology changes, industries change, and companies change. Take a look at a few of the jobs that didn't exist even twenty years ago:

- Desktop Publishing Specialist
- Internet Evangelist
- Network Administrator
- Senior Web Designer
- Webmaster

The job market changes regularly, too. The type of jobs that are considered "hot" today may be at the bottom of the list of jobs that employers are hiring for next time you job search.

That's why each and every time you start a job search you should spend time investigating career options and the type of jobs you might want to do. You may be surprised at what jobs are available, and you may generate some ideas for jobs that you had never thought of.

What's most important is to find the job that's right for you. I have a friend from college who took the first job he could find

ELSEWHERE ON THE WEB

▶ The Bureau of Labor Statistics (www.bls.gov) is an excellent source of occupational and career information. Information is available on the top industries and jobs, including the training and education required for each type of job, and the prospects for employment.

▶ The lists at http://about.
com/jobsearch/topjobs of the
fasting growing occupations,
the job categories that will
need the highest number of
new workers, and where to
find job listings are a good
starting point for reviewing
job options.

after graduation. He started as a temporary mail carrier, then took the post office exam and became a mailman. After a few years, he regretted that decision. By then, he had a wife and a family and not much experience doing anything else. Unfortunately, at that point, it was very hard to make a change that would provide a comparable salary and benefits, both of which he needed. Perhaps he would have been better served to spend some more time on a job search. That way, he could have been sure that the first job he accepted was the right job.

Maybe you'd like help deciding what you could, or should, be doing. Luckily, there are free and low-cost services that can help. Public libraries often have job search classes and workshops. They also have computers and research materials available to use, free of charge. If you're a college graduate, check with your career services office. Many colleges and universities offer assistance, regardless of when you graduated. Even if you didn't attend, some colleges will let nonaffiliates utilize their career library.

Career OneStop Centers, which are run by state Labor Departments, offer job search and career transition services, as well as training programs, to residents. Offices are available in many local communities. Use the OneStop Locator (www.servicelocator. org) to search for an office by zip code or city/state, or call 1-877-US-2JOBS for assistance.

Career counselors offer personalized assistance and the fees may be more reasonable than you anticipated. Counselors can help you explore both work and life issues. A career counselor can also help you plan and conduct a job search.

It may sound overwhelming, but we spend a good amount of our lives working. If you can find a job that you enjoy, that provides you with the salary and benefits you need to live comfortably, and that provides you with the opportunity to grow your career in the direction that you want to move, you will have succeeded in your job search.

You have probably read the quote from Confucius about work: "Choose a job you love, and you will never have to work a day in your life." If you think about it, it makes good sense. If you are working at a job you enjoy, and you like your working environment and coworkers, it doesn't feel like work.

Personality and Career Tests

There are a variety of personality tests and career tests that you can take to help you figure out what type of job you would like. There are tests that help you analyze your skills. These tests will then connect your skills to appropriate jobs and careers. Other tests will measure your aptitude for a certain profession, or a certain type of work.

Counselors can use career tests as part of the career-counseling process. Tests administered by a counselor will help you and the counselor determine the best career options for you. Tests are also used as part of the hiring process. If a company is hiring salespeople, for example, they may want to ensure that the candidates they are interviewing have the type of personality necessary to achieve the goals the company is trying to reach.

Career tests measure a variety of abilities, skills, and personality traits. They are designed to assist in the career-planning process and to generate ideas for career options. Some tests are simple and fun, while others are more complex. Some are free, while there is a fee for others. All of them are designed to help job seekers measure their skills and relate them to job options. The different types of tests include:

- **Aptitude tests:** These tests gauge your ability to do a certain job or your ability to gain the skills necessary to do a job.

ASK YOUR GUIDE

I need help with deciding what career I'm interested in. How can I find assistance?

▶ I always refer people with this question to the National Career Development Association (www.ncda.org). Their site can provide a list of career counselors in your location. They also have information on what a career counselor does, as well as guidelines on how to choose a counselor.

- **Career tests:** These tests can help determine what type of position is suitable for someone with your personality.
- **Career inventories:** These measure how what you are interested in matches what is required to work in different occupations.
- **Career personality tests:** Career counselors use **career personality tests** to analyze the type of personality you have and to connect your personality to related career options.

Keep in mind that no test is a perfect indicator of what you should do. However, career tests will give you an idea of the types of positions that might be a good fit for your skills, experience, and background. At the very least, they will give you a starting point for narrowing options and for focusing your job search. At best, they can help you define, quite specifically, the type of position you want.

Here is a sampling of career tests that are available for job seekers, along with information on what each test will measure. I've included a fun test, or two, because it's important not to be too serious about your job search, even though it's a serious endeavor. Job searching is hard work, and it's good to take a break every now and then and focus on something a little lighthearted, like the test that will tell you if you are a good candidate for circus employment.

Even if a career test isn't scientifically validated, it might give you some ideas. Those ideas can generate job options or ideas that are interesting, and perhaps even feasible. Here are some examples of tests that can help you:

- **The Myers-Briggs Type Indicator (MBTI)** determines your personality type. Knowing your personality type can assist in every stage of career development, from choosing a college major to considering retirement options. The MBTI will help determine the most popular careers that match your type of personality.

- **The Strong Interest Inventory** matches your interests to possible careers. It also provides information on what learning environment is best for you, your leadership style, and your preferred style of work.
- **The Keirsey Temperament Sorter** analyzes your temperament and tells you if you are an Artisan, Idealist, Guardian, or Rational. Your temperament can then be correlated to career possibilities.

Free career tests, including a selection of both scientifically validated and fun quizzes, available online include:

- Color Quiz: www.colorquiz.com
- Is This the Right Career for Me Quiz: http://about.com/careerplanning/occupationquiz
- Monster's Discover Your Perfect Career Quiz: http://tools.monster.com/perfectcareer
- The Princeton Review Career Quiz: www.princetonreview.com/cte/quiz/career_quiz1.asp
- What's Your Circus Skill: www.ringling.com/activity/aptitude (my favorite fun survey!)

There's no guarantee that career test results will be perfect, or right, but, they can help you generate ideas and give you options to consider that you might not have otherwise thought of. Sometimes, the results are surprising. In other cases, they will reinforce what you already know. That reinforcement can be worthwhile when you're not sure whether you are in the right job or career field.

WHAT'S HOT

▶ The top career tests (http://about.com/jobsearch/careertests) include the Myers-Briggs Type Indicator, the Strong Interest Inventory, and the Keirsey Temperament Sorter.

Investigating Career Options

The next step in your job search is to spend some time reviewing options to see what type of positions are available and to consider what it is you might want do in your next job.

You probably want to get right to the job listings, but it does make sense to spend time researching up front. It will save you time in the long run, because once you start looking at job openings, you will be able to limit your search to the type of positions that meet your criteria. In fact, many job sites require users to select a type of position or an industry to search. If you aren't specific, you will get more listings than you can possibly weed through.

That's because almost every employer posts jobs online. There are almost too many job sites to look at. There are sites for just about every geographic location and type of job that you can think of. The more you know about what you want, the quicker you will be able to search for job openings.

There are jobs available in every career field from advertising to zoology, and every job you can imagine in between. The careers/employment section of your local library is a good source of books on career options. *What Color Is Your Parachute*, also known as the job hunter's bible, has provided advice on how to find out what you really want to do, before looking for a job, for over thirty years. The advice is still timely and relevant for those who aren't sure what they want to do.

Check the periodical section of your local library or bookstore as well. There are many business magazines that provide insight into occupations and the world of work. *Inc.* magazine, for example, is an excellent source of information on new and growing small businesses, as well as advice on growth and niche industries.

The Internet is a very good place to explore jobs and careers. There is a wealth of information available from career

Web sites, professional **associations**, education institutions, employers, and from people who simply have an interest in the field. These are excellent online resources available to help you start exploring career options:

- **Monster's Major to Career Converter** (http://content. monstertrak.monster.com/tools/careerconverter) is a handy tool for college graduates. Select your major, and then click Results for a list of positions and information on how to search for related jobs.
- **The Occupational Outlook Handbook** (www.bls.gov/oco) provides information on hundreds of different types of positions.
- **WetFeet.com** (www.wetfeet.com/content/industries.aspx) has information listed by industry. You'll find industry trends, the major employers, job descriptions, and job listings.
- **Vault** (www.vault.com) provides inside information on many careers, as well as career information categorized by industry, company, and career topic.

Once you have narrowed down your career options a little, start looking for companies within those industries. Hoovers.com lets you search by **keyword** for industry and company information. Select the company you are interested in learning more about from the list to get detailed information.

Discussion Forums and Bulletin Boards are another good way to get inside information. Vault.com has Message Boards dedicated to individual companies and to industries. There's information on who's hiring, and who is laying off employees. You can find information on salaries, open positions, hiring, and get interview advice. There is even advice from employees who are actually working at the firm.

I've been working in the same career field for years. Should I spend time looking at other options?

▸ There's a school of thought that says that you should start from scratch and consider options every time you begin a job search. I typically take it one step further, advising visitors to my About.com site to look at career options even when they are not seeking employment. That's even more ideal, because you have no time constraints, and you're not rushing to get your resume done. It's always wise to consider alternatives and to have some ideas about what you would like to do. Sometimes the most perfect job comes along when we're not looking for it!

Forbes.com has lists of the best big companies, the best small companies, the largest companies, and the fastest-growing companies. Detailed information is available for the companies on the lists, which you can use to determine if some of them belong on your prospecting list of potential employees.

Once you have narrowed down your list of job possibilities, begin researching. In the past, you had to find company brochures or use reference materials to investigate potential employers. All that information is now available online. Company information is available in the About Us and Careers sections of **company Web sites**. Use Google to find the company's Web site by searching for the company name. It will typically show up in the first few results.

If the company has a Web log, commonly called a **blog**, read it. A Web log is an online journal that is available to the public. In some cases, companies even use blogs to recruit. The Microsoft Technical Recruiting blog, for example, is a good way to find out more about the type of positions Microsoft has available.

After you have researched which industries and companies might be good prospects, spend some time conducting **informational interviews** with people in careers of interest. An informational interview is a meeting with someone working in a job that interests you, which is conducted to gain information from an insider perspective. You can find people to interview in a variety of ways. If you belong to a professional association, check to see what networking resources are available. Attend a mixer, a meeting, or a seminar. They are ideal ways to make professional connections. Universities often have alumni career networks with volunteers who are glad to assist fellow graduates. Ask around—family, friends, or business colleagues may be able to provide you with a connection. Another way to find contacts is to reach out directly to companies to ask if there is a possibility of scheduling a brief informational meeting with an employee.

Transferable Skills

The skills you have learned in one job can be used in another. It could be a similar job, or it could be something completely different. If the skills are generic enough (not company specific), they can be transported between jobs, between companies, and even between industries.

The skills that can be transferred across industries and types of positions are called **transferable skills**. The skills that you learn in other ways, outside of the workplace, by volunteering, for example, can also be used to help qualify you for jobs that you might not have considered.

Here's a list of transferable skills:

- Decision-making
- Goal setting
- Management and leadership skills
- Mechanical/technical skills
- Meeting deadlines
- Planning and organizing
- Problem solving
- Project management
- Research and planning
- Verbal communications
- Written communications

Transferable skills can be used in a variety of ways. Take Peggy, one visitor to my About.com site, for example. She spent years working as an administrator for a large insurance company. During the same period, she volunteered on a regular basis for a local animal rescue group. When a job coordinating volunteers became available at a nearby animal shelter, she was able to use the skills she had acquired volunteering to help her get the job.

ELSEWHERE ON THE WEB

▸ Check out Technical Careers at Microsoft: http://blogs.msdn.com/jobsblog. This is a good example of how employers use blogs to recruit. It's a way to gauge interest in a job opening and to line up candidates to interview without getting overwhelmed with applicants. It also lets the recruiter know who's paying attention to the nontraditional ways of recruiting.

▶ To learn more about transferable skills, visit http://about.com/careerplanning/transferableskills. **Your transferable skills are the abilities you have that can be used in different jobs. It is important to learn how to identify your transferable skills and how to sell them to prospective employers.**

In a similar case, another career changer, Rosanna, spent a few hours a week volunteering for hospice. She did have a degree in social work, but she hadn't used it because she was a stay-at-home mom raising a family. When she was ready to go back to work, a job opened up at hospice and she was the first person interviewed. She was hired on the spot.

To assess your transferable skills, spend some time looking at what you have done. Make a list of the jobs you have had, the volunteering you have done, and the clubs and organizations you belong to. Have you helped out at school or church? How about summer jobs and activities? Then consider what you have done in each of those roles. Many of these skills may be able to be used effectively in the workplace.

Everything you have accomplished, work related or not, has provided you with skills you can use in a new job or career. Those can be incorporated into your resume and your **cover letters**. Just because you weren't paid for what you did doesn't mean that it doesn't qualify as work.

As your career progresses, you will be able to grow your list of transferable skills. All your daily activities have the potential to give you a new skill or ability you will be able to use in the future. It's important not to minimize what you have learned along the way. One job seeker, for example, told me that he didn't have any skills. He'd worked in construction for years. However, he had spent a lot of spare time skiing and was able to use the knowledge he had acquired to get certified as a ski instructor. That certification led to a seasonal position at a ski resort, and eventually led to a permanent career change.

We all have transferable skills, whether or not we think so. It's simply a question of figuring out what they are, then using them to define what it is we want to do with the skills we have.

Changing Careers

There's a difference between changing jobs and changing careers. Changing jobs is typically defined as moving to a similar position at a different employer. Changing careers is more involved and usually means moving to a completely different type of position or to a different industry.

A career change may mean retraining, additional education, and even starting over at a low-level position and beginning a new career path, from scratch. It's not always easy, which is why I am sometimes surprised by the number of people who successfully change careers, especially later in life. It isn't always easy to do, and sometimes it takes a leap of faith and a good amount of bravery. It's very easy to get set in your ways and to think that because you have always had this job or worked in that industry, you can't do anything else. That's not true. We can all make a change, if we want to. The timing needs to be right and the foundation for making a move needs to be set, but it can be done. The hardest part is convincing yourself that you're ready to do it.

In some cases, we're not even aware that we need a change. We're bored or tired or simply don't feel like going to work. We use every excuse we can think of to take time off and cringe at the thought of going back to work. Even worse, we simply don't like our job and would rather be anywhere else than at the office. That can happen to anyone. When it does, these warning signs should be an indicator that it's time for a change.

The following are some signs that it's time for a career change:

- Burned out
- Tired or bored
- No interest in the job

TOOLS YOU NEED

▶ Use this Transferable Skills Survey (www.d.umn. edu/student/loon/car/self/ career_transfer_survey.html) to score your transferable skills. The results will give you a list of your skills in five categories: Communication, Research and Planning, Human Relations, Organization, Management and Leadership, and Work Survival.

- Any excuse for not going to work will do
- Inability to focus on tasks
- Low productivity
- Poor work performance

If some of those symptoms describe you, keep in mind, your boss has probably noticed too. You may want to start thinking about finding a new job before your boss thinks of it. It's easier to job search when you have a job than when you just got fired. It's easier to explain that you want to advance your career than it is to explain why you lost your job because of poor performance.

That leap, I mentioned earlier, by the way, doesn't have to be a big one. Sometimes it makes sense to start with baby steps. Keep your full-time job, for example, and gain some experience volunteering in the career field you would like to explore. Or start out by working part-time at a new job, until you are ready to commit to a change. Taking steps in an alternative or new direction can also help you tolerate a job that you probably shouldn't be working in anymore. When you have other things to focus on, your situation at work may not seem so tedious or hopeless.

Other options include taking a college course, or two, to gain some new skills or to update your skills that are a little out of date. Seminars and short programs (often offered as Adult Learning programs by local school districts) are a good way to brush up your skills, or to get started learning something new.

Consider different roles within your current industry. Many companies hire internally before they hire publicly. If you are qualified for a different job at your company, apply for it. Discuss alternatives with your Human Resources Department. Most companies want to keep good employees and will do their best to find another position, or may even be willing to carve out a

ELSEWHERE ON THE WEB

▶ The Recruiter's Studio (http://therecruitersstudio.com) is a good source of real-world advice and tips on how to find your dream job from someone who helps people transition. Listen to the Webcasts to hear how clients have been able to achieve success pursuing their dream career and to hear advice from industry experts and hiring managers on how to successfully make a change. You can then review the career resources and job opportunities that are available.

new position, for workers they want to keep. The one common characteristic most career changers have is a willingness to take a risk. Another commonality is that they don't view their salary as a critically important factor. They are able to look beyond present circumstances to the future potential of a new job. That isn't always easy, but it can be done. An unemployment check or a temporary job can be used to supplement income. College tuition assistance or students loans can be obtained. Government funding may be available for retraining or learning new skills.

If you really, really want to make a change, you'll find a way. It may not be as quick or as easy as you would like, but it can happen. The following is a brief overview of the steps you will need to take to change careers:

1. Decide that you need a change.
2. Itemize your career interests and values.
3. Consider career options.
4. Create a short list of possible career alternatives.
5. Research the career options on your list.
6. Develop the skills you need to make a change.
7. Incorporate those skills into your resume.
8. Set short-term and long-term career goals.
9. Start a job search.

Discover Your Perfect Career

The job or career that's perfect for you may not be the job that's perfect for someone else. Everyone has his or her own expectations of what a job should be like. Some want different things out of life and work than others.

Consider Bob, who spent a good part of his working life driving a school bus. It wasn't because he didn't have other qualifications. He took the job deliberately because it gave him time to think and

WHAT'S HOT

▶ 10 Steps to a Successful Career Change (http://about.com/jobsearch/10steps) will help you explore career options and choose a new career in your current industry or in a new career field. If you consider your career change a step-by-step process, it won't seem nearly as daunting. It will also be much easier to make a smooth transition if you take it one step at a time.

▶ We all spend a good part of our day juggling a busy schedule, including things like work, appointments, errands, and other activities. I've always found that having a wall calendar with appointments noted on it, as well as a portable planner, really helps to keep me organized. I can see where I need to be at a glance and then review the details in my day planner.

to write poetry. What he wanted most out of life was to be a poet. He didn't expect to make a living writing poetry. Unfortunately, those people are few and far between. However, this job gave him plenty of time to write the poetry he wanted to—in his head while driving, and on paper when he wasn't working.

Another example comes to mind. Jean, overqualified by most standards, is happy to work at a part-time job in a local doctor's office. Why doesn't she want more out of her job? She's an aspiring actress and that low-key day job gives her time to audition and time to rehearse for plays and movies. It also pays the bills, which would be tough to do on the uncertain income she makes acting.

Then there's Sam. He was one of the best employees who ever worked for me. He couldn't read or write. Sam brought his wife with him to fill out his **job application**. He was dedicated, and he never missed a day of work. He was innovative and came up with ideas that saved the company money. Sam dressed like a college professor, topped off with a jaunty Irish tweed cap, but he was our office cleaning person. Hiring Sam was one of the best decisions I ever made, even though, on paper, he didn't have many qualifications.

Sam's story reminds me of the wise words of Martin Luther King, Jr., who said "If you are called to be a street sweeper, sweep streets even as Michelangelo painted, or Beethoven composed music, or Shakespeare wrote poetry. Sweep streets so well that all the hosts of heaven and earth will pause to say, 'Here lived a great street sweeper who did his job well.'"

It's important to consider those words and determine what career is perfectly suited to you—not what you *think* your perfect career should be, or what the career expectations of your family, your friends, and society are. After all, it is your career and that's what is most important.

Curt Rosengren is a Passion Catalyst, which means he helps people figure out what they want to do and how they can get there. He offers some valuable advice: "Make a commitment to yourself. In the next seven days, identify one thing you can do to begin pursuing your passion—and start doing it!" Curt also notes that it can take time, even years, to actually achieve your goals.

That's fine, as long as you get started. Even if you aren't able to start work at your perfect job today, you will be able to find jobs that will help you move in the right direction. If you play your cards right, you will also be able to achieve what you want, out of work, and out of life.

The most important steps to follow in order to find your perfect job are, first of all, to decide what it is you want to do by exploring career and job options. Next on the list is to research and narrow down the alternatives. What sounds good at first glance might not really be as good as it sounds. Carefully consider what's involved in the day-to-day activities you will be doing and decide whether you are sure it's something you are interested in doing.

Once you have a good sense of the type of job that interests you, the next step will be to consider how you want to work. Do you want to work full-time or part-time? Do you want a professional career or would you rather work at an hourly position? How about pay? How important is it to you and how much do you need to earn to pay your bills? Flexibility and benefits are important too.

Needless to say, job searching isn't a simple endeavor. If it were, we could all go online and post our resume, get an interview, and get the job. The problem with that, though, is that if we're not applying for jobs that we're qualified for and if our resume doesn't even come close to matching the job requirements, we're not going to get called for an interview. I can guarantee it.

Employers can afford to be selective; there are more people searching than ever before (Monster's database currently has 61 million job seeker accounts and 52 million resumes), so in order to be competitive you need to be focused, targeted, and prepared.

ELSEWHERE ON THE WEB

▶ What does passion have to do with careers? It actually has quite a lot to do with your work, as well as your life. Curt Rosengren's Web site and blog (www.passion catalyst.com) can help you define what it is you're passionate about, as it relates to careers. He also provides good advice on how to make meaningful change in your life, and how to find jobs that you care about and will enjoy.

The most important thing to remember when choosing job and career options is to follow your dreams so you are seeking employment that will mesh with who you are and where you want to go. Once you have accomplished that, the rest of your job search will fall into place.

Get Linked

At my Job Searching site on ABOUT.com, you can find more information on the topics I've discussed in this chapter. Check out the following links.

DISCOVER YOUR PERFECT JOB QUIZ

When you need help finding that perfect job, this simple and quick quiz will help you find the job that's right for you.

 http://about.com/jobsearch/perfectjobquiz

HOW TO FIND COMPANIES

Here's how to find companies with job openings, as well how as to find the inside scoop on companies you are interested in working for.

http://about.com/jobsearch/findcompanies

Chapter 2

Managing Your Job Search

Getting Organized

Before you start looking for a job, you will need to get orga-nized. It takes a little time to get organized and you may need to invest in some tools to help you start your job search, and keep it on track. It's time and money well spent because the better organized you are, the faster you will be able to find a job. Your job search will run much more smoothly if you have all the equipment you need in place before you start.

A telephone system where a message can be left for you at any time of day is essential. You can't look for a job if you don't have a working e-mail address, because most employers use the Internet to recruit, in one way or another. So, you need an e-mail account, too. Access to a computer to write resumes and cover letters is a necessity. If you don't own a computer, check with your local public library or see if a family member or friend will let you use his or her computer. Many libraries have computers and printers that patrons

A fax machine is a bit too expensive for my budget. Is there a more affordable alternative?

▶ An alternative for faxing that I recommend is an inexpensive fax machine that you can hook up to your phone line. These are available at most office supply stores and major retailers. Prices start at under $100. Free fax services are also available online. Monster, for example, offers a free fax receipt service via e-mail. You can sign up online (http://fw.monster.com/monster/clients/efax/form.ptml) for the service, which is provided through eFax.com. For sending faxes, there are fee-based services that let you send faxes directly from your computer.

can use for free. Either way, you will need to be able to access a computer on a daily basis.

There are also companies, such as FedEx Kinko's, that provide technology services, including computer workstation rentals, printing, wireless Internet access, and faxing, for a fee. You can search online (http://fedex.kinkos.com/locations/index.php) by zip code, or city and state, to find a store near you. Or call Customer Relations at 800-254-6567 to find a location that is convenient.

You will also need an appointment book or a PDA (personal digital assistant or hand-held computer) to schedule interviews and to track when you need to follow up with job search contacts.

The following is a checklist of everything you will need to get started on a job search:

- ○ E-mail account
- ○ Calendar
- ○ Computer
- ○ Copier or fax
- ○ Interview attire
- ○ Phone
- ○ Planner or organizer
- ○ Word-processing software

In this age of technology, it's almost impossible to job search if you're not computer literate. In some cases, employers only accept online applications. In others, they will want to communicate with you via e-mail or the Web. You will want to be able to apply online for jobs, post your resume online, send application materials via e-mail, and communicate with employers electronically. So, in most cases, you will need to have or be able to access all the items on the job search checklist.

Office space is essential. Take some time to put together what you need and to set up a workspace where you can work in an efficient manner. Because I work from home much of the time, I have a room set up as an office in my house. My office is full of equipment, including several computers, a printer (which doubles as a scanner), a phone, fax machine, several calendars, and a telephone answering machine.

I have a supply cabinet of copy paper, envelopes, stamps, business cards, labels, along with a well-organized file system for all my correspondence and paperwork. I may have too much in my office, but it saves time and a trip to the store or the post office when you have everything you need at your fingertips.

Depending on your living space, there may not be room to set up an office. If it isn't feasible, a table in a quiet corner will work just as well. As long as you have a quiet space to talk on the phone, access to the materials you need, and a computer to work on, you'll be fine.

What you're doing sounds a lot like work, doesn't it? That's because it is. Job searching is work, and if you consider your job search a part-time job (or full-time job if you're unemployed) and dedicate time and resources to it, you will be successful.

Tracking your job search is very important. I have folders set up on my computer for every component of job searching. I save a copy of every version of my resume I create. The same holds true for cover letters.

The easiest way to set up a new folder is to use "My Documents" in Microsoft Windows. Click on "My Documents," then click on "Make a New Folder." Create a folder called "Resumes" and another called "Cover Letters." Each time you create a new version of your resume, save it in the Resumes folder. Similarly, save

TOOLS YOU NEED

▸ Day-Timer (www.day
timer.com) has an excel-
lent selection of calendars,
appointment books, desk-top
calendars, and blotter-style
desk notepads that are ideal
for writing notes and jotting
down numbers and mes-
sages. You can even create
your own personalized cus-
tom Day-Timer by choosing
the style, binding, format,
and accessories. I like my
leather Day-Timer because
I can order refills for it each
year, rather than having to
order a new planning book.

I work full-time and I'm looking for a job. How can I return e-mails and phone calls in a timely manner?

▶ I always remind those who are juggling a job and a job search to think creatively. If you have a computer with a wireless Internet card, you can use your lunch hour to visit a library, bookstore, or coffee shop with Internet access. Check your e-mail, search, and apply for jobs, and respond to any correspondence you have received. Don't forget to check your voice mail for messages during your lunch hour and breaks from work.

the cover letters you write in the Cover Letters folder. That way, you'll be able to find all your job search correspondence fast.

I keep copies of all the employment-related e-mail I send and receive. You should do the same. Like you did with the folders for your documents, create a new mailbox or two specifically for your job search. I have a folder where I keep a copy of all the e-mails I have sent and received related to job searching. I have another folder where I keep all the e-mail related to my About.com site and another for personal correspondence.

Keeping copies of your job search correspondence enables you to check back to see what you said to a prospective employer and how they responded. A calendar to track when you need to follow up is also very useful. Unfortunately, not every employer will respond to you as quickly as you would like, so, you will need to follow up.

In addition, it's critically important to conduct your job search in a businesslike manner. There is nothing much worse, if you're a recruiter, than calling to schedule an interview and getting a voice mail message that says something very inappropriate. It's happened to me and, needless to say, I didn't leave a message. Instead, I moved on to the next candidate.

Given the competitiveness of the job market, you will want to make sure that all your job search communications are not only professional, but perfect! The reason is because the first impression you give an employer is the most important one. If the electronic or paper communications you send aren't perfect, and if you don't remember what you said to whom, your application will not be considered for employment.

Phone and Voice Mail

A phone, of course, is essential to your job search. A cell phone is ideal, because you can carry it with you, and you can check and respond to messages frequently. It also provides a history of calls you have made and received so you can easily find phone numbers for contacts you need to call.

Cell phone service doesn't have to be expensive. There are a variety of low-cost prepaid plans available. A quiz (http://about.com/cellphones/cellphonequiz) from the About.com Cell Phones Guide helps you instantly find out which company will cost you the least money.

When using your cell phone for job searching, make sure you include the phone number on your resume and in your cover letters. Include your phone number in your e-mail signature as well, because some hiring managers may want to call you rather than contacting you by e-mail.

If you don't have a cell phone, use your home phone. If you're using your home phone for job searching, you will need an answering machine or voice mail system so you don't miss any calls. Be sure that you can access the answering machine or voice mail when you're away from home so you can check for messages regularly. It's important to be able to return calls in a prompt manner.

When you're in the midst of a job search, make sure that an adult answers the phone. You don't know who may be calling—it could be a recruiter or a networking contact. Despite how cute your child sounds on the phone, it's annoying to listen to baby talk if you're a recruiter trying to schedule an interview or a contact who has been referred by someone else to help you find a job.

On a related note, have a quiet place where you can answer the phone. Some employers call to screen candidates over the phone. Others may call you to conduct a first-round telephone interview and they may not notify you about it in advance. So, you need to be prepared to discuss employment matters, regardless of what else is happening at home.

It's really hard to concentrate if the television is blaring, the dog is barking, and the kids are playing. When it's not a good time

WHAT'S HOT

▶ PDAs (personal digital assistants), which keep track of your interviews and networking appointments, are on the "hot" list for high-tech job seekers. Most models have a date book, memo pad, calculator, address book, e-mail capabilities, and even a "to do" list. Your PDA can be synchronized with your computer, so you can have all your data in both places. Besides being a cool toy, for those of us who like technology, it definitely saves on paper.

to talk, it is perfectly acceptable to ask the caller to hold on for a moment while you move to a quieter area. It's also appropriate to ask if you can return the call at a more convenient time. It's better to take the time to collect your thoughts and call back than it is to try and carry on a conversation in the midst of chaos.

Keep a notepad and pen next to your phone. That way you can jot down the name and number of who is calling. Try to get the job title and company name, as well as the job title of the position that the caller is hiring for. It's easy to think that you'll remember, until you hang up the phone and the information is gone from your mind.

Voice mail is an essential job search tool. You will want employers to be able to reach you to leave a message anytime of day. Your voice mail message needs to be polite and professional. It also needs to include your name, so callers know they have reached the right party, and instructions on how to leave a message.

I cringe at some of the voice mail messages I hear, especially when I'm calling younger job seekers. One that sticks in my mind is a message that talked about where the person was partying and was full of words I wouldn't use in polite conversation. Remember, if your resume has been distributed properly, you may not know who will be calling you. A networking contact could have passed on your resume to someone who would like to talk to you about employment.

If your message is less than professional, take a few minutes to record a new greeting that simply says that you are not available and you will return the call as soon as possible.

Calendar or Planner
Even though some people have to have the latest technology, it's not absolutely necessary. Expense can be an issue, and some of

us—including myself sometimes—are set in our ways. To be honest, I usually keep track of my appointments the old-fashioned way. I have a calendar where I list my family's appointments and an appointment book with a memo pad where I track where I have to go and what I need to do each day.

For me, it's quickest to glance at my appointment book to see where I need to be. I also carry a notepad and pen with me everywhere I go. It's useful to be able to jot down a note when I remember someone that I need to call or something that I need to do. I have a nice leather address book that has a spot in the back for a memo pad that I can use to write a quick reminder.

Basically, it's up to you whether your job search is high-tech or low-tech. If you are more comfortable with electronic communications, and you can afford it, consider adding a PDA to your job search tool kit. If not, paper works just as well, and you will still be able to keep track of your job search outreach without a problem. What matters is that you do keep track. How you do it isn't as important as the fact that you are doing it.

As an aside, some job search expenses are tax deductible. Your appointment book is a good place to track those expenses while you're job searching, rather than trying to recreate them after the fact. I make a note of the expense on the date I incur it, and I save the receipts in a file so I have backup documentation. By the end of the year, my appointment book is rather cluttered, but I have a good picture of what I did, when I did it, and what it cost me. Again, it's easier to itemize everything as it happens, rather than trying to remember later on.

Word-Processing Software

There are several options available when it comes to software you can use to write resumes and cover letters. Microsoft Word is the industry standard. When employers request a resume sent

WHAT'S HOT

▸ Most people I know who are conducting a job search use their cell phone as their primary means of communicating with recruiters and job search contacts. The reason for this is that it's easier to check messages and to return phone calls when you can store all the information on your cell phone than it is to use your home phone, especially when you're out and about much of the day. Most cell phones come with voice mail service. If yours doesn't, check to see if it's available.

▶ Check out Yahoo! Calendar (http://calendar.mail.yahoo.com) if you are interested in a free online calendar. Registered users can view a daily, weekly, monthly, and yearly schedule. You can also set up lists of tasks you need to do and events that are on your schedule. Set up reminders so you don't miss an interview or other appointment. Reminders can be sent to your cell phone, via e-mail, or by Yahoo! Messenger. Users can even share their calendars so other people can view it.

as an attachment (that's a file sent with an e-mail message), they typically request that candidates send the resume as a Microsoft Word document.

That could be an issue, because even though most computers come with some software applications, they don't necessarily come with Microsoft Word. However, in most cases you should be able to save the file as a Word file. For example, if you create your resume in WordPerfect, choose "File," then "Save As" from the menu to save your file as a Microsoft Word document. You will be able to select the file format, the name, and the location where you want to save the file.

Word-processing software includes:

- Microsoft Word (PC and Mac)
- Corel WordPerfect (PC)
- Apple iWork (Mac)
- Open Office, AbiWord, and other free programs (http://about.com/wordprocessing/freeprograms)

Many word-processing packages have resume templates built in (http://about.com/jobsearch/resumetemplate) to the program. That's important to keep in mind when reviewing software options, because it can save you time in writing and formatting your resume.

You will need different versions of your resume for different jobs. So, also use "Save As" to save different versions of your resume. If, for example, you are sending a resume for a technical job at General Electric, its focus should be different from one sent for a marketing job at a local publishing firm. Save both copies but under different names.

Resume writing software is also an option. If the thought of writing your own resume is daunting, and it can be, there is resume-writing software available that will do the job for you. With these types of software programs you fill in the blanks in a step-by-step organized fashion. You enter your educational background, experience, skills, and contact information. The program then creates a resume for you, typically in a choice of formats. Most packages will also proof your resume and check for grammatical errors.

Some resume-writing packages do more than just create a resume. They can help you write cover letters, manage your contacts, e-mail your resume, and even help you practice interviewing. Prices, depending on the software you purchase, range from $20 to $40.

The top resume-writing software includes:

- **ResumeMaker** (www.resumemaker.com) has a Professional edition and a Career edition. The Career edition comes with career planning and assessment tools. There is also a Web-based version that enables you to create a resume online and save it in several formats.
- **Resume Works Pro** (www.individualsoftware.com/new/consumer/details/rs7_details.htm) starts you out with a step-by-step guide to creating a resume. There's a contact manager you can use to outreach to the companies you want to pursue and assistance with cover letter writing as well.
- **WinWay Resume Deluxe** (www.winway.com) has a resume-writing wizard that writes your resume for you. It also has several resume formatting themes to choose from, as well as a Resume Auditor that checks your resume for mistakes and fixes them.

TOOLS YOU NEED

▶ The last thing you want to deal with is a computer crash where you lose everything. I use an external hard drive to back up my files. My Maxtor (www.maxtor.com) drive plugs into a USB port on my computer. Once I installed it, which only took a few minutes, it showed up on the list of drives under My Computer. I save my work daily, both to the hard drive on my computer and to my external hard drive, so I always have backup copies.

Regardless of how you choose to create your resume, either by writing it yourself, by buying software to do it, or by using a resume-writing service to write it for you, you will need a professional resume that will impress potential employers. There's absolutely no reason why anyone, with the right tools, can't put together a polished and professional resume. If you use the right software, take plenty of time, and carefully choose your words and the layout, you will be able to create first-class job correspondence yourself.

Resumes that don't look professional and aren't perfect won't make it into the interview pile. There is too much competition out there, and employers are not hesitant to reject a resume that isn't top-notch. One of the most important pieces of advice I can give you is to make sure that all the job search correspondence you send is perfect, absolutely perfect.

E-mail

E-mail is an integral part of today's hiring process. Recruiters contact prospective candidates via e-mail. Employers ask candidates to send resumes via e-mail. Hiring managers schedule interviews by e-mail and conduct follow-up conversations that way, as well. E-mail is an ideal way to network because it's a fast and simple way to connect with people who can help you with your job search. It may not be impossible to job search without e-mail, but it's close to impossible.

If you think it's too hard, think again. If you start with the basics and don't try to do too much at once, you'll be fine. Even my mom, who is seventy-five years old, is getting good at e-mail, though it took her a while to learn.

In addition to using your e-mail program for sending and receiving messages, you can also use it to be notified of new job postings by the online job sites. It's also how those job sites may notify you that a prospective employer has viewed your resume.

E-mail is also a good way to thank an interviewer for the time spent with you, as well as to reiterate your interest in a position. E-mail is also useful for following up on your status in the hiring process. You can check whether the company has your application and whether you are under consideration for the job.

It's very important not to use your work e-mail account to apply for jobs. Many employers can, and will, read e-mail that has been sent or received on their computer systems. Many employers also have company policies that prohibit using company equipment for personal business.

Another really good reason for not using your work account is mistakes that you could inadvertently make. John, a visitor to my About.com site, wrote to me after mistakenly sending an e-mail cover letter, along with his resume, to a colleague in another department at his company (some e-mail programs start filling in the "To:" field automatically when you start typing). Luckily, the colleague was also a friend and overlooked the message, but what if John had sent it to the boss? That has happened, and it's one of the job search scenarios that makes you cringe.

I haven't sent my resume to the wrong place, but I have sent a message to the wrong person, simply by clicking the Send button a little too quickly and not confirming I was sending it to the right person. So do be careful what you send to whom.

Set up a job search e-mail account. Setting up an e-mail account specifically for your job search will allow you to keep your job search communications separate from your personal correspondence. It also helps to prevent mistakes like the one I just mentioned.

Most computers come with an e-mail program like Microsoft Outlook. My personal favorite is Eudora, because I've found it easy to set up a variety of personalities, which I need for my various responsibilities, along with signatures to match each personality.

There are a variety of free and low-cost e-mail programs available:

- **Eudora** (www.eudora.com) has a free version, if you don't mind ads. There's also a free lite version, which has fewer features. The paid version comes with built-in SpamWatch and BossWatch.
- **Microsoft Outlook** (www.microsoft.com/office/outlook) has good options for organizing your e-mail files and managing your contacts and calendar.
- **Thunderbird** (www.mozilla.com/thunderbird) is a free download from Mozilla. It will import your other e-mail settings and has built-in junk mail filtering and scam protection.

Whichever e-mail program you choose, set up folders just for job searching so it's easy to find the e-mails you have sent and received. Enter your job search contacts in your address book so you won't have to dig through old e-mail messages to find them. In most cases, you can enter more information than an e-mail address. In Eudora, for example, I can include the home and business addresses of my contacts, as well as several phone numbers and alternate e-mail addresses.

As an alternative to using e-mail on just one computer, there are a variety of free Web-based e-mail programs available. Using online e-mail means that you can check your e-mail from any computer, which is very handy for job seekers. It's especially helpful if you don't have one computer you use all the time and/or if you are using a library computer or borrowing one.

Top Web-based e-mail programs include:

- **Yahoo! Mail** (http://mail.yahoo.com) is one of the top free e-mail programs. You will need to register with Yahoo! and choose an e-mail address to use when you sign up for Yahoo! Mail. Once you pick an e-mail address, you can log in to your e-mail account to send and receive mail. Yahoo! has good spam filters and, in addition to free e-mail, you get a calendar, notepad, and address book—all of which are useful for job seekers.
- **Gmail** (http://gmail.google.com) is Google's version of Web-based e-mail. When you set up a Gmail account you will be able to import your contacts from other e-mail programs, set up filters to help manage your mail, and check and send mail from your other e-mail accounts.
- **Hotmail** (www.hotmail.com), provided by MSN, was one of the first free e-mail services. It's still a good product, with a generous amount of storage space for your e-mail messages and built-in spam filters to help reduce junk mail.

Speaking of junk mail, if you have folders set up for spam, double-check them once a day or so. I find legitimate e-mail that somehow has ended up in my junk mail folder by mistake every once in a while. The last thing you want to do is lose a valuable message from a potential employer.

When setting up online e-mail and job search accounts, keep a list of the user names and passwords you create. It's easy to forget them, especially when you have a different one for each online account you set up. If you do forget a user name or password, you should be able to have it sent to you by e-mail. You will need to remember the answer to a security question so the system can verify that it is actually you requesting a lost password.

ELSEWHERE ON THE WEB

▶ The Top 10 Free E-mail Services (http://about.com/email/freeemail) is a list of free Web-based e-mail services. These services allow anyone to set up a personal e-mail account that can be accessed from any computer connected to the Internet. Once you have set up an e-mail account, you can access your e-mail by visiting the Web site that hosts it. Log in to your account to view and send e-mail messages.

I'm not that computer literate. Do I really need to use all these applications?

▶ No, you don't need to use everything. Instant message, for example, is helpful but not essential. I always tell visitors to my About.com site that e-mail and access to the Internet are a must for anyone who is job searching online. On the other hand, if you are looking for a job at a local retail store, you won't need much more than the ability to fill out a job application correctly.

Remember those old words of wisdom that it's not so much what you say, but how you say it that is important? Well, how you say it is also very important when communicating via e-mail.

Think before you hit the Send button, especially if what you are about to send isn't positive. For example, a hiring manager contacted me after she had, very politely, notified a candidate that she wasn't going to be hired for an open position. The candidate hit Reply and sent a two-word response: "your loss." This was particularly unfortunate, because the hiring manager was considering the candidate for another position. She just hadn't mentioned it yet, because she wasn't sure when it would become available. The candidate, because of her hasty and rude response, ensured that the employer wouldn't be considering her for any job opening.

Spell check and proofread your e-mail just like all your other correspondence. One client I worked with had the wrong phone number in her e-mail signature and on the resume she had sent out in response to many job postings, but hadn't proofread well enough to catch her mistake. She corrected it, but may have lost out on a good opportunity because employers weren't able to reach her. She was also embarrassed because it was an employer who informed her by e-mail that the phone number wasn't correct.

Instant Messenger Services

Instant message (IM) isn't essential, but it can be very handy to use when job searching, especially when networking. It can also be used to get job search assistance. Skidmore College's Career Services Office, for example, uses an instant-messaging system to answer quick questions and inquiries from students and alumni. It's much quicker than phone or e-mail and clients can get an immediate response to their inquiries.

Some online networking services, like Monster Networking, include IM addresses in member's profiles, so you can contact referrals via instant message. There are quite a few free instant-messaging services available and some, like AOL's Instant Messenger service (AIM), include free e-mail.

Top instant-messaging systems include:

- **AOL Instant Messenger (AIM)** (www.aim.com) is available as a free download or via the Web. You will create a screen name and password when you sign up. Once you have set up an account you can access it from any computer with Web access.
- **GoogleTalk** (www.google.com/talk) requires a GMail user name and password. It's a free download and your GMail contacts are automatically loaded into the system. You can talk to your contacts by instant message, phone, or e-mail.
- **Yahoo! Messenger** (http://messenger.yahoo.com) provides free computer-to-computer phone calls and voice mail, in addition to an instant-messaging service. Users can chat and even use the service on their cell phone.

When you set up your instant-messaging service, be careful what you choose as a screen name. A couple of good examples of instant message screen names *not* to use are *kissesalot* and *imacutie*. I really did get instant messages from people with those screen names. It, of course, really wasn't the best way to make an impression on someone who might be able to help with your job search. Being creative is fine when you're using IM for social activities, but it's better to be boring when you're job searching.

ELSEWHERE ON THE WEB

▶ AIM (AOL's instant-messenger service) is a free download. There are versions available for Windows, Mac, Linux, and for your PDA or cell phone. Download from www.aim.com. There is also an Express version that you can use to access AIM from any computer, which is handy if you're away from home or using someone else's computer.

Get Linked

At my Job Searching site on **ABOUT**.com, *you can find more information on the topics I've discussed in this chapter. Check out the following links.*

HOW TO FIND A JOB

This article will step you through the process of finding a job. It includes a list of everything you need to do to get started on a job search. It will help you cover all the bases and get your job search off to a good start.

 http://about.com/jobsearch/findajob

JOB SEARCH TOOL KIT

Review my job search tool kit to make sure that every impression you make is the best impression. It's important, because the first impression you make on a prospective employer is the one that matters the most.

http://about.com/jobsearch/toolkit

JOB SEARCH ACTION PLAN

Taking the time to write a job search action plan will speed up your job search. You can review my job search action plan to create a plan to help you implement and manage a job search.

http://about.com/jobsearch/actionplan

Chapter 3

Resume Writing

Resume Basics

Your resume is the most important document you will use in your job search. Your resume is what makes the first impression on a prospective employer. It will either get you an interview or get you a rejection letter. The resume you send only has about thirty seconds to make an impression on the person reading it. You will want that impression to be not just a good one, but even better, a great one. Your resume needs to be the one that makes the best impression on the person who might be hiring you for your next job, so spending time and effort on it will definitely pay off.

We create resumes in order to showcase to prospective employers what we have accomplished in our lives as it relates to work and careers. Your resume is the way you will highlight your professional accomplishments, your educational achievements, and the skills that are relevant and specific to the type of job for which you are applying.

▶ Invest in a dictionary and a thesaurus so you can quickly look up words when you aren't sure of the spelling or meaning. Keep them on your desk and use them frequently. It's easy to take a quick look in your dictionary while you're writing to check on spelling or usage. I have well-worn copies of Webster's College Dictionary and Roget's Thesaurus that I use often. If you're not sure about a word, double-check it. I can guarantee the recruiter will notice misspelled words on your resume.

There are several types of resumes. A chronological resume is the most familiar type and the one used most often. It lists your work history in reverse chronological order, with your most recent job listed first. A functional resume highlights your skills and experience rather than the jobs you have held. A combination resume highlights your skills (usually with a section at the top of the page), followed by your chronological employment history.

I prefer chronological resumes. First of all, a functional resume can be a red flag to a potential employer who may wonder if you aren't including your employment history because there is a problem with it. It's also annoying, to me, to have to figure out where someone worked, what they did, and when they did it.

It's best to use a functional resume when there are gaps in your employment history. That way you can focus on your skills rather than the gaps or glitches in your work record.

If you have a strong work history, use a chronological resume, with a statement at the top that highlights your skills. If you have been out of the work force for a while or are changing careers, consider a functional or combination resume.

Keep your resume formatting simple. First, take some time to think about how you are going to construct your resume—not what it says, but how it looks.

Visualize how your resume looks on paper, the bigger picture of how it's formatted and laid out, rather than the specific words you are including. Leave plenty of white space on your resume, because you don't want it to look crowded or cluttered. Keep your resume to one page if possible, but don't worry if it is longer because you have lots of experience. Use standard letter-size paper (8.5" × 11").

Using the standard job searching protocol is always better, in my opinion. The person who sent me a resume on legal-size paper didn't impress me. It was too big to fit tidily into the pile of resumes I was reviewing, too long to file with the other resumes I received, and it took extra time to process.

Don't write too much. Short sentences and paragraphs work much better than longer ones. Write clearly and simply. Your resume should be written simply and should be easy to read. As one visitor to my About.com site told me recently, "Job search correspondence ought to be fluent and easily taken in, especially in resumes and job letters."

It's important to tell the truth and not to exaggerate your qualifications when you write your resume. Here are a couple of reasons why. First of all, many employers check. They check your references, they check your transcripts, and they verify employment with prior employers. If you haven't told the truth and the company finds out, you can be fired later on.

A second reason is that not telling the truth usually comes back to haunt you. One visitor to my About.com Forum (http://about.com/jobsearch/forum) decided to inflate her GPA (grade point average) on her resume, just a little bit. She thought it would make her more competitive. She did really well on an interview. The employer then asked for copies of her college transcripts, and she had a difficult situation on her hands because the GPA on her resume didn't match her transcript. She was grappling for an excuse that would make sense so she could cover up her lapse in judgment.

I honestly think there is nothing to gain, and a lot to lose, by not telling the truth on your resume. When you tell the truth, you don't have to worry about getting caught in a lie, you don't have to remember which details you stretched or enhanced when you put them on your resume, and you don't have to stress over a potential employer asking difficult questions about your resume. The wrong answer could cost you the job opportunity.

When choosing fonts, keep the number of fonts you use to a minimum. Do choose a font like Arial or Times New Roman that's easy to read. Use bolding and bullets to highlight your job titles and responsibilities. But, don't overuse formatting. A resume with too much of a good thing, like too much capitalization or italicization, is hard to read. On a similar note, tiny fonts cause eyestrain, so make sure the font is large enough to read (10-or 12-point).

After you write your resume, look at it again to see if it looks appealing. Make sure that your fonts and point size are consistent throughout the document. If you use several fonts and sizes, be sure that each section is correct, as you want it to be formatted.

Creating Your Resume

The creation of a resume involves several steps. Your goal should be to create a clean, simple resume that is easy to read and clearly explains what your objectives are, what your background is, and what skills you have.

Compile the information to include in your resume. Regardless of the type of resume you choose, you will need to gather the information to include before you start writing. Use this resume checklist to compile the information you will need to have ready. You will need to make a list of all your employment information, your school and college information, and the relevant skills you have. Here's the information to include on your resume checklist:

- ○ Contact information
- ○ Summary and objective
- ○ Work history
- ○ Education and training
- ○ Skills
- ○ Additional information

How much work history to include depends on how many years you have been working. If you have been in the work force for years, you don't need to include all the experience that you have. If you're an older worker, also consider leaving off the dates when you went to college.

Why does how many years you include on your resume matter? When I wrote about the "gray ceiling" (http://about.com/job search/grayceiling) on my About.com site, and I was surprised by how many job seekers felt that they were discriminated against because of their age. It wasn't only older workers. In some cases, it was people in their thirties and forties who felt that they were considered too old for the job they were applying for. Age does matter, even though it shouldn't. However, you can prevent some age-related issues by strategically deciding what to include and what to leave off your resume.

Use a resume template as a guideline. Using a resume template is an ideal way to make sure that you include everything you need on your resume. Here's an overview of a resume template, with optional sections for an objective and career highlights.

The first section in your resume should include information on how prospective employers can contact you:

- Name
- Home address
- City, state, and zip code
- Home phone
- Cell phone
- E-mail address

The next section of your resume is the Objective. This is optional, but taking the time to write a customized objective that

ASK YOUR GUIDE

I have been working for thirty years and I'm afraid that I'm considered too old. What can I do?

▶ Many visitors to my About.com site share your concern. The AARP Web site (www.aarp.org/money/careers) has information and advice for older workers. There is information on what you can leave off your resume, how to interview effectively, how to deal with job loss, and how to balance work and life issues.

matches the job you are applying for will definitely help you stand out from the other candidates. This section should contain a sentence or two describing your goals for employment.

If you are seeking a professional position, include a section called Career Highlights/Qualifications. This section is also customized to the job you are seeking. List your relevant achievements and skills. This can either be a paragraph or a bulleted list of your skills as they match the job description.

The Experience section of your resume is a list of your work history. It should include the companies you worked for, dates of employment, the jobs you held, along with a list of responsibilities and achievements.

The following is an example of the Experience section:

- Company
- City and state
- Dates of employment
- Job title
- Responsibilities and achievements

The Education section of your resume should include a list of the colleges you attended, your degrees, as well as honors or awards you received:

- College(s) and degree(s)
- Awards and honors

If you're a college graduate or have been in the work force for a while, you don't need to include high school information. If you're a student seeking a part-time job or an internship and you're still in school or have just graduated, it's fine to include high school on your resume.

The Skills section of your resume comes next. It should include information on the skills that you have that are specific to the type of job you are applying for (i.e., Microsoft Office, HTML, or foreign languages). If you're applying for a job as a social worker, where being bilingual is an asset, certainly include the foreign language skills you have and your level of fluency. On the other hand, if you have advanced C++ programming skills and you are applying for a job as an editorial assistant, there is no reason to list them. In fact, you may appear to be overqualified for the position if you list high-level skills that aren't related to the job.

The last section of your resume is the Additional Information section. Use it to list professional memberships, publications, volunteering, and other related activities. Do make sure that what you include is relevant. For example, if you have taken piano lessons for years and teach piano as a side job, but you aren't applying for a job in the music field or as an educator, there is no need to list your ability to play the piano on your resume.

The rule of thumb to remember is that if it's related to the position you are applying for, include it on your resume. Consider whether the skill adds value to your credentials, and if not, leave it off your resume.

There is no need to include references on your resume. Instead, have your references on a separate list, ready to give to an employer on request.

Microsoft Word templates are another option. If you use Microsoft Word, you can use the templates that came with your software to compile the information that you need to include on your resume. Here's how to open the templates: Open Microsoft Word, click on File, New Templates or New from Template. Then, click on Templates in My Computer, Other Documents. You will find a selection in the Templates section there.

ELSEWHERE ON THE WEB

▶ Microsoft has a large selection of resume templates available on its Web site. (Go to http://office.microsoft.com, visit the My Careers section, click on Templates, then on Resumes.) There are templates for basic resumes, job-specific resumes, and resumes for a variety of employment situations, like career changing, looking for an entry-level job, or returning to the work force after an absence.

Once the template file is open, you can type over the existing information with your personal information. Save the file with a new file name so you still have the original template for future use. I usually save my resume with a file name that includes my name and what it is, to make it easier for the employer to recognize and file it. For example, my most current, general resume is saved as doyleresume.doc.

If you use a template, do take some time to edit the template so your resume looks unique. Even though it's easy to use a template, and they are helpful in getting started, you will want to do the best you can to make sure your resume stands out from the crowd and doesn't look like every other resume the recruiter receives.

Carefully proofread your resume. Use the following checklist to make sure you have checked, and double-checked, everything on your resume:

- ❍ Use a dictionary as you write.
- ❍ Your current position should be described in the present tense (manage staff).
- ❍ Previous positions should be described in past tense (managed staff).
- ❍ Use periods at the end of all full sentences.
- ❍ Make sure your punctuation is consistent.
- ❍ Double-check all the dates of employment.
- ❍ Double-check your contact information.
- ❍ Spell check your finished resume.
- ❍ Ask a friend to proofread your resume.

There are some things that should not be included on your resume in the United States. In fact, it is illegal for employers to ask for some personal and confidential information. The information you do not need to include on your resume is:

- Age
- Gender
- Marital status
- Number of children
- Salary history
- References

One visitor to my About.com site wondered whether he should include his IQ and the fact that he was a member of Mensa on his resume. The consensus from the experts in our Discussion Forum was that he shouldn't include it because it wasn't relevant to the jobs he was applying for and because it sounded a bit like he was bragging.

In general, don't include anything on your resume that isn't relevant to the specific job search you are conducting.

It's also important to keep your resume simple. The resume I received on glow-in-the-dark hot pink paper didn't impress me. The fluorescent green one didn't make a good impression either. Even the lovely calligraphy used to address one envelope I received didn't help the candidate. Employers aren't impressed by candidates who include extraneous information that wasn't requested, like copies of every diploma they ever earned.

Targeted Resumes

In the past, job seekers created one version of their resume and that was it. You sent the same version of your resume in response to each and every help-wanted ad that you read in the daily newspaper. Now it's necessary to have at least several versions of your resume. You will send out a different version depending on the job. The job applicants who are getting the most interviews are the ones who take the time to write a targeted resume for each and every job they apply for. Take the time to review the job posting carefully, and edit your resume so it reflects what the employer is seeking in a candidate.

Writing a targeted sample resume isn't hard. Start by reviewing the job posting. Then write a customized objective that matches the job posting. Here's an example:

- **Job Posting:** This position provides technology leadership and direction for the company's software systems. This includes technology evaluation, new product architecture and delivery, management of software engineers and developers, as well as interfacing with sales and corporate administration.
- **Resume Objective:** To apply my unique combination of technical expertise, managerial experience, business acumen, and sales support to direct the delivery and acceptance of mission-critical software systems.

Also include a section called Career Qualifications on your resume. This should include a bulleted list of the experience, skills, and key accomplishments from your employment history.

Using the technology position as an example, here are career highlights that relate specifically to the job posting.

Qualifications:
- Directed development teams and implemented software delivery, achieving 100 percent on-time delivery of three enterprise software products.

WHAT'S HOT

▶ When writing your first resume, creativity will impress employers. Don't limit yourself. Instead of thinking that you haven't done anything, consider what activities you have participated in that you can include. Have you volunteered? Do you belong to a youth group? What classes have you taken? How about awards you have received? All these can be listed on your resume. So can the personal characteristics that are related to the jobs you are seeking.

- Managed all product delivery activities for software services provider, ensuring all products were delivered in advance of scheduled release.
- Managed developers, database administrators, and product architects responsible for product design and development in order to streamline all software development activities.

The recruiter will appreciate the fact that you have taken the time to understand what the company is looking for, and that you have taken the time to identify how you are the candidate with the qualifications for the position. Not only have you saved the recruiter some time reading through your resume, you have also promoted your candidacy by highlighting your specific relevant qualifications.

It can be time-consuming to edit and rewrite your resume for every job you apply for, but in the long run, it's well worth the effort you put into it.

How to Mail Your Resume

An important word of advice is to mail your resume to the person mentioned in the job posting. It is fine to send another copy to a networking contact who may be able to help, but don't bypass the person responsible for reviewing the applications.

Follow the instructions. If the help-wanted ad says to mail your resume to a post office box or a Human Resources Department, do exactly what the ad says. There's a reason that the employer wants all the resumes in one place. It makes it much easier to review them when all the candidates follow the same guidelines.

When my department was hiring a summer assistant, one candidate sent a resume to my boss and to the company president. She never bothered to apply via human resources, as stated in the ad. She thought circumventing the hiring process would get her an interview. Instead, it knocked her out of consideration.

About.com's Human Resources Guide, Susan Heathfield, notes, "When applying for an advertised position, applying directly to the CEO is the death knell for your application. You tick off the human resources people, who are the monitors and caretakers of the hiring process. They build the pool of candidates that managers interview. They schedule the interviews. And, believe it or not, respected human resources people have a serious influence on who gets hired."

How to Upload Your Resume

Uploading your resume to a jobs site like Monster (www.monster.com) or CareerBuilder (www.careerbuilder.com) is simple. The job site will walk you through the process and will explain to you, step-by-step, what you need to do.

First of all, you will need to create a resume and save it on your computer. You will need to know where you have it saved (for example, in the Resumes folder you created in My Documents). You will also need to know the file name.

If you haven't ever visited the site where you want to upload your resume, you will need to register. You will choose a user name and password, then enter your contact information, including your name, address, e-mail address, and phone number. There is some optional information, like your date of birth, gender, and ethnicity, which you can opt out of including. Keep track of the various versions of your resume and your user names and passwords for each site where you upload your resume.

Once you have created an account, you will be able to upload your resume. In most cases, you will be able to choose how you want to upload your resume:

- Build your resume online
- Upload your resume
- Copy and paste your resume

When you build your resume online, you will be entering the information from your resume into boxes, which will then create a resume for you. You can either cut and paste or type in the information.

If you choose option two, you will select the resume (Microsoft Word) file on your hard drive and click the file name to upload it.

The third alternative involves copying and pasting the information from your resume into a text box. In this case, there may be a limit to the number of characters that can be included, so be prepared to edit your resume for length. There's typically a spell check option. Use it to spell check your resume before you save the file and upload it to the job site.

You may be able to upload multiple copies of your resume, which is ideal for sending targeted resumes to specific types of employers or companies in certain industries. America's Job Bank and Monster, for example, both allow users to upload five different versions of their resume.

It's important to protect your privacy. If you are currently employed, you may want to block your resume from being viewed by certain companies, like the one you work for.

I know one job seeker whose company was searching a job site for candidates for employment. His resume showed up on the list of prospects. The company had no idea he was seeking employment and they weren't thrilled to get the unexpected news that he was planning to leave. He had no other offers pending, so it wasn't a strategic move on his part.

TOOLS YOU NEED

▶ When sending paper copies of your resume it's important to print them on good-quality paper. Invest in white, off-white, or ivory paper that has a watermark, a weight between sixteen and twenty-five pounds, and at least 25 percent cotton fiber. Fold your resume (neatly, in thirds) so it fits into a 4⅛" × 9½" envelope or mail it (flat) in a 9" × 12" envelope. Don't forget to include your return address and sufficient postage on the envelope.

How to Submit Your Resume Online

There are a variety of ways to submit your resume online. Options include applying for job postings you see on **job banks**, submitting your resume to apply to job postings you find on company Web sites, and posting your resume so employers can find it, and can find you.

The most important thing you need to do is to follow directions. I frequently get resumes from people who think that I can help them find a job. My About.com site specifically notes that I am not in a position to hire, or to review resumes or cover letters. You wouldn't think that reading and following the directions would be hard, but it seems to be for many people!

When employers say that they prefer that you apply directly via the job site where you find the job ad, do so. It's appropriate to follow up on your application using e-mail or by calling. In fact, it's a good job search strategy to check whether your application has been received and to ask whether the employer needs more information. However, the first step should be to submit your resume the way the employer wants to receive it.

In some cases you will have a choice. Here's an example of a sample job posting: A professional services firm is seeking an administrative assistant to work in their corporate headquarters. Send resume to *abc@xyc.com* or apply online by clicking the "Apply Now" button.

If you use the "Apply Now" feature, the system will automatically send the resume you have stored in your account to the company. Or you can upload a customized version of your resume that you have created to apply for this job and send that instead. You will also be able select or upload a cover letter to include with your application.

When there is a choice, I recommend sending the resume yourself via e-mail. When you do, you will be able to customize

TOOLS YOU NEED

▶ The Privacy Rights Clearinghouse's tips (www .privacyrights.org) for job seekers who post their resumes online are important to read. Suggestions include reading the Web site's privacy policy, being able to delete your resume, not including references, limiting the personal information you include, and never divulging financial data. There is also advice on how to safeguard your social security number. Additional advice on how to investigate and select a resume writing service is also included.

the subject line of your e-mail message by listing the job title and where you found the listing. You will also be able to send a personal message to the hiring manager. Plus, you will have a record of your correspondence so you can follow up on your submission.

Apply online via company Web sites. Not all companies, especially smaller ones, post on the major job sites. Rather, they list job openings only on their company Web site. In some cases, they get more than enough applicants without advertising. In others, recruiting budgets are limited and they don't want the additional expense of paying for job listings.

Most major companies do list jobs on their Web site, even if they post on job banks. So, if you have a particular employer in mind, check out their Web site. The URL is typically the company name or a slight variation followed by dot com (for example, fidelity.com). Searching Google by company name is another way to find Web addresses. Once you're at the company site, check the "About Us" section. That's typically where job openings are listed.

Some employers have recruiting systems in place and will want you to create an account, just like you did for the job sites. You will be able to post your resume online for human resources personnel to view and submit your resume for specific job openings. You may also be able to apply via e-mail for openings.

For example, if you are interested in applying online for jobs at Wal-Mart, you will need to register and create an account. Registered users can apply online for jobs that interest them and sign up to receive job alerts by e-mail advising them of job postings that match their preferences.

JPMorganChase is another example. Their job postings are on a dedicated, secure Web site at https://careers.jpmorganchase.com.

ELSEWHERE ON THE WEB

▶ A resume-posting service can help you get your resume online if you're short on time. Resume Rabbit (www.resumerabbit.com) and similar services will post your resume to many job sites for a fee. In this case, you fill out a simple five-minute form and your resume is posted to over seventy-five job sites. In addition, you can log in to your account to get a list of where your resume is posted, plus a list of your user names and passwords.

I've heard about resume-blasting services. What exactly are they, and are they something I should pay for?

▶ I get many inquiries from visitors to my About.com site who have the same question. There's a difference between resume posting, where a service will upload your resume to many job sites at once for you, and resume blasting. Resume blasting sends your resume to hundreds or thousands of recruiters or employers via e-mail. Unfortunately, in many cases, unsolicited e-mail like that ends up being trashed instead of read. I wouldn't recommend spending money on a resume-blasting service.

Job seekers are encouraged to create a job profile in order to receive e-mail notification about job opportunities and to submit resume information into the employment database, which company recruiters search for candidates.

Take the time to make sure that you are submitting your resume to employers, and to jobs, for which you are qualified. I can't count the number of resumes I've received from candidates when I don't have any job openings or when they are not even remotely qualified for the job. Given the amount of e-mail most people get today, all you are doing is wasting the employer's time—and your own time.

How to Send Your Resume via E-mail

Many smaller employers don't have the technology in place, or the resources, to set up online recruiting software systems. Others prefer to receive all the resumes in a similar format or prefer that all the resumes be sent to a specific recruiting contact or to a general hiring e-mail box (for example, jobs@company.com).

When the instructions in the job postings say to e-mail your resume, follow these tips to make sure you do send it correctly.

First of all, send the resume from the e-mail account you are using for your job search. That way, you will receive a response at the e-mail address you are checking frequently.

Make sure you fill in the subject line of the message. Use the job title, and the job ID if there is one, as the subject. For example, if you're applying for an Administrative Assistant job that the company lists as Job ID 012345, the subject of your message should read "Administrative Assistant, Job ID 012345".

Set up an e-mail signature that includes your name, phone number(s), and e-mail address. Even though your e-mail address is included in the "From" section of your message, it's good to include it again in your signature so the employer can refer to it.

If a cover letter is requested, include it in the body of your e-mail message. Attach your resume to the message formatted as a Microsoft Word file (with a .doc extension).

Don't fill out the "To" section of your message yet. You're going to send the message to yourself first in order to test it to make sure that it looks, and reads, the way you want it to. Once you receive a copy of the e-mail and it's perfect, you can resend it to the employer.

When you receive the e-mail message you send to yourself, check both the e-mail message itself and the attachment. Proofread and check for formatting errors. Edit as necessary to make sure everything is perfect.

After you are sure both the e-mail message and your resume are in order, send the message to the e-mail address listed in the job posting (you will be able to "send as new" or "send again" in your e-mail software). You're less likely to make a mistake if you copy and paste the e-mail address from the job posting into the e-mail message, rather than typing it. It's easier to make a mistake when you're retyping.

Copy yourself on the message by entering your e-mail address into the Bcc: (blind carbon copy) field. That way you will have a copy of exactly what you sent and a confirmation that it was sent to the employer.

Do check your e-mail to make sure that the message went through. If, for some reason, the message bounces you will receive an "undeliverable" message in your e-mail inbox. If that happens, double-check to make sure you have correctly entered the e-mail address where you are sending your resumes and try again.

ELSEWHERE ON THE WEB

▶ Sometimes you will need to send a text (unformatted resume). Monster's article on how to e-mail a text resume (http://resume.monster.com/print/?article=/articles/email/index.asp) explains how to create a plain text (ASCII) resume, how to test to make sure the file is converted properly, and provides step-by-step instructions on how to make sure that your message is formatted correctly. The article also includes tips to make sure your resume isn't garbled and isn't discarded by the employers to whom you send it.

Get Linked

*At my Job Searching site on **ABOUT**.com, you can find more information on the topics I've discussed in this chapter. Check out the following links.*

RESUME SAMPLES

These resume examples will give you a good sampling of resumes for a variety of employment situations. There are samples for job seekers looking for internships and summer jobs, for entry-level candidates, and for midlevel and experienced professionals.

 http://about.com/jobsearch/resumesample

RESUME AND COVER LETTER GUIDE

This guide provides resume-writing assistance and includes advice on how to write a resume, how to choose a resume-writing service, as well as formatting, styles, printing, and resume-writing tips and techniques.

 http://about.com/jobsearch/resumeguide

TEN TIPS FOR AN INTERVIEW-WINNING RESUME

Do you want your resume to shine in the eyes of the employer you want to attract? Follow these ten tips to create an interview-winning resume that is head and shoulders above the crowd.

 http://about.com/jobsearch/10resumetips

Chapter 4

Writing Cover Letters

Why Your Cover Letter Must Be Customized

Do you need to send a cover letter with your resume? Well, it's not an absolute requirement, but it is probably what will make the difference when it comes to your resume ending up in the "no" pile or the "interview" pile.

John, a visitor to my About.com site, wrote to me because he had sent out hundreds of resumes. He didn't understand why he wasn't getting any calls from employers. The problem was that he hadn't taken the time to write cover letters to send with his resume. When he started sending cover letters too, he ended up getting interviews—and a job that was just perfect for him.

Like your resume, a cover letter only gets seconds to make an impression. Therefore, you need to get the employer's attention fast. In order to get your cover letter noticed, you will need to customize it. That means taking the time to inform the employer about how well your credentials match the qualifications listed for the position for which you are applying.

I'm struggling with writing cover letters. How can I get help?

▶ Don't be discouraged if writing cover letters seems like a challenge. They aren't easy, even for people with lots of experience writing them. If you're a college graduate, check with your career office to see if they can review your cover letters for you. If not, review samples to get an idea of what an effective cover letter looks like. There are also companies like ResumeEdge (www.resumeedge.com) that will write cover letters for you, for a fee.

When you use your cover letter to demonstrate to the hiring manager that you have what she's looking for, you will definitely enhance your chances of getting called for an interview. Your cover letter shouldn't duplicate what you have on your resume. Rather, use your cover letter to highlight your relevant skills and to let the employer know why you are a strong candidate for employment.

The purpose of writing cover letters is to interpret the facts on your resume, to pitch your experience and skills to a prospective employer, and to add a personal touch to your candidacy for employment. It's often your first contact with an employer, so it's critical to make a good impression.

Keep in mind that you only have a brief amount of time, and space on the page, to make that impression on the employer. That's why customized cover letters are so important. No employer wants to read more than a page; the hiring manager wants to know right away why you are a strong candidate.

Don't send form letters. Sending a generic letter to every employer you can find is a waste of time, for a couple of reasons. If the company doesn't have job openings, your resume will end up being filed away. In fact, some employers only accept applications for advertised openings and don't even keep resumes on file. It's easier to review resumes and cover letters that come in response to a specific job posting than it is to search resumes and follow up with candidates who applied in the past to see if they are still available.

Another reason for not sending form letters is that they are generic. They do not provide the employer with any information on what you can do, why your credentials are important to the company, and why they should consider you for employment. Most employers receive hundreds of applications for every position they post on a major job bank and they don't have the time or the energy to spend (or waste) on mediocre cover letters.

Don't use a standard template for writing a cover letter either. It's different when you're writing a resume. There are only so many ways that you can format employment history and education. However, you will want your cover letters to reflect your personality and your style, without being flamboyant or overselling yourself. Your cover letters should provide the employer with a glimpse of who you are and how you might fit into the company culture, as well as why you are the right person for the job.

How to Write a Customized Cover Letter

There are several types of cover letters that are used depending on why you are contacting the employer. The ones used most often include the following:

- **An application letter** is used to apply for posted job openings.
- **A prospecting letter** is sent when you are inquiring about the possibility of employment, but aren't applying for a specific job opening.
- **A networking letter** is sent to ask someone you know or someone you have been referred to for advice, information, and job search assistance.

Each type of letter can be sent on paper or by e-mail. How you send it depends on what the employer asks for and how fast you need to get in touch.

Your cover letter should include at least three paragraphs. You will want to cover the following points:

- ○ The reason you are writing
- ○ Why you are qualified
- ○ How you will follow up

TOOLS YOU NEED

▶ When you need help writing cover letters, and we sometimes do even if we've had a lot of practice writing letters, there are a variety of good cover letter books that will help you with the process. See my Top Picks (http://about.com/jobsearch/coverletterbooks) for books on cover letter writing and products that will give you a hand. The list also includes information on a service that can assist you with writing cover letters if you really need help.

Review this sample job posting, then take a look at how the job seeker customized her cover letter to show how her qualifications matched what the employer was seeking.

Editor: Responsible for writing, editing, and proofreading print and online copy. Develop editorial standards for print and online publication. Hire and oversee freelance writers, reporters, design team, and editorial staff, working on daily online news Web site and weekly newsletter. Assign and edit freelance copy and manage freelancers. Must enjoy working on multiple projects.

The following letter reflects the qualifications listed in the job posting:

Dear Hiring Manager,

I am writing to express my interest in the Editor position advertised on Monster.com. My unique combination of creative talent, technical expertise, and experience managing both people and projects makes me the right person to help your team thrive.

I have a great deal of experience managing creative people and motivating them to create copy. I am also responsible for hiring, training, and supervising editorial and administrative staff, as well as freelance writers.

I have developed editorial standards for style and quality that are used by the editorial and writing teams. In addition, I have not only managed editors and writers, but have written numerous newsletters, headlines, and other copy under tight deadlines.

I would be thrilled to use my diverse talents to help your team. My resume is enclosed. If I can provide you with any

ELSEWHERE ON THE WEB

▶ When you want to inquire about job openings, you will need a letter that will impress the employer, because the company may not necessarily have a current opening. You will also need to pitch why the company should be interested in you. Check out About.com Job Searching Technical Guide's collection of sample inquiry letters at http://about.com/jobsearchtech/inquiryletters.

further information on my background and qualifications, please let me know. I look forward to hearing from you.

Sincerely,

Signature

As you can see, the job seeker took the time to carefully review the job posting. She then showed the employer why she was qualified for the job—and why she should get an interview. The employer can quickly and clearly see why the candidate appears to have the qualifications for the job.

Notice that I said "appears" to have the qualifications. Some candidates embellish their cover letters in order to get an interview. The problem with overselling yourself is that the employer is going to find out as soon as you sit down for an interview that you don't have the right skills. You'll be out of contention for the position anyway, regardless of how wonderful your cover letter sounded.

If you aren't qualified for the job, don't spend time writing a cover letter that sounds like you are. Instead, spend the time applying for jobs that do fit your qualifications, or work on improving your skills so that you will be qualified in the future.

A well-written cover letter has several parts. The first part of your cover letter is the contact section. It should include your name, address, phone number(s), and e-mail address. Double-check the information for accuracy. If you have a typo in your phone number or e-mail address, the employer isn't going spend any time trying to track you down. Next, list the date you are writing the letter.

If you know the employer contact information, include it in your cover letter:

ELSEWHERE ON THE WEB

▶ When you're writing letters to network with contacts, rather than applying for specific job openings, you will want to write letters that are different in content and tone. Monster's article on Networking 101 (http://resume.monster.com/articles/networking) provides help with who to contact, what to write, how to sound professional and friendly, as well as how to ask for help.

- Contact name
- Contact job title
- Company
- Street address
- City, state, and zip code

Include a salutation, but don't make it too personal. When applying for a job, "Dear Jill" is not appropriate, even if you know the person to whom you are writing. Rather, start your letter with "Dear Ms. Smith."

Many employers don't list a contact person in the job posting on purpose. They don't want phone calls or e-mails, so they advertise the job without listing a contact. If you can find a contact person by researching the company on the Web, write directly to that person. If not, write "Dear Hiring Manager."

The first paragraph of your letter should include information on why you are writing. If you have a contact at the company, this is a good place to mention it. Also note the position that you are applying for and where you noticed it. If you found a job posting in your local newspaper, say so. For example, write: "I am interested in the Marketing Assistant position recently advertised in the *Times Union*."

Next, describe what you have to offer the employer. Either use bullets to highlight your qualifications or write several short paragraphs that describe your skills and how they match what the company is seeking. This is where you need to sell the employer on why the hiring manager should interview you. Don't repeat your resume. Instead, highlight the appropriate experience and abilities from your resume to impress upon the employer that you are a strong candidate.

If you are applying for different positions at the same employer, send separate cover letters and resumes for each position. They will probably be screened separately and it will save the hiring manager from making copies of your correspondence to pass along to different departments.

Here's an example of a cover letter that includes a list of the job requirements mentioned in the help-wanted ad, followed by the candidate's experience:

Key Holder Requirements:
- Assist the management team in all aspects of store operations, including sales, customer service, payroll, inventory, receiving, and visual merchandising
- Assist managers by opening and closing store and by scheduling store staff
- Encourage exceptional customer service

My Skills and Experience:
- Assist with store operations, including sales, payroll, scheduling, reports, and inventory management
- Place orders to restock merchandise and handle receiving of products
- Extensive work with visual standards and with the merchandising of high-ticket items
- Provide excellent customer service to all clientele, including scheduling private shopping appointments with high-end customers

As you can see, the candidate itemized the job requirements, then constructed his resume to match his skills to those requirements.

It is important to be consistent when describing your background. When writing about your current position, use the present tense. When writing about positions you previously held, use past tense. That way, the employer is clear as to what you are doing and what you have done. Inconsistencies and omissions are a red flag to a prospective employer.

Finish your cover letter with a final paragraph thanking the employer for considering you for the position. Ask if there is any other information you can provide and reiterate that you are available for an interview at the employer's convenience.

Also, if you're editing and rewriting an existing cover letter, be very sure that you have changed the contact information, the job title, and the qualifications to match the position for which you are applying. An employer isn't going to readily forgive getting a cover letter addressed to a different company or one that mentions a position the company doesn't have available.

One human resources manager told me that the cover letter mistakes that annoy her most are:

- Candidates who tell her that they want to work at ABC Company (which is not her company).
- Candidates who say they are "perfect" for the job without including any reasons why.
- Cover letters that only say, "The enclosed resume is submitted to apply for XYZ position advertised on ABC Web site." Why bother?

What not to include in your cover letters. There are some things that you should not include in your cover letter:

- Don't include personal information like your marital status or date of birth.
- References should not be included in your cover letter.

ELSEWHERE ON THE WEB

▶ The question of whether or not to include salary information in your cover letter comes up often. If the employer specifically asks for your salary history, definitely include it. If the employer asks for your salary requirements, include a range. That said, there are differing opinions on what to include. ResumeMagic's article at www.resumagic.com/cover _letters6.html explains the issues, pro and con, of listing salary and gives examples on how best to address them.

- Don't send a photo unless you are applying for a modeling or acting position, for example, and the employer requests it.

The employer has no need to know personal and confidential information. In fact, employers would rather not know it. They want to judge all candidates on an equal playing field without considering personal characteristics.

In addition to pitching your candidacy for employment, you can also use your cover letter to explain gaps in your resume. For example, if you took some time off from work to raise a family or to return to school, mentioning it in your cover letter is a good way to alert the employer as to why there is an interruption in your work history. You can also let the employer know that you are returning to the work force and are willing and able to commit to employment.

How to Mail Your Cover Letter

To get a cover letter ready to mail, proofread it, then have a friend proofread it again before you print the final version. One typo or grammatical error is one too many and may be enough to get your cover letter rejected.

Use a good-quality ink jet or laser printer so that your letters look like they have been printed professionally. Ink jet printers are available in office supply and department stores for under $50, while laser printers start at about $250. Have extra ink cartridges on hand so you don't run out of ink in the middle of getting a cover letter and resume ready to mail. Also have envelopes, postage, and other office supplies on hand.

Choose a font that matches what you used on your resume. Once you include a cover letter, your resume and letter become a package, and you want the hiring manager to view them that way.

ASK YOUR GUIDE

How do I find contact information to send personalized cover letters? It's usually not listed in the job posting.

▶ I'm asked this question a lot on my About.com Job Searching site, because I recommend sending a personalized cover letter whenever possible. There are several strategies you can use to get the information. Visit the company Web site and check the "About Us" section for a list of staff. Use a directory like Hoovers (www.hoovers .com) to search by company name, then click on People for a contact list. If need be, make a phone call to find out who the hiring manager is.

The formatting, the fonts you use, and the look and feel of your documents need to be consistent.

Use plain paper (copy paper) to print the drafts of your cover letter. When you are sure it's perfect, print the final version on good-quality bond paper that matches your resume (white, off-white, or ivory). Print your cover letters on standard-size 8.5" × 11" paper. Using off-size paper or odd colors won't impress any prospective employer.

Don't forget to personally sign your cover letter and also remember to enclose your resume with your cover letter.

If the employer asks for other materials, like a writing sample or transcript, enclose them also. If you don't include the materials that the employer requests, your cover letter and resume will end up in the "no" pile for a couple of reasons. First of all, you didn't follow the instructions. Secondly, the employer isn't going to take the time to follow up with you to request the materials you forgot to include. Unless you are truly unique, there will be too many other candidates who did follow the directions for every job that is posted.

Don't staple your cover letter to your resume. Place your cover letter on top of your resume so the person who opens the envelope sees that first.

Here's a checklist you can use to make sure your cover letter is ready to go:

- ○ Company name, job title, and contact person's name are correct
- ○ Salutation is correct
- ○ Your contact information is accurate
- ○ Writing is concise, clear, and focused
- ○ Cover letter contains action verbs
- ○ Your qualifications are tied to the job

- Letter has been spell checked and proofread
- You have thanked the employer for considering you
- Letter is signed
- Envelope is sealed
- Envelope contains your return address and sufficient postage

You will make a good impression, especially if you have other attachments, by sending your cover letter and resume flat in a 9" × 12" envelope. Also, the employer may want to scan your documents. If you use a smaller envelope, fold your cover letter and resume neatly into thirds.

Take the time to print a mailing label with the employer's contact information. Print a supply of labels with your name and address to have on hand so that you get your materials in the mail right away. Be sure to put sufficient postage on the envelope.

As I've mentioned before, there is no need for gimmicks to make an impression. I have received cover letters and resumes that were sent by overnight delivery, hand delivered by the candidate, and sent by courier service. One person even sneaked into the back door of my office building (bypassing the reception desk) to hand me his resume. In all cases, these special-delivery packages ended up in the same pile of resumes as did the ones sent by regular mail. It wasn't worth the job seeker spending the time or the extra money.

How to Upload Your Cover Letter

You will be able to upload your cover letter to both job banks and company Web sites. At some sites, you will be able to upload multiple copies of your letters. You will also be able to access the letters you have created to edit them or to replace them with a new letter.

TOOLS YOU NEED

▶ In order to write a good cover letter you will need to write creatively. If you don't have a thesaurus available, consider adding Dictionary.com's free toolbar to your browser. The toolbar includes a dictionary, a thesaurus, and a word of the day. You'll be able to look in the thesaurus to help you find words to use and to polish up your cover letter so it sounds professional.

Don't upload your cover letter when you upload your resume. Instead, wait until you have found jobs to apply to, and then upload the cover letter you have created specifically for that position.

The first step in uploading a cover letter is to log in to your account on the site where you want to put your letter. Most job banks allow users to upload at least one copy of their cover letters, usually more.

At sites where you are limited in the number of cover letters you can store, upload a new cover letter or edit your existing one each time you apply for a job. It will take a few minutes, but you will be applying with that customized cover letter that is so critical to effective job searching. It's worth taking the extra time to apply with a letter designed to impress the employer.

Registered users of Monster (www.monster.com), for example, can create up to five letters. There isn't an option to upload your cover letters. Instead, you will write your letter in your word-processing software, then copy and paste it into a text box. Up to 4,000 characters are allowed, and there is an option to spell check. There are also optional entry-level and experienced candidate templates you can use.

Other job banks work in a similar way. Yahoo! HotJobs (http://hotjobs.com) lets you create one cover letter by typing or pasting into a text box. You can edit the letter at any time in order to customize it for specific job postings. America's Job Bank (www.ajb.org) allows you to save five different cover letters, and when you apply for a job you can select which of those cover letters to include.

Follow the directions. CareerBuilder (www.careerbuilder.com) suggests that you only upload Microsoft Word or text-only documents, while other job banks have different restrictions. If your cover letter isn't formatted correctly it will be garbled, so do follow the instructions.

There's a preview option that allows you to view your cover letter before you save it and after you edit it. Take advantage of it so you can see your cover letter the same way that your prospective employer will.

How to Submit Your Cover Letter Online

Submitting your cover letters and your resume online via a job bank is easy. It doesn't get complicated until the company requests you to send it in a different format or you opt for an alternative way of applying.

Each job site will walk you through the directions of how to apply. In most cases there is an "Apply Now" button you can click to automatically submit your materials to the employer.

Sometimes you will be given an option of how to apply. In many cases it will depend on how the employer chooses to receive applications. In one recent job posting on CareerBuilder.com, for example, candidates have two options:

- Apply online with a posted resume
- Apply instantly via e-mail

In the first case, candidates will apply with the resume and cover letter that they have uploaded to CareerBuilder. In the second, clicking on the e-mail button will open a new e-mail message addressed to CareerBuilder with the subject line of the message filled in for you.

A third option is faxing your materials. If you are registered with a participating fax service, you can do that automatically, directly from the job bank's Web site with a simple click of the Fax Now button. If you haven't signed up for the service, and you may not want to if there's a fee, there should be a fax number in the job

WHAT'S HOT

▶ The most popular content on my About.com site is my Cover Letters Samples section (http://about.com/ jobsearch/coverletter samples). You will find samples for a wide variety of positions, including sample letters to submit online, in many career fields. Use the samples to get ideas about what to write, then write your own cover letters that match your skills to the requirements listed in the job posting.

posting. Fax your cover letter and your resume to the number listed in the ad.

Again, follow the directions in the job posting. If the employer says to include a specific job title or code in your fax, list it. They may be tracking where applications are coming from, and that code will give them the information they need. It will also let them know what job you are applying for if they have many openings.

I prefer sending my e-mail directly to the employer when it's listed as an option. The reason is because I want to make sure that the e-mail actually went, I want to make sure I have a copy of what was sent, and I use my copy of the message as a reminder to myself to follow up.

There are benefits to using the "Apply Now" button though. The hiring manager will be expecting to receive applications online, so the materials will be sure to get to the right person. There is also a greater danger of your message ending up in a spam mailbox when it's sent from a personal e-mail account, especially if you forget to include information in the subject line of your message. Just about every message I receive without a subject ends up in my junk e-mail folder.

When you apply online the employer will be able to view it in the company's online account at any time. Plus, you will have a record of the jobs you have applied to using the Apply Online button.

Monster, for example, has an Apply History section that shows you all the jobs you have applied for in the past eighteen months. It also lists which resume you used to apply to each job.

Another benefit to using online application systems is the fact that all your application materials, including all the versions of your resume and cover letter that you have created, are available from any computer. You can access everything you have on file at the job site by logging into your job seeker account.

How to Send Your Cover Letter via E-mail

Some job postings will ask you to send your cover letter and resume by e-mail. The employer will typically specify how you should send them.

One option when sending your cover letter by e-mail is to paste your letter into the e-mail message, rather than writing directly in your e-mail. Write the cover letter in your word-processing software so you can readily edit and proof it. Don't forget to spell check and to check your grammar, capitalization, and formatting. They are just as important in e-mail cover letters as they are in paper cover letters sent by mail.

Make sure you include a signature with your e-mail address and phone number. Include the title of the position you are applying for in the subject line of your message.

Also be sure that your e-mail address is correct. I have received e-mails from visitors to my About.com site that I spent time responding to, only to find out that I couldn't reach them because they didn't have a valid e-mail address or they had a typo in their address.

If the e-mail you send to a prospective employer bounces, they aren't going to try to figure out what your correct e-mail address should be. You will be out of contention for the job.

If the job posting asks you to send an attachment, send your cover letter as an MS Word document or in a different format (PDF or RTF, typically) if that is what the employer requests.

It's easy to attach a file to your e-mail message. When the message you are writing is open, click on Message, then Send File (or Insert File) at the top of the screen. You will be prompted to find the file on the hard drive of your computer. Open the directory where you have saved your cover letter, then click on the file name to attach it to the message.

TOOLS YOU NEED

▶ The About.com Job Searching Resumes and Cover Letters that Work Class (http://about.com/jobsearch/onlineresumeclass) is a free online class. It provides step-by-step instructions for writing cover letters that will get your job applications noticed. You will receive lessons via e-mail and will be able to ask questions as you progress through the class material. The class covers all facets of writing and submitting your cover letter to employers.

There are several alternatives for sending your cover letter. It's more up to the employer than it is you as to how you are going to send your cover letter and resume.

Employers request many different types of formats and attachments. Here are some examples:

- Please attach a current version of your resume as a Word attachment.
- For consideration, please e-mail *abc@xyz.com* and attach your resume.
- E-mail your application to *abc@xyz.com*. In the e-mail, briefly describe your experiences and qualifications, and attach your resume in any PC compatible format.
- Please do not attach resume. Click below (the Apply Now button) to apply.
- You will need to attach PDF samples to be considered.

As you can see there are lots of different ways that employers want to receive materials from interested candidates. Take the time to read, and understand, what the company wants before you click the Send button in your e-mail program.

Before you send your cover letter to the employer, first send the message to yourself to test that the formatting works. Once the message and attachments you have included appear to be in order, resend the message to the employer.

Every time you send your cover letter by e-mail send a copy to yourself using the Bcc: (blind carbon copy field) in your e-mail program. That way you will have a record of all your job search correspondence.

You can use your copy of the e-mail message as a reminder to contact the employer if you don't hear from them in a timely manner. (Create a file in your e-mail box titled "follow up" and save it there.)

In a similar vein, if you use the Apply Online button, save a copy of the job posting so you can follow up if need be. Either save the job to the Saved Jobs section of your job seeker account or copy and paste the job ad and save it in a file on your computer.

Use caution when sending networking letters. When sending a networking letter, be careful that it goes to the right person. I have lost count of the number of people who have sent unsolicited cover letters and resumes to my About.com Job Searching e-mail address. Sometimes they send attachments without even writing anything in the e-mail. Other times, they ask me to find them a job doing something or doing anything.

At the least, if you are writing to someone who you think will be able to help you with your job search, explain who you are, why you are writing, and why you think that person might be able to help you. Otherwise, those unsolicited letters are only going to end up being trashed.

ELSEWHERE ON THE WEB

▶ Sending a follow-up letter to reaffirm your interest in the position is a good strategy. Employers typically receive hundreds of cover letters and resumes, so sending a follow-up letter is a good way to remind the hiring manager that you exist and you're an excellent candidate for the employer. Check out the selection of follow-up samples on CareerLab at www.careerlab.com/letters/chap14.htm for good information on when and what to write.

Get Linked

Here's some more information from my **ABOUT**.com *Job Searching site that will help you write compelling cover letters and secure an interview.*

CUTTING-EDGE COVER LETTERS

This offers advice and suggestions on how to make your cover letter the one that is chosen out of the many letters employers get for each job they advertise.

↗ http://about.com/jobsearch/cuttingedge

E-MAIL COVER LETTERS

This step-by-step guide will walk you through the process of creating and sending an e-mail cover letter. It includes advice on what to include, as well as what not to do when sending letters by e-mail.

↗ http://about.com/jobsearch/emailcoverletter

HOW TO WRITE COVER LETTERS

This resource will teach you how to write and format an effective cover letter and also includes samples of various types of cover letters.

↗ http://about.com/jobsearch/writecoverletter

Chapter 5

Job Applications

Preparing a Job Application

You may be surprised at how often, and when, you are required to fill out a job application. Job seekers expect to fill out an application when applying for jobs at retail stores, like Target or Wal-Mart, for example. However, some companies require every candidate for employment, regardless of the job level, to complete a job application. This can be the case even if you have already submitted a resume.

Be prepared to complete a job application either as part of the initial application process or when you are interviewing. It's important to have all the information that you need to complete the application ready to include, because it may require more information than you have on your resume.

The application for employment could be a paper application or you could be asked to complete an online job application. In both cases, it is important to fill out the application completely. Don't leave anything blank or leave any information off the form.

I'm applying for senior management positions. Why am I being asked to fill out job applications?

▶ I'm frequently asked this question on my About.com site. Many job seekers are surprised to learn that they have to fill out an application, regardless of what position they applied for. It could be an online application or a paper one, but the employer wants consistent data on file for all applicants. It's also a way to get your verification, by ink or electronic signature, that the information you are supplying is accurate.

You will be asked to list your contact information, your employment history, and your education. You may be asked to include the skills and qualifications you have that are related to the job you want. In addition, you may be asked when you are available to work and whether you have been convicted of a crime.

Never write "see resume" when you are asked to complete a job application. The company wouldn't be asking you to fill out an application if it wasn't necessary, for one reason or another. At one company where I worked, we required all applicants to fill out a paper application for employment. One candidate for a sales manager position took offense. He thought he was too important for our application process and believed he shouldn't have to comply. His complaints took him out of consideration for the job. We thought that if the candidate was this difficult when applying for a job, he wouldn't be cooperative and a team player if we hired him. It isn't a smart move for any employer to hire someone who will be difficult to work with.

Applicant tracking systems are used by many companies.
Job applications can be completed the old-fashioned way—on paper. Or, the company may utilize a hiring system, which includes a job application. It depends on the technology utilized by the company.

For example, some companies use **applicant tracking systems**, which allow them to manage the entire recruiting process, from receiving applications to hiring employees. The information in the database is used for everything from screening candidates to checking references to completing new-hire paperwork. These systems are also used for regulatory compliance and to track candidate sources. Sourcing is how the candidates got to the job posting, from a search on the Web, from a job site like Monster, by going directly to the company Web site, or from reading a help-wanted ad in the newspaper, for example.

Once applicants upload their background information into the database it can be transferred from one component to another. For example, company recruiters can review the applications, the hiring manager can schedule interviews, and human resources personnel can use the same information to put individuals on the payroll once they are hired. These integrated systems streamline the recruiting and application process and make it much easier for companies to handle hiring.

In fact, more and more companies, especially larger ones, are no longer accepting paper resumes. They only want to receive online applications. According to Taleo (www.taleo.com), the number of companies accepting only online applications has increased significantly over the last five years. In 2000, only 27 percent of the Fortune 500 companies required online applications. By 2005, 77 percent of the Fortune 500 companies required applicants to apply online.

The same holds true for smaller companies as well. Many don't want to manage paper anymore. It's easier to have technology that will manage their recruiting programs than it is to review, handle, and file paper resumes and applications. It's also much easier to track and manage a database of applicants than it is to review piles of paper applications.

Review tips for preparing job applications. The following tips will help you complete your job applications correctly:

- Write neatly and legibly (printing is preferable to cursive).
- Request a new copy of the application form and start again if you make a mistake.
- Use black ink (no fancy purple gel pens!).
- Complete every section of the application.

ASK YOUR GUIDE

Will a company really check everything I put on my job application?

▶ In a word, yes. I get many inquiries about whether it makes sense to leave items off job applications. For example, I'm asked about leaving off bad jobs, criminal convictions, and poor educational experiences. The problem with doing so is that up to 80 percent of employers conduct background checks. The Privacy Rights Clearinghouse (www.privacyrights .org) has information on what employers can check and your privacy rights when job seeking.

- Proofread your application, checking for typos and gram-
  matical errors.
- List jobs and education in reverse chronological order (most
  recent first).
- Check with references before you use them.
- If this is your first job search, use personal references.
- Sign and date your application.

If you have a photocopier available, bring a copy of the application home. Copy the application, then fill out all the information
you need on the copy. That way, if you make a mistake you haven't
made it on the original. Once the job application copy is perfect,
carefully write the information on the original application.

What's most important is to follow the directions. If the company says to apply in person, don't call or e-mail. When the job
posting says to mail your application, do so. Don't call or stop in. If
the job listing says to apply online at the company Web site, do it.

Sometimes job seekers think that applying creatively can help
their candidacy. It doesn't. In fact, it usually has the opposite effect.
So, take the time to carefully review the requirements for the jobs for
which you are applying. When you aren't qualified, move on to the
next job listing. Carefully read that job listing to determine how the
employer wants to receive applications, keeping in mind that there
isn't one standard way that companies want candidates to apply.

Every company has a different process, and even companies that
use online systems don't all use the same system. So, every time you
apply for a job you will have a slightly different experience. However,
the information that you will be asked is usually standard information
that you can prepare in advance. That's the one thing that is consistent about applying online; there are few variations in the information you are asked to provide. What's different is the way you will get
the information into the employee's recruiting system.

Every employer wants to know your employment history, your educational background, and your skills and qualifications. They may need to know why you left your last job and what you expect to earn. In all cases, the employer will want to know where you live and how to contact you, typically by phone and by e-mail, if you have an e-mail address.

Review Sample Job Applications

Before you apply for jobs, it's a good idea to review sample job applications so you're not surprised by the information you are asked to provide. In addition to giving you a good overview of what you will need to put on your application, samples can also be used to itemize the information you will need to fill in. If you have all the information filled out on a sample application in advance, it will be much easier to fill out actual job applications when applying for employment.

The same holds true when you apply for jobs online. If you have a list of all the information you need next to the computer you are using, you will be able to efficiently move through the online application process. The last thing you want when you're trying to submit an application is to waste time trying to remember when you worked where and how much you were paid. Gather all the information you need so you can get your applications completed fast.

The following is a sample of a job application. It's important to review all the information you will need to complete so you are prepared in advance.

Personal Information:
- ○ Name
- ○ Address, city, state, zip code
- ○ Phone number

- Social Security number
- Are you eligible to work in the United States?
- If you are under age eighteen, do you have an employment certificate?
- Have you been convicted of a felony within the last five years?

Education and Experience:
- School(s) attended, degrees, graduation date
- Skills and qualifications

Work History (for current and prior positions):
- Employer
- Address, phone, e-mail
- Supervisor
- Your job title and responsibilities
- Salary
- Dates worked
- Reason for leaving
- Permission to contact previous employer

References:
- Name
- Job title, company
- Address, phone, e-mail

Job/Availability:
- Job title
- Days available
- Hours available
- Date you are available to start work

At the end of a job application there is usually a certification that you must sign and date. A certification will usually sound something like this:

I authorize the verification of all the information listed above. I certify that the information contained in this employment application is accurate. I understand that false information may be grounds for not offering employment or for immediate termination of employment at any point in the future.

By signing the certification you are attesting to the truth of everything you have written on the job application. If the application is online, you will click a box to acknowledge that you are submitting complete and accurate information. That checked box will count as your signature.

The certification is important because if you deliberately omit something from your application (like a job you got fired from or a school you dropped out of), it is, at the least, grounds not to hire you. Even worse, if the employer finds out at any time in the future that you lied, even by omission, you could be fired.

Some of the other information required by the application may necessitate you providing additional information. For example, if you say you have an employment certificate (working papers), the employer may ask for a copy. If you have been convicted of a crime, state laws vary as to what the company can legally ask you, but you may be asked to provide additional information.

Another important part of the job application to consider is the "Permission to Contact Your Employer" section. If you are currently employed, your boss may not know that you are job searching and you certainly don't want him to get a phone call to check your references.

ELSEWHERE ON THE WEB

▶ The sample job application form (www.state.hi.us/dlir/rs/loihi/CKJSA/PRTJBAPP.HTM) covers just about everything you may need to fill out when applying for jobs. Print out a copy, fill it out, and use it as a guide when filling out other job applications. That way, you will have all the information you need ready to go.

When that's the case, check "no" and advise the hiring manager that you would appreciate your boss not being contacted until you are in serious contention for the position. That way you can protect your current employment status as long as necessary.

How to Apply Online

One of the benefits of applying online for a job is the speed at which your application is received. Aimee, a visitor to my About.com site, wrote to me because she was amazed at how quickly she got a response from an employer. She applied online early one morning. She received a phone call to schedule an interview within an hour of applying. She interviewed after lunch and got a job offer later that same afternoon. What helped expedite the process was the fact that Aimee was checking the Web site frequently for new job postings. As a result, she was ready to apply as soon as she saw a position that was a good fit. The employer wanted to fill the job fast, so it worked out perfectly for both of them.

When applying for employment via a job site like HotJobs or America's Job Bank, the process of how you apply is directed by how the employer wants to receive applications. First, you will need to log in to the account you created when you posted your resume and cover letter. If you haven't created an account, you won't be able to apply for jobs automatically until you do.

Once you are logged in, you will see a Find Jobs button or a Search Jobs button. Use that to locate jobs in the industries and location(s) that interest you. When you search, you will generate a list of job postings. Review the listings. When you find a job you would like to apply for, read the job description carefully. The employer will tell you exactly how to apply and the system will step you through the process.

One option is to apply directly online. If the employer is accepting applications that way, you will see a button that says Apply

Now, Click Here to Apply, or something similar. Click the button and you will be prompted to apply, typically by choosing one of the resumes and cover letters that you have uploaded earlier. If you haven't yet uploaded a resume, you will be able to choose a resume from your computer to use. You will save the resume, then use it to apply for the job.

Your resume will be sent directly to the employer by the job bank. It will also be available for the employer to view online. At some sites, you will have a list of the jobs you have applied for, so you can check the status of your applications.

Alternatively, you will be sent directly (via the same Apply Now or Click Here button) to the employer's Web site to complete an online application. Or you may be asked to e-mail or fax your resume, cover letters, and other requested information directly to the company.

In all cases, the most important thing to do is to follow the instructions in the job posting. Otherwise, your application may not be considered. If the job posting asks for additional material, like a cover letter, a transcript, or a writing sample, be sure to include that too.

Some employers do not consider applicants who don't follow all the directions or who do not include requested application materials. It will even say that in some job listings. For example, one company says, "For consideration, e-mail your resume, writing sample, and salary requirements." If you forget to include something, resend your application materials with everything included. The employer isn't going to take the time to contact you to tell you what you neglected to include.

Track your job applications. When you're applying for jobs online at the major job sites, the application process is simple. It's keeping track of where you have applied that can be cumbersome.

WHAT'S HOT

▸ Some companies are now using kiosks rather than paper application systems. Candidates for employment can still visit the company to apply, but they complete an online application in a free-standing booth, or kiosk. Candidates can also apply at kiosks set up in high-traffic public areas like malls or train stations. In addition, some kiosks have searchable job databases, and applicants can apply online for specific job openings.

You don't want to put yourself in a dilemma where you get a call for an interview, but you have no recollection of applying for the job and you don't recall anything about it.

Use the job site's Apply History section to track your applications or set up a spreadsheet to create a list of the job applications you have submitted.

Your spreadsheet should include the following information:

- Job title
- Employer name
- Contact person, if available
- Web site address and e-mail address
- Site where you applied
- How you applied
- The version of your resume and cover letter you submitted
- Date applied

When you are using multiple job sites to search for and apply for jobs, use your browser to help keep track. Internet Explorer users can use the Favorites menu to create a "Job Search" folder. Bookmark all the job sites you are using and add them to the folder. That way it will be easy to manage what sites you are using for your applications.

How to Apply at Company Sites

It can be a little cumbersome, depending on the company, to apply online at company sites. It's much easier to upload your resume at a site like CareerBuilder or Monster and apply via their recruiting system. Unfortunately, not all employers post on the job banks. They don't need to—they have more than enough applicants without ever posting a job anywhere other than on their own company

▶ Spreadsheet software templates are excellent tools for keeping track of your job applications. Microsoft Office Online (http://office .microsoft.com) has Excel templates that you can tweak slightly to use to track your job applications. The Web site also has advice and tips on how to use Excel to manage information in lists, like the list of employment applications you have submitted.

site. In other cases, even if they do list jobs online, they want to receive applications through their own applicant tracking system.

Many sites require users to register, create a user name and password, and build a profile that includes your experience and education. You will need a valid e-mail account to register and a phone number.

On the plus side, if you are interested in working for a specific company, the online systems are terrific. Applicants can select career fields, positions, and geographic areas where they want to work. **Job search agents** will send you new listings that match the criteria you selected by e-mail, and you can apply online for available jobs.

At some companies, recruiters actively review the applicant database to find candidates. That, in and of itself, is a good reason for spending the time to create an account at a company site. There may not be an available position today, but your application is on file so the company can notify you about a job when it becomes available.

In some cases, how you apply depends on the type of job you are applying for. At Wal-Mart, for example, candidates for office positions can apply online, while candidates for employment at Wal-Mart stores must complete and submit a job application at that facility.

At General Electric you can either upload your resume to apply or type in the information. Your cover letter can be typed into a text box. On Home Depot's Careers Web site, job seekers can search for jobs at a specific store location. Once they have found a position that interests them they can create an employment profile and apply online.

Employers in a wide variety of career fields and industries accept online applications. Individuals who are interested in spending time overseas volunteering for the Peace Corps will start the

ELSEWHERE ON THE WEB

▶ If you are applying for a job with the federal government, the application form will be different from the forms used by private companies. Before you apply for a federal job, check to see if you can use a resume or if you can use the Optional Application for Federal Employment—OF 612. If you need the form, you can download it from the Office of Personnel Management at www.opm.gov/forms.

▶ When applying for positions within your company, you may need to complete an internal job application. Your employer will want to know why you are qualified for the new position, what your qualifications are, and why you want to change jobs. The Internal Job Application at http://about.com/human resources/internalapplication will give you a good idea of what you need to know to apply and how to go about applying.

application process by applying online. On the opposite end of the spectrum, job seekers who want to work for the Internal Revenue Service or the FBI can search for jobs and apply online for many openings. Regardless of the industry you want to work in, start the job application process by checking the company Web site for information on how to apply.

Just to add another twist to online job applications, some companies partner with a job site to accept applications. Disney, for example, lists employment information on its careers Web site. When you search, though, it is through Monster's search engine. You can then apply via Monster if you have an existing account or create a new account to submit your application.

As you can see, there are a variety of ways employers want you to submit an application. The best rule is to check the guidelines before you apply. In most cases, instructions for how applications are accepted are listed on the company Web site or in the specific job posting.

One timesaver is to have all the information in your computer. Copy and paste from your resume or create a new document that you can use to copy from to enter your data into the job application form. That's faster than typing, and there's less chance of making a mistake.

Conduct company research. There are Web sites where you can look up companies and get advice and tips on how to apply. Profiles of top companies and Web sites that provide company profiles are available on my About.com site at http://about.com/jobsearch/companyprofiles.

Using company profiles is a good way to find out how the company wants to receive applications, as well as to find companies where you might want to work. Sometimes you can click around a company Web site for quite a while to get to the right section.

These company profiles will get you directly to the right section. Some sites listed, like WetFeet.com and Vault.com, for example, also give you insider information and hiring tips, as well as basic company information. That's useful to have, especially when the company has an extensive employment process.

In-Person Job Applications

Many employers, especially retail and hospitality establishments, encourage applicants to apply in person. They may have specific days and hours when they accept applications or you may be able to stop by anytime to apply.

An option is to stop by the store or the company to pick up an application. Bring it home, complete it at your leisure, and return to the establishment with a completed application. That's often less stressful than sitting there filling out an application with someone watching over your shoulder.

When you apply in person for a job, it's important to make sure that your job application is presentable.

I have actually received job applications that I couldn't read. It was impossible to follow up with an interview, because I couldn't decipher the phone number or the person's name. If you have trouble writing clearly, ask someone with good handwriting to fill out the application for you.

You also need to dress appropriately when applying for a job in person. How you dress when applying for employment is a reflection of how you will dress for work, so it's important to make a good impression.

I have seen applicants show up in skirts that are way too short, blouses that are way too low-cut, pants that are ripped, and shoes so ancient that they shouldn't have been worn in public, for any reason. I've also seen applicants in stiletto heels, others in running suits, and even job seekers who applied wearing old T-shirts and

ELSEWHERE ON THE WEB

▶ Vault's Company Research Web site (http://vault.com/companies/searchcompanies.jsp) is an excellent resource for finding and researching companies. There is even a Why Work for Us section where featured employers will give you a pitch on why you should go to work for them. There's a Contact Info section for each employer that you can use to apply for job openings. There is also a Message Board where you can ask questions and seek advice about the company.

worn-out jeans—none of which made a good impression. If there is any doubt in your mind about it being appropriate attire, don't wear it. If you have any questions, ask for a second opinion before you start your job search.

What to wear when applying for a job in person:

- Business casual dress, which means khakis and a collared shirt or sweater
- Sensible, closed-toe shoes
- Hair and fingernails must be well groomed
- Minimal makeup, jewelry, and perfume (or cologne)

On a related note, some companies have policies that prohibit employees from having visible tattoos, body piercings (other than earrings), and other body art. I know one student who was told to remove her eyebrow ring and to cover up her small tattoo before starting student teaching. The school thought it was a bad example to set for the children. The student felt discriminated against, and she wasn't the only one who has had that happen. Over 50 percent of the people who responded to a survey on the About.com Tattoo site believed they were discriminated against in their career because of their tattoo.

In most cases, body art policies aren't considered discriminatory as long as they are enforced equally. It could be considered discriminatory, for example, if male employees weren't allowed to wear jewelry but women were.

Unless you are applying for a position where it doesn't matter what piercings or tattoos you have, consider removing some rings and covering up. It will give you a better chance of getting the job.

Be prepared to interview. When you apply for a job in person, be prepared for an interview. Some managers prefer to interview

TOOLS YOU NEED

▶ When you are applying for a job in person, bring a quality leather notepad holder or portfolio with you. Use it to carry a few copies of your resume, a couple of pens, and a list of the information you will need to fill out your job applications. See my Top Picks: Pad Holders and Portfolios at http://about. com/jobsearch/toppicks for a selection of pad holders that will impress, regardless of the position for which you are applying.

applicants immediately, if time permits, rather than calling them to come in for an interview.

Give yourself plenty of time, just in case you do spend time interviewing. It's important to have a brief synopsis of your background that you can discuss, as well as a good idea of when you are available to work. Be honest. If you have baseball practice three times a week and sing in the church choir on Sunday, say so. If you need to pick up your daughter from child care at a specific time each afternoon, mention it.

Employers are often willing to work around your schedule, especially when you are applying for a part-time job. What's important is to let the employer know when you are available and to be able to commit to a schedule. They may be flexible up front, but they won't be as accommodating if you tell them after the fact that the schedule you already committed to isn't feasible.

Also know when you will be able to start a new job. If you are leaving one job to start another one, it's definitely appropriate to let your new employer know you need to give two weeks' notice. If you aren't employed, consider how much time you need to get ready to start a new job, and plan accordingly.

When you apply for jobs in person, you need to be prepared with all the personal data you will need to be considered for employment. Bring the following information with you when you apply in person:

- Contact information
- Social Security number
- Driver's license (if you have one)
- Schools and dates attended
- Names, addresses, and phone number of previous employers
- Dates worked at prior employers
- List of references (name, job title, company, phone)

ELSEWHERE ON THE WEB

▶ What's legal to ask on a job application and what shouldn't you be asked? The overview from New Hampshire Employment Security at www.nhes.state .nh.us/esb/application.htm provides good information about what employers can ask and what they cannot. There is a list of legal questions, as well as lists of illegal and discriminatory job application questions. The site also provides tips on completing your application.

- Days and hours you are available
- Resume (if you have one)
- Notepad and pen

All-Important Follow-Up

Following up, when done correctly, is important when you submit a job application. If you have applied in person, it's simple. When you apply, ask the hiring manager when you might expect to hear about an interview. If you don't hear within that time period, call the manager and ask about your application status. It's also appropriate to make a return visit to the company to check on your application. There could be any number of reasons for a delay, but calling or stopping in will remind the manager that you are interested and motivated to get hired.

Follow-up becomes more complicated when you have applied online either through a job bank or directly on a company's Web site. There may not be a contact person listed with whom you can check. Many companies intentionally don't list a contact person in a job posting, because the company may not want phone calls from applicants.

Many human resources professionals don't have the time to field calls from applicants and would rather applicants didn't call. In fact, some job postings specifically say "No phone calls, please." Others even mention that phone calls will not be returned. If they don't want you to call, don't. Save both yourself and the hiring manager time.

I know that you have probably read that you must follow up to check on the status of your application, but it is best not to if the company requests that you don't. Otherwise, it is a good idea to follow up, but you should do so in the appropriate manner. If you have a contact person at the company, offer to provide additional information and to answer any questions about your application.

WHAT'S HOT

▶ On-the-spot interviews are happening more and more often. So, when you are applying for jobs, be prepared for a quick interview to take place as soon as you hand in your application. You will be asked about your work history and your education. Prepare answers to interview questions, including why you want to work at the company and why you are qualified. You'll make a really good impression if you are prepared for an interview.

That way, you are offering something positive rather than just bugging human resources personnel to see if they have your application. They probably do, and if you applied electronically you may have received a confirmation that your application was received.

When you do follow up, use e-mail rather than phone. I am more likely to respond to an e-mail (it's quicker and simpler to answer) than I am to spend time on the phone with an applicant.

Another option is to use a referral person, if you have one, to put in a good word regarding your application. Anthony, one visitor to my About.com site who was applying for Web designer positions, applied for a position at a local museum. A friend of a friend had a contact there, and she mentioned to the hiring manager the fact that Anthony had applied. She also noted that he was very talented and would make an excellent employee. The hiring manager was thrilled to get the referral, and Anthony's resume moved to the top of the "yes" pile, without him having to pick up the phone, send an e-mail, or do any kind of follow-up.

Follow-up, when done correctly, can enhance your application prospects. However, if you overdo it, you can jeopardize your chances of getting an interview. Hiring managers don't like candidates who they consider too pushy or obnoxious. Repeated inquiries will most likely knock the candidate out of contention.

TOOLS YOU NEED

▶ When you want to follow up, but you don't know what to write, review the sample follow-up letter from the About.com site at http://about.com/jobsearch/follow-up. It reiterates the candidate's interest in the job and offers to provide more information upon the employer's request. When you don't know the hiring manager's name, address the letter to "Dear Hiring Manager." You can send the letter via regular mail or by e-mail.

Get Linked

*Here are some resources from my **ABOUT**.com Job Searching site to assist you in completing job applications and applying for job openings.*

JOB APPLICATION CENTER

This guide to job applications includes how to complete paper, online, and employer direct job applications. It provides step-by-step instructions on how to apply for employment using all methods of application.

↗ http://about.com/jobsearch/jobapplications

EMPLOYMENT APPLICATION OPTIONS

Should you apply online or submit a resume when applying for employment? Which option will get your application noticed? Here are the pros and cons of both alternatives and how to decide what will work best for you.

↗ http://about.com/jobsearch/applicationoptions

SAMPLE JOB APPLICATIONS

Review sample employment applications, including the federal application for employment, sample job application letters, and follow-up letters.

↗ http://about.com/jobsearch/sampleapplications

Chapter 6

Looking for Job Listings

Focus Your Job Search

Focusing your job search means taking the time to target specific types of jobs in certain locations. Why do you need to do that? The reason is that the number of jobs posted online is overwhelming. There is no way you can look at all of them, or even a significant number of them. And you don't want to. Your valuable time is better spent looking for jobs that meet the specific criteria you select and applying for jobs that meet your interests and for which you are qualified.

Take a look at the number of jobs posted on the major job sites to get an idea about why you need to be selective. Though the numbers may vary, currently America's Job Bank has close to 2 million jobs listed, Monster has over 1 million job postings, and CareerBuilder has over 400,000 job listings. That's a lot of jobs. It's too many to weed through without setting up specific search criteria to narrow down the list into a workable number.

Even the niche job sites that focus on a particular type of job or specific location have a lot of listings to look through.

My article on the Top Job Sites at http://about.com/jobsearch/topjobsites is always on the list of content that visitors to my About.com site read most often. It provides information on the top job banks, when to use them, and when to look elsewhere for job postings. There's also advice on how to successfully diversify your job search.

Mediabistro.com, one of my favorite niche sites, has over 1,100 media job postings. Another favorite, Cool Works.com, the summer and **seasonal job** site, has thousands of listings. SnagAJob.com has over 100,000 part-time and hourly job postings.

Company sites can have a lot of listings too. Citigroup's careers Web site currently has over 1,000 jobs listed, while Home Depot and Bank of America also have thousands of open positions. Other companies have many openings too, some in the hundreds, some more. Even when the company doesn't have a huge number of listings, it only takes one to be the right job for you.

It's a competitive job market. In addition to there being a lot of job listings, there is a lot of competition from other job seekers. America's Job Bank has almost 700,000 resumes posted. There's even more resumes—millions—on some of the other sites. Monster has 52 million resumes and over 61 million job seeker accounts!

In addition to those who post resumes, there are candidates who are finding job openings at companies and applying directly. That's lots of competition for every single job that is posted.

The competition is why you shouldn't limit yourself to online job searching. You can spend all day posting your resume and submitting job applications and you may not get the response you would like. In most cases, the reason you don't get contacted isn't your lack of credentials or qualifications; it's because there are so many applicants that the company can afford to be picky.

The competition is also why it is important to use all the job sites, not just the top ones, in your job search. It's also why it's a good idea to integrate traditional job-searching tools, like networking, into your job search. Networking is still the primary way job seekers find jobs, though today it can include networking online and by e-mail, as well as networking in person and on the phone.

How can you focus your job search? The best way to start is to consider geography. Do you want to work in your hometown? Would you prefer to relocate? Or does it make a difference one way or the other? If you are willing to work anywhere, put aside location when you start searching. Instead, focus your search on the type of position that you want or the industry that interests you.

The job sites will let you limit your search to a specific category, and on some sites you can even visit Web pages with listings for specialty users. For example, Monster and CareerBuilder have targeted lists for entry-level job seekers. There are also targeted listings for job seekers interested in health care, hospitality, finance, diversity, and science, just to name a few of the special-interest Web pages. If you are interested in jobs in a specific industry, check the targeted job listings first.

Types of Job Searches

There are a variety of ways you can search for jobs. Options include searching by location, company name, type of job, industry, and/or keyword. You can search by any one item or by any combination of options. The following list is a quick overview of the searches available on most sites:

- City and state or zip code
- Distance from a city
- Company name
- Date posted
- Employment type (full-time, part-time, contractor)
- Industry
- Job category
- Keyword

I know what I want to do. Where should I start looking for jobs?

▶ Don't worry. Everyone gets confused when they start a job search. Even people like me, who have been looking at jobs online for years, can get confused unless they are organized and keep track of their job search. The best way to start is to start small. Don't try to look everywhere at once. Start with one job site and get familiar with how it works by posting your resume and applying for a job or two. Then add another to your list, and so on.

There are also options for viewing the results. You can order the results by date listed (to see the new postings first), by company name, or by location. I usually sort results by date so I can review the most recent job postings first.

Use keywords to search. Another useful job search tool is the keyword option. All the top job sites let users search by keyword. A keyword is a word that is relevant to the job you are seeking. When you search by keyword, all the positions that contain the term you entered will be listed. The reason this is so effective is that a keyword search looks at the entire job posting. The term may not necessarily be listed in the job title or in the description. The search results will include it, regardless of where it appears.

Here are some examples. If I were interested in a customer service manager position in Chicago, I could click on Customer Service as a job category and then narrow down my search by location. However, since I know exactly what I want, because I determined the focus of my job search in advance, I can simply enter my search term and location to get a list of jobs with one click of my mouse.

Running a similar search on Monster worked well too. I decided that I didn't want to work more than ten miles from my hometown. So, I went to Monster's Instant Search, entered my zip code, selected a ten-mile radius, and entered human resources (because I was looking for jobs in human resources) as a keyword. Again, I got a list of jobs that met my criteria with one click of my mouse. The list gave me all the related positions, for example, Human Resources Manager, Human Resources Administrator, and Human Resources Consultant.

The best way to do this is to make a list of keywords relevant to your job search. Use specific keywords to describe what you are looking for. For example, don't just use a general term like *sales*, because it will get you more listings than you need. If you are interested in sales management, use that as a term, or if you are interested in sales representative jobs, use that term as your keyword.

The more specific you make your search, the more relevant the search results will be.

While you are using keywords, do one more search. Rather than entering terms that match what you are qualified to do, just for fun, enter some terms that match what you would like to do if you could. You may be surprised that there are listings that match, and you may be even more surprised to learn that you may have the right experience to apply for the jobs.

To add a slightly different twist to the results, you will also get listings that advertise that the company, or the location, offer your favorite activity as a perk.

For example, I enjoy sailing. When I entered that as a keyword, I got not only listings for sailing jobs, but also listings that advertised the community where the job was located as an excellent place for sailing and other activities.

Searching by different (not necessarily job related) terms can be a good way to find job openings that match your interests as well as your skills.

As you can see, refining your search can be a real time-saver. Taking the time in advance to focus your job search will enable you to get right to the job listings that meet the specific criteria that are important to you.

Job search agents can speed up your job search. Job search agents are another good way to expedite your job search and to find out about new positions as soon as they are listed. Once you have job search agents in place, you will receive e-mail

TOOLS YOU NEED

▶ The Job Searching Forum (http://about.com/jobsearch/forum) section of my About.com site has a Job Listings folder and a Jobs Wanted folder. It's a good place to check for new listings because many employers post openings as soon as they know they may need candidates. You can also post information on the types of positions you are interested in, so employers can contact you directly. There's also a section where you can request job search help and advice.

messages when the system finds new jobs that match the criteria you selected when you set up the agents.

In order to set up a search agent, you will need to be registered with the job site you are using. Depending on the site, job search agents may be called:

- Job Alert (CareerBuilder)
- Job Search Agent (Monster)
- Job Scout (America's Job Bank)
- Saved Searches (HotJobs)

To set up job search agents, log in to your account, then click Create Job Search Agent (or the term used by the site you are on). You will be prompted to name your search, to select career fields and locations to search, and you will be asked how often you want to run the search and receive results by e-mail. I recommend having the searches run daily so you get new job postings as soon as they are listed.

Monster lets you set up five different search agents, while America's Job Bank lets you set up ten job scouts. Other sites offer a similar amount, while some of the job search engine sites (like SimplyHired.com) also allow users to save searches and set up e-mail alerts. Larger company Web sites also provide job search agent services so you can set up alerts to send you new postings just for that company. If there is a certain company you would love to work for, this is a great way to stay on top of the jobs that are available.

CareerBuilder's Matching Jobs Service will even send new listings to your cell phone. Once you have uploaded your resume and registered for the service, it will scan your resume to find jobs that best match your resume. It will then send text messages (up to five a day) as the system finds jobs that are a match.

Job Search Engines

Job search engines are a relatively recent technology. Unlike the job banks where employers list jobs directly, these sites allow users to search the top job banks, association sites, online newspapers, company Web sites, and other job sites by location and keyword. Some job search engines generate a list of matching results in your browser, while others send you listings by e-mail.

These sites typically provide some extras along with the job listings. Both Indeed.com and SimplyHired.com let you map the location of the job. Most have advanced search options that include the type of job, type of company, keyword, location, and the date the job was posted. As a bonus, if you're a dog lover, like I am, you'll be pleased to know that SimplyHired even lets you search for dog-friendly companies.

I wouldn't use job search engines as my only job search tool. The reason is that, for the most part, you still need to go to the actual site where the position is listed to apply and because there are more bells and whistles, which are useful, on some of the top sites.

That said, the job search engine sites are resources that should be included on your list of job search sites to be checked regularly. Bookmark them in the Job Search folder you have set up in your Favorites menu.

Job Sites

Job banks are an essential part of your job search. There are the top job banks, like Monster, HotJobs, and CareerBuilder, and there are thousands of smaller job sites covering every career field and geographic location you can imagine, and then some. There are also sites that focus on something else but include job listings as a benefit to their users.

WHAT'S HOT

▶ My article on using the job search engines (http://about.com/jobsearch/jobsearch engines) is read frequently by visitors to my About.com site. In addition to reading about how the job search engines work, you can check out the results I got when I tested the top job search engines. I found that some worked better than others. Some generated excellent results, some were okay, and others didn't work well at all.

Jobs are big business on the Internet, and it's amazing how many job sites there are. In 1998, according to Interbiznet.com, there were 2,500 sites providing job postings. Today, there are thousands more sites, with millions of job postings.

There are sites that list only summer jobs, while others list only hourly jobs. There are sites dedicated to work-at-home jobs, and others that list volunteer opportunities. There is even a site that only lists jobs that pay over $100,000 a year.

As you can see from the numbers, there are almost too many job sites. There can be a tendency to try and visit every job site you can because you don't want to miss out on what might be the perfect job.

On one hand, that can make sense. The dilemma is that not every job is listed everywhere and you want to make sure that you find all the jobs for which you are qualified. On the other hand, there aren't enough hours in the day to look at every site that might have a job that matches your requirements.

It makes better sense to limit your search, at least at first. You can then expand it to include more job sites if your first round of searching isn't successful. Take it one step at a time by starting out slowly then expanding your job search horizons. If you don't do it this way, job searching can become very overwhelming.

Start by reviewing job sites that contain the type of jobs that interest you. On my About.com site, I categorize job sites by the type of position they list and by the type of job seeker you are.

This list will give you an overview of what's available:

- Entry-level jobs
- Government jobs
- Part-time and hourly jobs
- Internships and summer jobs
- Job banks and job search engines

- Jobs listed by location or type
- Newspaper help-wanted ads
- Freelance and temporary jobs
- Teen jobs
- Work-at-home jobs

How do you determine which sites you need? If you're a high school or college student looking for a part-time job or a summer job, check the job sites that list part-time jobs and jobs just for teens and students.

If you are about to graduate from college or are a recent graduate, use the entry-level job sites. When you only want to work on a temporary basis, you will find job sites that list just temp positions. If you want to work at home or for the government, you will find sites that list those positions, too.

The same holds true if you are looking for a summer job or an internship. Start with the sites that specialize in the type of job you want. If you don't have success, expand your search to include more job sites.

Do you need an online profile? Most of the job sites let registered users create a personal profile in addition to posting their resume. You can put a lot of personal information in it, as well as information on your experience and the type of job you are seeking.

In most cases, a lot of the information is optional. You can include it if you want to, but it isn't required. The reason for the profile is to help employers find you and to help match you (on some sites) with job openings. I don't think you need to complete all the personal information the sites request. You also can keep your profile private, which is a good idea if you're employed. You don't want your employer to find your profile by mistake!

TOOLS YOU NEED

▶ If you need help getting organized and keeping track of the jobs you are applying for, there is software that can help. ResumeMaker Professional (http://resumemaker .com) has a Contact Manager where you can list targeted companies, set up a job search checklist, review a log of the jobs for which you have applied, review a to-do list, set up action items for each company, and create a daily and weekly schedule.

There are also job sites that offer upgraded services where your profile can be used for networking. There are still other sites that suggest that everyone should have a universal profile that will give you an online professional presence separate from your job-searching presence. It will, the companies say, give recruiters a snapshot of your background and experience. In both cases, these are fee-based services, so job seekers have to pay for the additional exposure.

Career expert and nationally syndicated newspaper columnist Joyce Lain Kennedy questions the value of paying for a separate profile: "Recruiters and employers want to hire people whose qualifications are a good fit for the job's requirements. If they decide to make the effort to check out a universal profile, they're already very interested because of a referral, or successful interview, or well-done resume. An inappropriate fact on a canned profile could cause reconsideration of your value."

I agree, and I wouldn't suggest paying a monthly fee for putting your personal profile online. In my opinion, the return on your investment simply isn't there.

Company Web Sites and Blogs

Company Web sites and blogs are another good source of job listings, and more. Most companies list job openings in the careers section of the company Web site, but you can find additional information that is very useful when job searching.

The company Web site can provide information on the products and services it sells. There is usually detailed information on the corporate officers and executive management team. You may find information on the company history as well as finances and growth. There are often even descriptions of the company culture that will give you an idea of how you might fit in.

For example, Quad/Graphics corporate Web site mentions that it is on the Forbes (www.forbes.com) 2006 list of the best companies to work for. A related press release mentions that Forbes "cites, among other areas of excellence, our family-oriented atmosphere (half of our employees are related by blood or marriage), as well as our onsite medical and child care centers, and recreational facilities."

Starbucks, another company on Forbes' list, provides similar information on their Web site. When I reviewed their site, I found that Starbucks offers health insurance, tuition reimbursement, savings plans, and stock option plans, just to mention some of the benefits provided to employees.

Check the benefits section of the company Web site to find out what benefits are available at the companies you are interested in. Most companies provide an itemized list on what is offered, as well as eligibility guidelines.

A blog (formally know as a Web log) is an online journal that is available on the Internet. Companies use blogs to provide information about the company and its products and services. Job and career sites use them to provide advice and to promote their services. Some job seekers use personal blogs to promote themselves.

Read job search blogs on a regular basis. Blogs created for job seekers to provide advice, information, and job search assistance are useful too. Most of the top job search sites have blogs, as do sites that provide career change assistance, resume-writing services, and job search advice.

I update my blog on my About.com site (http://about.com/jobsearch/blog) almost every day. I share job search tips and techniques, insight into job searching, and success stories contributed

ASK YOUR GUIDE

Creating blogs doesn't seem like an efficient way for companies to recruit. Can reading them really help me find a job?

▶ When new technology comes into play, visitors to my About.com site always wonder if it will be effective. I do too. Some new technology works and some doesn't. Blogs are becoming an effective recruiting tool. Though they typically get the employer less candidates than a help-wanted ad, that's a good thing for many employers. However, they are also a way to get the more focused candidates who have taken the time to read the blog.

by the visitors to my site. I also read other job search and career blogs daily. They are an excellent source of good career advice. The following is a list of some of my favorite career blogs:

- BostonWorks Job Blog: http://bostonworks.boston.com/blog
- BlueSky Resumes Blog: www.blueskyresumes.com/weblog
- Monster Blog: http://monster.typepad.com/monsterblog
- Recruiting.com Blog: http://recruiting.blogs.com
- The Occupational Adventure: http://curtrosengren.typepad.com/occupationaladventure

A blog can help with your job search. Job seekers have used their blogs to showcase their experience and background, and to chronicle their job search. It's an additional way to get visibility and to market your candidacy to potential employers.

A blog is also a way to show what you know. For example, I know one person who has created a blog that highlights his technical-writing skills. Another acquaintance, who is a human resources manager, has a blog that discusses benefits and compensation. These weren't specifically created to use for job searching, but they do show what the writers know about their career field and gives them exposure in their industry.

Do be careful what you write. Some of the things I've read on blogs would knock the person right off the list of potential candidates. One person wrote about how she lied on interviews. Another wrote about how she spent her lunch hour enjoying (too many) cocktails. Yet another wrote about how she had called in sick on several occasions to go on interviews. None of these are going to compel a potential employer to contact you. They will actually have the opposite effect. Here are some personal job search blog do's and don'ts:

▶ More and more businesses are using blogs for informal (and sometimes formal) recruiting. They provide Web site visitors with information on what's happening in the company, they let potential employees know the company's vision and culture, and they are a way for the company to have a voice, rather than just providing static information. From the company's point of view they are easy and simple to update, and they provide the company with a way to communicate in a more casual and informal manner.

- Be discreet. Don't write that you hate your job and your boss.
- If you write it, someone will read it. Many employers will use Google to find information on prospective employees before they make a job offer.
- When you create a job search blog, make sure it is relevant and focused to your job search.
- Leave your blog off your resume unless it is relevant to your job search.
- Be careful. There are employees who have been fired for blogging, either for divulging confidential company information or for bad-mouthing the company.

If you are interested in setting up a blog, you can do so for free. The About.com Web Logs site has a list of the top free Web log platforms at http://about.com/weblogs/freeblogs. The list includes:

- WordPress
- Blogger.com
- Moveable Type

Setting up a blog is straightforward and quite simple. You will register with the site, then choose a name for your blog. All the writing and editing can be done online. Do spell check and proofread your blog posts (most blog software has a built-in spell checker). Your blog needs to be as professional as your other job search correspondence.

Just one word of advice: Don't start a blog unless you are willing to keep it up. The point of blogging is to be timely and current. Nobody is interested in reading old information, and blogs can get out of date really fast. A blog that hasn't be updated in a week or two will be considered stale and old news.

ELSEWHERE ON THE WEB

▶ I don't think anyone would be amazed at Google having a blog. Of course they do, and you can read it at http://googleblog.blogspot.com. You would expect Microsoft to have blogs as well. Microsoft's recruiting blog is available at http://blogs.msdn.com/jobsblog. However, you might be surprised at some of the more traditional companies that have blogs. GM is a good example. The GM Fast-Lane Blog (http://fastlane.gmblogs.com) has posts from executives, as well as other General Motors employees.

On a related note, don't include a link on your resume or in your blog to any questionable personal material. I've seen some Facebook and My Space profiles that certainly shouldn't be seen by any prospective employer. In fact, some of them have made me cringe. The last thing you want to do is advertise them to the person who is screening your resume.

Be very careful what you write online and what you advertise, inadvertently or not, to prospective employers. One rule of thumb I have is to remember that my mom might be reading it!

Newspapers and Associations

Newspapers and professional associations are another good source of job listings. Even though the number of help-wanted ads in newspapers has dropped quite a bit since the Internet became a prime recruiting venue, employers still use them to recruit.

For candidates with a specialization, professional associations can be an excellent source of focused job leads. Member employers post jobs to recruit candidates who belong to the association because they know that they will most likely have the appropriate credentials. It saves fielding numerous inquiries from candidates who aren't qualified.

Don't forget to check the newspaper. I know that some people consider reading the newspaper help-wanted ads an old-fashioned way of job searching. However, more people than you might expect have found jobs in the newspaper. Cecilia, a visitor to my About.com site, was interested in finding a part-time job for when her kids were in school. She didn't want anything complicated; rather, she wanted to earn a little extra money and fill some hours during the day. She checked her local daily newspaper and her weekly PennySaver paper on a daily basis. Within a week or so she had two offers for part-time jobs.

Some companies only advertise in the newspaper. They don't need the volume of candidates that they would get if they listed jobs on a national, or even a regional, job site. In addition, they aren't interested in paying relocation expenses or coordinating interview logistics for job seekers who are out of the area.

This doesn't mean that you have to buy your local newspaper every morning. Most newspapers have online classifieds on their Web site where you can search for jobs. I do subscribe to a couple of local papers, though—not because I am looking for a job, but because I want to see what listings are available. I usually have clients who aren't specifically looking for a job, but who may be interested if the right job came along.

Angela, for example, works as an administrator at a local accounting firm. She's also very health conscious and spends a lot of the time at the gym. She's been able to earn some extra money by working as a personal trainer. She's found listings by word of mouth and found them by glancing through the help-wanted ads in her local paper. She didn't really need those jobs, but they were available and she was qualified. If she hadn't been reading the paper regularly, she wouldn't have found them.

Use association Web sites to job search. Some association's sites may seem small and not very useful, but you will discover that they can work well. Because they are smaller they typically don't get the traffic larger sites do and there is less competition. The openings are usually current, immediate openings and job seekers typically get a good response when using them.

Our local chamber of commerce provides a free job listing service for local employers who belong to the association. There aren't tons of job listings, but there are usually some in every employment area listed. I know several people who have found jobs on the site.

ELSEWHERE ON THE WEB

▶ Some companies still list jobs only in their local newspaper. When hunting for jobs in a certain city or state, you will need to check the newspaper's Web site for job listings. NewsVoyager (www .newspaperlinks.com) is a good way to find newspapers in the locations where you want to be. Either click on the map to get newspapers listed by city and state or search by the newspaper name, if you know it, and/or the location.

One of my clients, Paul, had recently moved to this area and asked for my help with his job search. He had retail experience and he was a connoisseur of fine wine. I check job sites daily because I never know when I will see a position that might be a fit for one of my clients. I noticed a listing for a new wine store specializing in fine wine that was about to open in our town. Paul e-mailed his resume to the contact in the job posting. He also stopped by the store just to say hello to the owner and to mention he was interested in the job. The owner gave him a quick verbal quiz to discover what he knew about wine and hired him on the spot.

There are more associations than those for local businesses. If you are a professional, there will be numerous associations you can join. At one company I worked for our sales manager belonged to an association of local sales executives. The weekly luncheons were an ideal way to make networking and business contacts. A friend who is a CPA belongs to the American Institute of Certified Public Accountants. In addition to information on publications, continuing education, and the CPA exam, he is also able to view job listings on the association Web site.

Some associations require membership to access job postings, while other sites make job listings available to anyone who is interested. In both cases, associations in your career field(s) of interest are a valuable addition to your job search.

If you belong to an association, check what resources are available to members. In addition to job postings, you may also be able to find lists of member companies, which will give you leads to investigate for job openings. If you don't belong to an association, check to see what resources are available for nonmembers. Many association Web sites provide information to all visitors to the site. Consider joining if the benefits will help with your job search.

Get Linked

*The following resources that are available on my **ABOUT**.com Job Searching site will provide you with additional resources for finding job listings.*

JOB LISTING DIRECTORY

This directory includes job banks, job search engines, niche job sites, jobs listed by location, job listings, for various types of job seekers, and additional job listing resources.

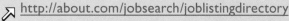 http://about.com/jobsearch/joblistingdirectory

HELP-WANTED ADS

Here you'll find international, national, state, and local help-wanted ads, job listings and employment classifieds from daily, weekly, and specialty newspapers.

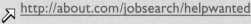 http://about.com/jobsearch/helpwanted

TOP TEN JOB SITES

There are a lot of job sites online, but I do have some favorites. Here is my selection of the top ten job sites. All of them are worth incorporating into your job search, because not all employers list on every site, even though it may sometimes seem that way.

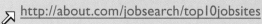 http://about.com/jobsearch/top10jobsites

Chapter 7

Shelton State Libraries
Shelton State Community College

Top Job Banks and Search Engines

The Top Job Sites

What are the differences between job banks and job search engines? There are actually quite a few differences and some similarities. The major difference is that a job bank (like Monster or CareerBuilder) contains jobs that employers have posted on the site for a fee. The job search engines search those job banks, and many other sources, like company Web sites, newspaper sites, and associations for job listings. So, when you use a job search engine, you will get job listings from all the top job banks, as well as from other Web sites.

Which job bank you should use depends on how you are job searching. If you absolutely need to find a job, I'd recommend registering with all the job banks and using them all to conduct a high-powered job search. Supplement that search by using job search

I've applied for lots of jobs, but I haven't received the response I expected. What can I do?

▶ I've spoken to many job seekers with the same problem. They apply for many jobs but don't get a good response. There are some things you can do to jump-start your job search and there's an article on my About.com site that details them. You can read it at http://about.com/jobsearch/jumpstart. The most important thing is to diversify your job search and not limit it to using one or two job banks.

engines to find additional listings. Also, use the job search engines as a quick way to search when you're short on time.

If you don't have to find a job but you are interested in knowing what the job market is like and in knowing what jobs are available that meet your interests, the job search engines are a good way to stay on top of what's out there.

The reason is that in many cases, once you find a job to apply for, you are going to need to register with the job banks anyway. So, it makes sense to register before you start a search if you are actively seeking employment. If you're browsing the job market, use the search engines to see what jobs are available, then register with the job banks when you find a job that interests you.

A job bank isn't necessarily better than a job search engine. They are different and both should be integrated into your job search. The top job banks are mammoth and have so many job postings and resumes posted that it's hard to keep track of the numbers. It does make sense to use the top job sites in your search.

There are several reasons why it's important to use the top job banks. First of all, not all employers post on every site, but almost every major employer posts on at least one or more of the top sites. Taking just a quick look at Monster showed me job postings from General Electric, JPMorgan Chase, Geico, and Apple Computer, just to name a few of the companies with current listings.

Despite the volume of resumes posted, employers can, and will, find you. Craig, a visitor to my About.com site, posted his resume on Monster and HotJobs. Two weeks later he started receiving e-mail from employers asking if he was interested in open positions. One position was an absolutely perfect fit, and he scheduled an interview and company visit. He was offered the job after the first interview.

I suggested to Samantha, another frequent visitor to my About.com site, that she should use MonsterTrak, which is Monster's site for college students and alumni. She posted her resume and got great results within days. By the way, when you post your resume on MonsterTrak you can choose to make it only available to your career office or available to employers as well. The option you choose depends on how actively you are job seeking and whether you want to be contacted directly by employers or would prefer to be contacted only by your career office.

Don't let the numbers scare you. Just because there are a lot of resumes posted (and there are) doesn't mean that yours won't be the one that will catch the eye of a recruiter, especially if it's well written and focused. Employers do use the job sites to actively recruit candidates, but because of the competition, you will need to make sure your resume and cover letters are absolutely perfect.

When job searching, it's important to use all the resources you can, because there's no way to know which job site will have the listing that's going to be the perfect job for you. That's why job searching is work, but if you are willing to spend time searching on all the top job sites, you will eventually find the right job.

The top four job sites include:

- **America's Job Bank:** www.ajb.org
- **CareerBuilder:** www.careerbuilder.com
- **Monster:** www.monster.com
- **Yahoo! HotJobs:** http://hotjobs.com

There are also a variety of smaller job banks you can use. There's a list that includes many of the small- to mid-sized job banks available on my About.com site at http://about.com/jobsearch/jobbanks.

TOOLS YOU NEED

▶ When you want to make sure that your current employer doesn't discover that you are job searching, there are steps you can take to ensure that your job search is confidential. Review these Stealth Job-Hunting Tips (http://about.com/jobsearch/stealthsearch) to make sure you have all the tools in place to make sure that you don't get caught!

▶ Your State Department of Labor Web site is a good source of job listings and job search help. You might not expect it to be the place where employers go to post jobs, but in most cases there are no fees to list and many local employers use them. Also, you will find jobs that are close to home, as well as a good selection of regional and statewide job listings.

I wouldn't advise that you spend a lot of time looking for jobs on the smaller job banks, but they are worth perusing on occasion.

The reason I don't suggest spending too much time using the smaller job banks is because there are so many of them and there are only so many places that employers will list. Employers are most likely to use the job banks with more name recognition or to use niche job sites to get candidates with the specific background they need.

Employers only have so many recruiting dollars to spend on each job they hire for and they want to spend it wisely, at sites where they will get the most qualified candidates for the money they spend.

That said, it depends on how much time you have to job search. Job searching is a numbers game. The more time you have to spend, the more resumes you can post, the more jobs you can apply to, and the better chance you will have of getting interviews. If time is limited, spend it where your resume will get more visibility and where you will find more job leads, which means spending it on the top job banks.

Don't forget to save some of your job-searching time for offline activities. Very few job seekers find a job by posting on only one job bank. Networking is still one of the main ways people get jobs, and it's important to use your contacts, both personal and professional, whenever you can.

In fact, one of my About.com site visitors who is actively job seeking told me that he e-mails all his contacts once a month or so, just to touch base and say hello. That's a good way to stay in touch. I do the same thing. In fact, I just heard from my college roommate (from quite a few years ago!) and from a colleague I worked with years ago. They let me know how their careers were going and I did likewise.

How to Use Job Banks

The best way to use the job banks is to start in an organized and orderly manner. First of all, make a list of the sites you are going to use. Once you get to the site, you will need to register (don't forget to write down your user name and password) before you can post your resume and apply for jobs.

Here's a list of what you need to do for each site:

- ○ Register and create a user name and password
- ○ Post your resume
- ○ Post cover letters
- ○ Search for jobs
- ○ Check directions on how to apply
- ○ Set up job search agents to get new listings by e-mail that match your interests
- ○ Keep track of the jobs you have applied for

I've found that it's easier to stay organized if I work on one job site at a time. That way, I'm not switching back and forth between sites and forgetting what I need to do on what site. I can run through each of the sites on a regular basis to stay on top of my job searching activities.

Take the time to focus your job search. The most important step is to remember to focus your job search. Each job site gives you a wide variety of search parameters. Use them to narrow down your search so that it returns a reasonable number of listings. Running a broad search that generates hundreds of listings isn't really going to be helpful. Rather, you're better off running a more specific search and getting fewer job listings to review. Here are the standard job search parameters available on most sites:

TOOLS YOU NEED

▶ The About.com Job Searching newsletter is the best way to find out what's happening in the world of jobs and careers. It's a free weekly e-mail newsletter and you can subscribe online at http://about.com/jobsearch/newsletter. Each issue is full of advice, suggestions, and tips for job seekers, along with links to relevant information on my site. The newsletter is a great way to stay on top of what's new and what's newsworthy.

- **Company Name:** Either type in the company name or use it as a keyword
- **Job Category:** Type of position or industry
- **Keyword(s):** Words included in the job description or company information
- **Location:** City, state, zip code or region

Some of the job banks have additional search options, such as within a radius of a specific zip code, by multiple locations, salary range, or type of employment (full-time, part-time, contract, or intern).

Search selectively. When you search, search selectively and limit the options as best you can. If you want a job in New York City, for example, specify that, rather than searching for all the jobs in New York state. When you're looking for a job in a specific city, remember that many states have cities with the same name.

If you are interested in an SQL programming job, use *SQL* as a keyword; don't just use a general term like *programmer*. Here's why it matters. When I searched Monster using programmer as a keyword, I got over 1,000 job listings for all types of computer programmers. When I searched for SQL programmer, I got only listings that required the skills I entered.

Another good way to narrow your search is to use the targeted job search pages that are set up by some sites. Monster's Finance and Accounting section has specialized information on companies that are hiring, as do the other targeted job pages that are available. CareerBuilder's specialized job search section narrows down your search by only pulling listings that match the specific category you selected. For example, the Human Resources job search searches only HR jobs, while the Engineering job category only pulls responses from the engineering jobs section.

Here's how to find the focused job categories:

- **CareerBuilder Specialized Job Search:** Click on Show More Categories on the bottom of the CareerBuilder home page.
- **Monster Targeted Job Search:** The list is on left side of the job search page.
- **Yahoo! HotJobs Vertical Job Categories:** Click on Browse Categories on the bottom of the HotJobs home page.

Once you have accessed the focused job category page your searches will only generate results from that job category. So, you are only searching jobs that match your interests.

On the other hand, you only want to narrow your search when it's in your best interest to do so. If you are interested in a position that is available in many industries, like administrative assistant or customer service manager, for example, use the keyword search to find jobs in the location(s) that interest you. Don't limit your options, because you may find jobs that interest you in a wide variety of categories.

There are sites that focus on entry-level professional positions. If you're a college student or graduate, check with your college or university to see if they partner with MonsterTrak (www.monstertrak.com). If they do, you will be able to access jobs listed specifically for college students and alumni from your institution. There are other sites, as well, that focus on entry-level jobs. They are a good source of job listings for career changes as well as for recent graduates.

The following are the top sites for the college market:

- CB Campus: www.cbcampus.com
- College Grad Job Hunter: www.collegegrad.com

ELSEWHERE ON THE WEB

▶ Do you want to work for a big company? How about a fast-growing company or a tech company? Would you prefer a private company to a public one? Whichever type of company you want to work for, Forbes has a list for you. Forbes Lists are available at www.forbes.com/lists. Lists include the 200 Best Small Companies, the 400 Best Big Companies, and the World's 2,000 Largest Companies, to name just a few.

I'm not desperate to find a new job, but I'd make a move for the right position. How seriously should I job search?

▶ I often hear from job seekers who would change jobs for the right opportunity. You don't have to work as hard as someone who needs a job now, but you should be aware of the job market and available jobs. One way to do this is to set up e-mail alerts to notify you of new postings on the job sites you use.

- eRecruiting: www.erecruiting.com
- MonsterTrak: www.monstertrak.com
- NACElink: www.nacelink.com
- Student Jobs: www.studentjobs.gov

Some sites require that users be affiliated with a college; others are available to all job seekers. Check with your college career office to see which sites they partner with and to get a user name and password so you can access the job listings.

These sites are good resources for career changers too. If you are considering a different line of work, you will probably have to start with an entry-level job, even if you have years of experience in another field. These sites are a good way to explore opportunities in new fields.

The Best Job Search Engines

At first, the concept of creating a job search engine to search the Internet for job listings was a novel one. It was similar to when Google first arrived as a way to find information online. There were other search engines before Google, and more since, but none, in my opinion, have done what Google has done to make it easy to find information online, both quickly and simply.

The job search engine market, though a relatively new one, is as competitive as the job bank market. It seems like every few weeks brings a new job search engine, each claiming to work faster and better than the competition. Some of them are excellent; others give you mixed results.

Most of the top job search engines are integrated with other technology. For example, Indeed.com has options to research the company on Google, view all the jobs from the company, map the job location, and to find contacts at LinkedIn or

Ryze. SimplyHired offers similar services. You can see who you know on LinkedIn, view the job location on a map, e-mail the job to a friend, and even apply online for some listings.

The most competitive sites continue to add new features. As an example, David Parmet from Indeed.com wrote to tell me about innovations at that site: "We've added some new features at Indeed that I thought you would like to hear about. Our job trends tool at www.indeed.com/jobtrends allows you to track job titles or locations over the course of the year." This is a useful tool—you can see the volume of jobs listed for a particular type of position, which is a good indicator of how the job market is doing.

SimplyHired even added a dog-friendly company search. Their survey of dog owners showed that 49 percent of dog owners would switch jobs if they could bring their dog to work, and 70 percent of dog owners believe a dog-friendly workplace is an important employee benefit.

Top employers like Google and Amazon, along with many smaller companies, do allow dogs in the workplace. It may not be a requirement, but for dog lovers like me, being able to bring your dog to work is definitely a pleasant perk. Aside from pleasing dog lovers, the dog-friendly search is a good example of how the job search engines are responsive to both their users and to the need to remain competitive in a tough market by continually expanding their offerings.

The top job search engine sites include:

- **Indeed.com** includes job listings from thousands of Web sites, including major job boards, newspapers, associations, and company Web sites.
- **Jobster.com** provides job listings from thousands of employers and recruiters.
- **SimplyHired.com** searches thousands of job boards, classified ads, and company Web sites.

ELSEWHERE ON THE WEB

▶ If you're a Yahoo! member, you can access everything you need to job search in one place. You'll be able to view your saved job searches, saved jobs, your resumes, and log in to your mail account to check your e-mail, review your calendar, and your notepad. It's a good way to take care of all your job search needs in one online solution.

The job search engines can save you time by searching the Internet for job listings for you. In most cases they do a good job, but with one caveat—they don't always find every job listing. That's the reason that I don't suggest using a job search engine instead of using the job banks, though I do think they should be included in your job search.

Here's what can happen sometimes. When I did some test searches for a particular employer, the job search engines found all the jobs sometimes, but not always. In some instances it could have been because all the job postings weren't listed on the employer Web site, or because they were listed elsewhere. For example, when I searched for jobs at the Bronx Zoo, in New York, I discovered that jobs at the zoo were actually listed on the Wildlife Conservation Society Web site. I found that information by using Google, rather than by using the job search engines. Some jobs that were listed in the newspaper or on a job bank were included in results, but I found more listings by going directly to the employer Web site.

Here's another tip to ensure you are getting to all the listings. If you find jobs that interest you at a certain employer listed on a job bank, take a few minutes to visit the company Web site to make sure that you are finding all the jobs for which you are qualified.

For each of the sites you use, you'll need to register, where applicable, and set up job search agents to send you new job postings. Here's a list of the job sites you should be using:

- Job banks
- Job search engines
- Niche job sites
- Local job sites
- College/university job site
- Networking sites

Make sure that you are using all the sites that are relevant to your job search. You may even want to allocate a specific amount of time to spend on each site, and on your overall job search. That's important, especially if you are working and job searching. You don't want to spend every nonworking or waking hour on your job search or you will burn out fast.

Check your e-mail and your voice mail at least once a day, preferably more often. If you get a message from a recruiter or hiring manager, you will want to respond as soon as you can. Set up a job search system so you are checking job search engines one day, job banks the next, and niche and local sites the third day, for example. That way you will be checking all the relevant job sites for new listings in a timely manner.

How to Use Job Search Engines

The best way to use the job search engines is to search for a job in a specific location. For example, if you're interested in a Web designer job in Minneapolis, you can search quickly and get a good variety of listings that meet your query. I got a good sampling of listings from all the job search engines.

When you absolutely don't have to find a job, the job search engines are also a good way to stay on top of the job market without having to take the time to register with the job banks. If you see a job that interests you, you can go ahead and apply. Otherwise, you don't need to do anything.

Each job search engine site searches a little differently. The basic search on each site is by keyword and location (city, state, or zip code). You'll see an Advanced Search button on the front page of each site, and you should use it. It will help you refine your search and focus the results so they more closely match the type of job you want.

Advanced search options vary from site to site, but they all offer some unique, and useful, query options. The advanced search option on Jobster includes radius from a city, date posted, and multiple keywords or a phrase. SimplyHired's advanced search options include keyword and company filters to help you find jobs at specific employers. Indeed lets you search by company, a variety of keywords, or type of job (full-time, part-time, temporary, contract), and it also lets you decide if you want to search all the Web or just employer sites or job boards.

Here are some job search engine tips:

- **Search by city and state:** There are cities with similar names in various locations, so don't forget to specify your state.
- **Run your search on all the search engines:** Results vary and you want to be sure you get as many jobs as possible.
- **Use advanced search options:** You will be able to narrow your search criteria.

Again, it can be confusing when you're looking for jobs in all the right places. In order to be looking in the right places, you will need to be looking in a lot of places. So, do keep track of where you are searching. Bookmark each site in your Favorites folder in your browser; sort the list in alphabetical order, so you can check each site in a methodical and organized manner.

Use the tools provided by the job search engines. Like the job banks, the job search engines have additional tools that you should take advantage of. Indeed has a plug-in you can download to search right from your desktop. You can also set up my.indeed, which enables you to save individual job listings, track jobs you've looked at, and save and manage job searches. It's easy to save a job to review in the future if you aren't ready to apply—just click Save Job next to the position in the search results. SimplyHired has options to save searches and to create e-mail alerts to send you new job postings.

Jobster has a variety of search engines for job seekers. Users can register, create a profile that employers can search, and build a network of connections you can use to help with your job search.

Speaking of connections, most of the job search engines let you take full of advantage of your online connections. When you click on More Options under the job posting on Indeed, you will be able to see if you have any contacts at the networking sites LinkedIn and Ryze. At SimplyHired you can also search for contacts at LinkedIn.

Why is finding contacts important? Well, those contacts may be able to provide a referral for you or may know someone who can put in a good word for you at an employer. Having a contact at a prospective employer will increase the chance that the employer will look at your resume. It might even help you get an interview.

One client of mine happened to be interested in a volunteer coordinator job working at a local homeless shelter. The job was advertised on the shelter's Web site, and the client found it by using Indeed.com. A good friend of mine is president of a local nonprofit group that happens to work with the shelter. She was glad to refer my client, because she was sending a good prospect to the organization, and they were glad to consider the applicant, because they were always looking for qualified candidates.

By the way, this all happened by e-mail. It only took me a moment or two to e-mail my friend. It took her a couple of minutes to e-mail her contact to put in a good word for my client. That's why it's important to take full advantage of every connection you have. You never know when someone you know might know someone who can help.

Regardless of how you are applying for jobs, always use any connections you have. Even if they are remote, it certainly won't hurt. Your contact may even make a little money by referring you. Some companies pay bonuses to employees who refer candidates for open positions.

WHAT'S HOT

▶ Once you get your resume out there, and even before, you may be surprised to find headhunters approaching you. There are skills that are in high demand and recruiters are always looking for good candidates. Before you sign an agreement though, thoroughly check out what the headhunter is going to do for you and review the guidelines on how to choose a headhunter at http://about.com/jobsearch/headhunter.

In some cases, the referral bonus can be a few hundred dollars. For positions that are hard to fill, it can be significantly higher. So, don't feel like you are imposing by asking a family member, friend, or acquaintance to help. Most people are more than happy to help, even if they aren't getting paid.

In fact, at least one-third of job openings are filled by referral and never listed publicly. So, in addition to helping your resume get noticed, your contacts can help you find jobs that you might never have known were available.

Where to Find Job Sites

Finding job sites isn't always easy. There are lots of them—actually, too many—available online. As I've mentioned before, I always start searching on the top sites, then broaden my search as necessary.

There are some sites, including my About.com site, that categorize, review, and list job sites. Here is a selection of job guides you can use to find job sites:

- **About.com Job Searching** (http://jobsearch.about.com): My site includes directories of job sites organized by type of position, location, and type of job seeker.
- **About.com Job Searching Technical** (http://jobsearchtech .about.com): This About.com site is an excellent resource for job seekers looking for a technical position.
- **Job-Hunt** (www.job-hunt.org): This site lists job by location (U.S. and international) as well as by type of job.
- **JobStar:** (www.jobstar.org): JobStar has a variety of resources for job seekers interested in specific career options.
- **The Riley Guide** (www.rileyguide.com): The Riley Guide was one of the first Internet sites to provide employment information, and it's still an excellent resource.

I'd recommend using one of the sites listed here, because they have done most of the work for you. The resources have been collected, so everything you need is in one place. They are easy to navigate and will save you lots of up-front time researching job sites to use.

However, new sites are being added to the Web every day. There is always someone who thinks they have a new and better idea for creating a job search site. Some of the sites are excellent and others aren't, but they are worth a look.

So, if you're not finding what you need, search Google using the type of job you are interested in (accounting jobs or marketing jobs, for example) to see a list of job sites that match your search. You will have to weed through them, because in most cases you will get millions of search results, but you may find some good leads that way.

Explore the hidden job market. In some cases, you may be interested in a job that's in a very specific career field or in an industry that doesn't necessarily advertise online. Some employers don't advertise online because they get more than enough candidates through other channels or they aren't high-tech enough to recruit online. Believe it or not, that still happens.

This is called the hidden job market because it includes jobs that are never advertised online. That's why it's important to use a broad range of job search tools when hunting for a new job. Jobs could be filled by referral only, or simply listed on a Web site but not advertised or promoted. Sometimes employers will even create an opening or fill an opening sooner than expected if the perfect candidate comes along.

There are some estimates that say 50 percent, or even more, of jobs aren't listed. I'm not sure how accurate that is, but even if

TOOLS YOU NEED

▶ **When you need to find a job fast, my How to Speed Up Your Job Search class (**http://about.com/jobsearch/onlinesearchclass**) is a great way to expedite your job search. The class provides online resources and personal assistance, as well as advice on how to speed up your job search. The class covers self-assessment and the career-planning process, resume and cover letter writing, employer research, interviewing,** salary negotiations**, as well as how to job search effectively.**

the number is less, it's still a lot of jobs that you can't easily find by running a quick search.

It's important to save your money. Unfortunately, there are unscrupulous Web site operators who take advantage of job seekers. My most important rule is not to pay for job listings. There are so many good sites out there, you shouldn't need to pay to join a job site, pay to get job listings, or pay for newsletters or advice.

The only, very rare, exception would be if you are seeking employment in an industry that doesn't have many job openings and where employers typically don't advertise jobs online. These are few and far between, so before you pay a fee, thoroughly check out the Web site and ask for a sample of what you will receive. Also, ask for references from other people who have used the service. Here are some job site do's and don'ts:

- Don't give out confidential information when you register.
- Don't pay to register with the site.
- Do check out the companies you apply to.
- Don't pay for job listings.
- Don't believe it if the job ad says you will make millions.
- Don't pay for anything that says it will help you find a job in hours or days.
- Do use all the free resources available online.

It's also important to be very careful who you pay for job search help. There's a difference between paying an employment agency to place you in a job and using a recruiter to connect you with potential employers. I would not recommend paying for placement. Most recruiters are paid a percentage of the first year's salary or a flat fee by the company for whom they are finding candidates.

ELSEWHERE ON THE WEB

▶ Did you know that Monster has more than just job listings? There is a section of the Web site that provides career advice (http://content .monster.com). You'll find targeted advice for specific career fields and message boards where you can post questions. There are articles on job searching, interviewing, and resumes, as well as specialized advice like that for job seekers over fifty.

Using a career counselor is different and can be very helpful when job searching. There are career counselors who can help you with career planning and job searching. A career counselor can help you define what type of work you want to do and teach you the skills you need to job hunt. They can also help with resume and cover letter writing. When you use counselors, you are paying for the help they provide, not paying for placement in a specific position.

As I said, I wouldn't recommend paying for placement services. I have heard of too many people who have paid thousands of dollars to firms that have done nothing other than give them a list of companies to apply to. In most cases, they could have easily found the same list online.

The volume of scams related to job searching is a good reason to stick with the top banks and search engines. Even though they may not be able to review every listing, you will have a better chance of not being taken advantage of if you use the top sites.

ELSEWHERE ON THE WEB

▶ The Federal Trade Commission has information on job placement scams at www.ftc.gov/reports/fraud/busops.htm. It discusses the type of scams, what the FTC has done to investigate them, and how to avoid getting lured into a job placement scam. Take the time to review what might happen so it doesn't happen to you.

Get Linked

*Check out the following resources from my **ABOUT**.com Job Searching site for more job search advice and tips.*

ONESTOP JOB SEARCH GUIDE

The OneStop Job Search Guide includes all the resources you need for a successful job search, including how to write resumes, where to look for jobs, and how to conduct a job search.

 http://about.com/jobsearch/onestopjob

START A JOB SEARCH

If you are about to get to started on a job search, here is everything you need to know, including how to start your job search, where to find job postings, how to apply, and more employment resources.

 http://about.com/jobsearch/startsearch

JOB SEARCHING

This resource provides job postings, advice on conducting an effective job search, information on where to find search help, and tips on writing job search correspondence.

http://about.com/jobsearch/jobsearchresource

Chapter 8

Using Niche Job Sites

Jobs Listed by Type

A niche job site is a job site that lists only jobs in a specific career field or industry. For example, Dice.com lists only technical jobs, Playbill.com lists film and theater jobs, and Bio.com lists science job openings. When you are interested in a particular type of job, the niche job sites like these are excellent resources. Whether you are interested in jobs in advertising, jobs at the zoo, or any career field in between, you will find sites that list jobs in your field of interest. There are job sites for every type of job and for every type of job seeker.

If you are searching for an internship or a summer job, you will find sites that are dedicated to those types of positions. The same holds true for hourly jobs, part-time jobs, and work-at-home jobs. If there is a job doing it, there is a Web site for it. There are Web sites for anything and everything related to job searching. Besides sites dedicated to finding jobs, there are also sites that tell you how to quit your job, how to find information on working at specific companies or in certain industries, and how to find careers that will change your life.

Why are there so many Web sites? The main reason is that online job searching is a big business. There is money to be earned from employers paying to post jobs. Sites can earn money from ads, and revenue from offering services like resume and cover letter writing, job posting, personal salary reports, or interview coaching. Niche sites also get commission on services by offering links to discounted continuing-education classes, for example, or from offering classes and seminars to job seekers who sign up for these fee-based services.

Job sites also get income by offering premium services for job seekers. For example, Monster's premium service lets you post extra copies of resumes and cover letters, puts your resume higher in employer searches, and highlights your resume so it is more attractive to employers. Other sites offer similar services, also for a fee. CareerBuilder offers resume upgrades, background checks, and resume-posting services. Yahoo! HotJobs has partnerships with an assessment service, a resume-writing service, and a credit-reporting service.

As you probably know by now, I usually don't recommend paying for anything related to job searching unless it is something unique and not available elsewhere free of charge. That rule of thumb holds true for using the niche job sites as well. Before you spend a dime (and you probably don't need to), carefully research what is being offered and what you are getting for the money you are spending. Ask yourself if it is available elsewhere for no charge and take a few minutes to research what other options (besides ones that cost money) are available.

Because the niche sites are smaller, it's often harder for them to generate revenue than it is for the bigger sites where employers post jobs as a matter of course, so be cautious and carefully

ELSEWHERE ON THE WEB

▶ If you have a lot of job-searching phone calls to make, you may want to consider an Internet phone service. The About.com Wireless/Networking site (http://about.com/comp networking/internetphone) has information on Internet phones, including providers that offer free Internet phone services. You can make phone calls right from your computer and save on long-distance charges.

evaluate the site before you post. As with the other job sites, there are some that are a wonderful source of job leads, there are some that are not so good, and others that are simply awful. They also may be more likely to pitch products and services you probably don't need, because they are seeking all the revenue streams they can get.

A special word of warning about sites that list work-at-home jobs. Providing listings for jobs you can do from home is one of the biggest online moneymakers. It's also one of the areas where you find the most scams. Be very vigilant when searching for work-at-home jobs. In my opinion, legitimate jobs that allow you to work from home are few and far between. I know too many people who have been taken advantage of by scams, both work-at-home scams and general scams related to job searching.

Some of the scams related to job searches are really creative. One visitor to my About.com site wrote to me because she had received a letter in response to the resume she has posted online. She had recently posted her resume and the e-mail referenced a job that sounded a lot like the type of jobs she was seeking. I had to read the e-mail very carefully to interpret what the letter was saying (it was very long and very detailed).

To make a long story short, the bottom line was that the employer wanted her to send her bank account number so they could process her new hire paperwork. It, of course, was a scam, but I can see how she was taken in by it. The letter included very detailed information on how she would be paid, the vacation and benefits she would receive, when she would start, and other instructions. I had to send her a Web site that listed this type of scam to show her that it definitely wasn't real.

To complicate matters, in some cases the employer is a legitimate company, but the costs are significantly higher than the job seeker expected. Consider Nikole, for example. She wrote to me

TOOLS YOU NEED

▶ For job seekers on the go, a PDA (personal digital assistant) or cell phone with e-mail capabilities is a must. When you're job searching you will need to be able to check and respond to e-mail in a timely manner. You'll also want to check your job search alerts so you can apply to new job listings as soon as possible.

▶ If you are doing any kind of traveling while you're hunting for a new job, you will definitely need a laptop (notebook) computer so you can check the Web and your e-mail for new job postings and messages from employers. You will also be able stay in touch with your networking contacts, regardless of where you are. The About .com Guide to PC Hardware has good information on buying notebook PCs, at http://about.com/compreviews/notebooks.

to let me know about her experiences applying for call center jobs. She asked me to write about them on my About.com site to help others who might be taken advantage of by such companies.

You can read the article that resulted from our conversation at http://about.com/jobsearch/callcenterjobs. Nikole, like many other people seeking call center employment, didn't realize that she would be paid by the minute rather than by the call. She also didn't realize that she had to pay for training, pay for a background check, and pay a monthly fee for technical support. All the costs she incurred ensured that she didn't have much of a paycheck at the end of each month.

The lesson in all of this, regardless of the type of posting you are looking for, is to be very cautious when searching for jobs online—and offline. You'll see ads in the newspaper for "jobs" that will pay you lots of money without requiring applicants to have much experience. If it sounds too good to be true, it probably is.

Any mention of making hundreds or thousands of dollars for doing little work, or no work, should be a red flag to every job seeker. Companies don't pay employees to do nothing, for any reason. The only way you are going to make money is by working for it.

It's important to use the sites that focus on a specific career. When you are interested in a job in a specific career field or industry, be certain to use the job banks and search engines, but also use the sites that list the type of jobs that interest you.

There are a couple of reasons why. Some of the best places to find jobs in certain industries or niches aren't job banks. For example, the American Zoo and Aquarium Association has job listings from member zoos. The Union Jobs Clearinghouse lists union apprenticeship programs, as well as staff positions working for unions. USA Jobs is the federal government's job site and the site you should use if you are interested in federal employment.

In fact, you will find jobs at the organization as well as jobs listed by member companies. The American Bar Association, for example, has jobs listed at the association, as well as job listings from law firms. In addition, there is career advice and a job answer board for members.

When is a job not a job? Not all jobs are actually listed as jobs. If you are interested in acting or dance jobs, you won't find most of those types of openings posted on the job banks or even listed as jobs. Instead, they are listed as casting calls and auditions.

There's a list of sites that list casting calls for everything from Broadway shows to reality television auditions on my About.com site at http://about.com/jobsearch/castingcalls. These are fun to take a look at even if you're not interested in being the next American Idol or Survivor contestant, just to see what's involved in applying and what people will go through to get a chance at fame!

Check the job site directories. There are several sites that categorize jobs by type. You'll find easy-to-navigate lists of jobs sorted by type. They are an easy way to get directly to the listings in your field.

Here are some great job site directories:

- About.com Jobs by Career Field: http://about.com/jobsearch/jobsbyfieldlist
- Job-Hunt Job Search Resources by Industry: www.job-hunt.org
- The Riley Guide Audience-Targeted Sites: www.rileyguide.com/jobs.html#aud

The sites available in each category are too numerous to attempt to itemize or list, so do visit the sites that have done

ELSEWHERE ON THE WEB

▶ Craig's List (www.craigslist.org) is one of my favorite sites to find job listings. It's very simple—you click on the city where you want to work, then on the type of job that interests you. You will apply by e-mail to the jobs you choose. As I said, it's very basic, but it is a good source of job listings. There's also a jobs discussion forum where you can post your questions.

that work for you. It's worth taking the time to review niche sites, because you may find jobs that aren't listed elsewhere, especially in very specialized industries and for nonbusiness job listings. Non-profit organizations and the government may not list their open-ings on fee-based job sites. Remember that many nonprofits don't have budgets to pay for posting jobs, while many government jobs (both federal and state) are only listed on the government's Web site.

Part-Time and Hourly Jobs

If you're interested in a part-time job or an hourly job, you can find (and apply) for jobs online. However, that shouldn't be the only way you look for jobs. Small companies hire a large number of hourly workers and many don't post jobs on the Internet. Some large employers, like Wal-Mart, expect candidates for hourly employ-ment to apply directly at the store where they want to work.

Other employers, especially in retail, simply put a help-wanted poster in the window. Take the time to walk around your town or the mall if you're interested in an hourly job. Sometimes that's the fastest (and easiest) way to find a job. You won't have to wait for your online job application to be processed and filtered down to a store manager. You'll be applying directly to the person who is responsible for hiring.

Some of the top part-time and hourly job sites include:

- EmploymentGuide.com
- GrooveJob.com
- Indeed.com
- Monster Hourly and Skilled Jobs (http://hourlyandskilled.monster.com)
- SnagAJob.com

Another way to find part-time jobs is to search the top job sites by keyword and location. In this case, rather than searching by the category you are interested in, search using *part time* and *part-time* as keywords. Also, some sites, like Indeed.com, let you search for only part-time openings when you use the advanced search options.

You can search for hourly jobs by keyword, but also search by location and by the type of position you want. Here, use more general search terms, because hourly jobs cross industries. For example, use *retail* as a keyword to find jobs at stores, *manufacturing* to find related jobs, and so on.

The are a variety of ways skilled trade jobs are listed. Many trades and construction jobs are listed under hourly positions, so check those sites for these types of jobs. Monster bundles hourly and skilled jobs together into a category. That's another good place to look. To add another twist to your job search efforts, some hourly jobs will be listed as blue-collar jobs. There are sites like BlueCollarJobs.com that list just those types of openings.

If you are interested in working for a construction union, check the Web site to see how to apply. In many cases, you will need to go through an apprenticeship program. Those usually aren't listed on jobs sites, but information on how to apply should be available on the national union's Web site.

As you can see, there's something—often too much—online for everyone looking for a job. That's why it's easy to get overwhelmed and why it makes sense to stick with the sites that have the majority of listings that match what interests you. Otherwise, you can spend all day looking online and really not get anywhere. That's why it is a good idea to go offline to look for employment as well, especially in the case of a part-time job search.

WHAT'S HOT

▶ A new employment trend is for job seekers to opt out of the traditional employment path, where they worked full-time for the same employer for many years, often until retirement. Now, people of all ages are looking for more flexible work options so they can spend time with their families, spend time on hobbies and other activities, and work at jobs they enjoy, rather than at jobs that just pay the bills.

Internships

An internship is a preprofessional work experience that provides students, recent graduates, and career changers with a chance to find out more about a certain career or industry. An internship is also a good way for older workers, as well as younger ones, to move into a new field and to gain experience that will help their career progress. There are many benefits to doing an internship, even though you may not be paid:

- Gain work experience
- Get insight into prospective employers and industries
- Obtain college credit
- Get priority consideration for employment

You might think that internships are only for students, but that's not always the case. Many internship programs do accept older applicants. Michael, after many years as a union electrician, decided he was ready for a change. He went back to school for a master's degree. After graduating, he applied to a government internship program run by his state senate, and he was accepted. He was the oldest intern ever accepted by the program, but it was worth it. After completing the internship, Michael was offered a full-time job as a legislative director for a downstate assemblyperson and was able to change careers, just as he had planned when he started graduate school.

If you are a career changer interested in an internship, explain in your cover letter why you are interested in an internship position. Speak to why you are looking for a career change or want to learn about a new industry. Explain to the internship sponsor why you are interested in an internship, rather than a full-time job. Otherwise, your application may not receive much consideration.

If you're a student or college graduate, the best way to find an internship is to start with your high school guidance office or college career services office. Ask what internship resources are available for students. Also ask if the office staff can help you find internships to apply to and help you prepare your resume, cover letter, and other applications materials.

Some Web sites that list internships restrict access to constituents (students and alumni from that institution), while others are available to all candidates. If a password is required, check with your college or university to see if they can give you access.

Here are some top college internship sites:

- eRecruiting: www.erecruiting.com
- MonsterTrak: www.monstertrak.com
- NACElink: www.nacelink.com

You will be able to search specifically for internships, as a type of job, on these sites. Searching for co-ops, fellowships, and externships will also generate listings. Searches can further be narrowed according to whether the internship is paid or not paid. Some internships are paid, while others are not. Companies that offer internships don't always pay interns, because they believe they are providing you with a work experience, rather than hiring you for a job.

Other options to check on are whether the internship must be done for credit (which eliminates nonstudent candidates) or whether there is a stipend or expense reimbursement, if you aren't going to be paid.

Other internship sites provide open access to anyone who is seeking an internship. If you're not affiliated with a college, and even if you are, these are excellent resources to use to find internships.

ASK YOUR GUIDE

I'm a college student. Is it worth doing an unpaid internship?

▶ Absolutely! Even though an internship might not be paid, you may be able to receive college credit for it. In addition, you will learn new skills and have a chance to experiment with a variety of jobs and industries. Also, many companies use their internship programs as a way to screen and recruit future candidates for employment. Their interns are often the first to get job offers. They are also a great resume builder.

Some top open internship sites include:

- **College Grad Job Hunter:** www.collegegrad.com
- **Idealist.org:** www.idealist.org (nonprofit internships)
- **InternWeb:** www.internWeb.com
- **WetFeet Internship Search Engine:** www.wetfeet.internship programs.com

As with jobs, there are niche internship sites that list internship opportunities in a specific career field or location. For example, the Student Conservation Society lists environmental internship opportunities and The City of New York also has a large internship program. You'll find a selection of internship sponsors in specific categories on my About.com site at http://about.com/jobsearch/usinternships.

International internship opportunities also abound. There are sites that list international internships, volunteer opportunities, and work experiences. Check out the list at http://about.com/jobsearch/internationalintern. Check carefully before applying for an overseas opportunity to find out the visa requirements and the paperwork you will need to complete.

Search the job banks and use the job search engines to locate internship listings as well. Use *intern* or *internship* as a keyword. You'll find a good selection of internships there, too.

Brian Kruger, president of CollegeGrad.com, explained to me why he thinks internships are valuable: "The opportunity often exists to work for the company you interned with after graduation. That is, if you were a good employee. While accepting a position with your intern company can make your job search infinitely easier, it also limits your scope of opportunities to just one company. If the company is everything you ever wanted, if they provide you with opportunities for growth and advancement, go for it."

ELSEWHERE ON THE WEB

▶ For more information on internships, including where to search for internships, how to write internship resumes and cover letters, and how to interview for an internship, visit the About.com Internships site (http://internships.about.com). There are lots of resources to help guide you through your search for an internship.

Another way to explore career options is spending a day, or part of a day, job shadowing. National Job Shadow Day (www. jobshadow.org) is an endeavor (not just a day) established to provide young people with the opportunity to "job shadow" a career mentor so they have the opportunity to explore career options and to see how the skills they learn in school relate to work.

Like internships, job shadowing can be a way for adults to explore career change options, to make contacts, and to investigate work alternatives. If you're a college graduate, your career services office may be able to provide you with a list of alumni who are interested in having other alumni job shadow them at their place of employment.

Otherwise, if you belong to an association, like your local chamber of commerce, it may be able to set up job shadowing with a professional in the field you are interested in learning more about. Networking is another good way to find job shadow sponsors. If you know someone who is in a job you'd like to have, ask if you can spend some time visiting her in the office to learn about the position.

Seasonal and Summer Jobs

Interested in finding a summer job? How about a seasonal job? There's a difference between the two types of positions, and, of course, there are job sites dedicated to both. Summer jobs are typically offered when school is out (between Memorial Day and Labor Day). Seasonal jobs are offered for a long time period. For example, ski season jobs usually run from November into April. Tax jobs are typically available from January through April. At some resorts, high season is the summer; in other cases, winter is the prime time to find employment. The "season" depends on the type of position, the industry, and when there is a need to hire to fill jobs.

ELSEWHERE ON THE WEB

▶ If you're a student looking to spend time overseas, there are organizations that will help place you and help you with the paperwork. CIEE (the Council on International Educational Exchange) has programs in over thirty countries. Check it out at www.ciee.org. BUNAC (www.bunac.org) offers work and volunteer opportunities in a variety of countries. Like CIEE, they will help you with placement and paperwork.

There are some people who make a living combining seasonal jobs. Brett works as a ski instructor during the winter and as a carpenter during the summer. Joan, another visitor to my About.com site, works preparing taxes during tax season, works a retail temporary job during the holiday shopping season, and has a job at a summer camp from June to September. She's been able to combine several positions she enjoys into one career.

Of course, there are also lots of employers who hire students just for the summer. Check with your high school guidance or college career office for help finding job listings. You'll find listings the old-fashioned way—on paper (many camps still mail flyers)—and online.

Here are some top seasonal and summer job sites:

ELSEWHERE ON THE WEB

▶ One of the first places you should look for a summer or seasonal job is Cool Works (www.coolworks.com). There are thousands of summer and seasonal job listings, as well as a free weekly e-mail newsletter. You will find jobs in parks, at resorts, on the water, on the ski slopes, and at summer camps. Cool Works even offers a free e-mail account you can use, and check online, for your job search.

- **About.com Summer Job Listings** (http://about.com/jobsearch/summerjobs) is a directory of sites with summer job postings.
- **Back Door Guide to Short-Term Job Adventures** (www.backdoorjobs.com) has U.S. and international summer jobs, internships, and short-term positions.
- **Cool Works** (www.coolworks.com) lists seasonal jobs at parks, ranches, ski resorts, beach resorts, and amusement parks.
- **National Park Service** (www.nps.gov/personnel) lists summer jobs at United States National Parks.
- **SummerJobs** (www.summerjobs.com) includes United States and international summer jobs.

Before you start your summer job search, make sure you are organized. Either create a resume or have a list of the schools you attended and the skills you have so you can complete job applications. When applying in person, dress neatly.

Here are some summer job search tips:

- If you're under eighteen years old, check to see if you need working papers.
- Start your summer job search early.
- Be flexible in your job requirements.
- Have a list of references ready.
- Visit local companies to see if they are hiring.
- Consider your own small business (baby-sitting or pet-sitting, mowing lawns, etc.).
- Network—let everyone you know that you are looking for a job.

Summer camp jobs are usually listed separately from summer jobs, so start your camp job search with the sites that list just camp positions. If you have been a camper and are interested in returning as a counselor, check out opportunities at the camp you attended. Many camps are thrilled to hire alumni campers. In addition to hiring entry-level candidates and students, camps often recruit experienced professionals, like teachers, for specialized jobs and management positions.

When you want to work at a summer camp, start your search earlier. Camp management wants to hire staff well in advance of camp season so they know all their jobs are filled and can focus on planning camp activities.

Here are some top summer camp sites:

- CampChannel: www.campchannel.com
- CampDepot: www.campdepot.com
- CampJobs: www.campjobs.com
- CampPage: www.camppage.com

Before you apply for a summer camp job you will need to get prepared. Create a list of camps where you want to apply. Be flexible and have several choices, because jobs fill fast at some camps, especially those that regularly hire staff back from the previous year. Check to see if the camp requires a job application. If so, complete it carefully. It should be legible and error free.

Follow up if you don't hear back in a timely manner. Also, have a resume, cover letter, and references ready to send upon request.

Don't forget to check to see what the camp provides to employees in addition to salary. Is room and board provided? Do you get any sick time or days off? Do you need to commit to the entire season? Check with the camp before you accept the position, because salary and benefits vary from camp to camp.

Work-at-Home Jobs

Most people would love to work from home. There are, unfortunately, very few people who are actually making a living working at home. There are some companies that do hire off-site employees and other people who earn enough doing contract work or freelancing to make a living. In my experience, though, it takes more work to find a legitimate work-at-home job online than it does to find any other job. That's because there are more jobs listed that aren't legitimate than jobs that are.

The first and most important step to take before you apply for a work-at-home job is to check it out to make sure that it's not a scam. Use this checklist to make sure that the position isn't a scam:

- Carefully investigate every listing you review.
- Avoid listings that guarantee you will get rich quickly.
- Do not pay for leads, lists, or kits.

ASK YOUR GUIDE

I want to work from home, but I'm not having any luck finding a job. Can you help?

▶ It seems like everyone wants to work from home, and I get asked this question a lot by visitors to my About .com site. To be honest, legitimate work-at-home jobs are few and far between. There are some listings for "real" jobs, but you will need to weed through what you find to make sure the job isn't a scam.

○ Ask for references from the company and ask to talk to other employees.

○ Consider if it sounds too good to be true (if it does, it's probably not legitimate).

To find work-at-home jobs, use the sites that focus on those types of jobs. I have a list of these, as well as information and advice on working from home, at http://about.com/jobsearch/workfromhome. Search the job banks and job search engines using *work at home, work from home, freelance, home based* and similar terms. Review the listings very, very carefully, because many of them won't be legitimate. Even though the job sites try to check the postings that are listed, it's easy, because of the volume of listings, for scams to fall through the cracks.

Regardless of the type of job you are looking for, work at home, professional, temporary, summer, seasonal, contract, or internship, it's very important to keep your personal information confidential. Monster has valuable information on keeping your job search safe at http://help.monster.com/besafe. It's important reading for anyone who is using the Internet, and especially important for those of us who spend a lot of time online researching careers and applying for job opportunities. It's better to be safe than sorry and err on the side of divulging too little information, rather than too much.

How to Find Niche Job Sites

Finding good niche sites is difficult. I do have lists of them on my About.com site and there a few other sites, like Job-Hunt.org and the Riley Guide that categorize them, too. However, there are other new sites to check out, and older sites that fall off the radar and no longer have many listings.

There are some perennially good niche sites that continue to provide quality job listings in their niche. At Media Bistro, for

WHAT'S HOT

▶ My article on Work at Home Scams (http://about.com/jobsearch/homescams) is a must-read for anyone interested in working from home. It includes tips and advice on how to evaluate job listings, how to find out if an ad is too good to be true, and where to look to find out if the company you are interested in is on the scam list.

▶ Job sites that cater to a specific audience are becoming very popular. For example, Women for Hire (www .womenforhire.com) has live job fairs and online career advice and job postings just for women. Experience Works (www.experience works.org) provides training and employment for low-income senior citizens and RecruitABILITY (www. disabledperson.com) lists jobs posted by companies who are recruiting candidates with disabilities.

example, there is always an excellent selection of communications/ media jobs, along with career and networking information.

The 6FigureJobs.com Web site lists jobs for those in the $100,000+ salary range, while SnagAJob.com lists only hourly positions.

Check with the people you know, especially people in the same field as you, to see what job sites they use. Sometimes I'm surprised to learn which sites job seekers have success on, and it's always good to have variety in your job search. Job seekers you know may have discovered sites that you haven't heard about, and it can never hurt to explore as many resources as possible.

I spend quite a bit of time trying out the various job sites because I don't want to recommend sites I haven't used. I also want to make sure that I know the best way to search each site and what does, and doesn't, work on at least most of the sites I look at on a daily basis. There aren't enough hours to check every single site, but I do try them out as often as I can.

When you have time, it's good to do the same thing—experiment to see which sites work best for you. Not all sites are created equal and you'll have better success, depending on your interests, with some sites than with others.

I've compiled a list of my favorite job sites, which you can check out at http://about.com/jobsearch/bestjobsites.

Do make your own list of job sites to use, as well, because everyone has different interests and different career goals. So, you'll want to come up with a targeted list of your own favorite sites. Check it every once in a while, even when you have found a new job, because you never know when another position that will be your next step up your career ladder will come along.

Get Linked

The following links will direct you to more job search advice and information from my ABOUT.com site. These links will point you toward more online resources that will help you use niche job sites effectively when job searching.

JOB LISTINGS

This directory contains job sites categorized by type of site, including job banks, niche job sites, local jobs, help-wanted ads, and employment opportunities listed by career field.

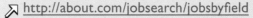 http://about.com/jobsearch/jobsitedirectory

ONLINE JOB SEARCHING

Here's advice on how to search for jobs online, including information on searching job databases and finding resources that target your interests.

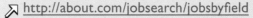 http://about.com/jobsearch/jobsbyfield

JOB FAIRS

There are virtual career fairs where you can participate online, as well as live job fairs in most major cities. Here's information on how to participate, how to find job fairs, and how job fairs can help with your job search.

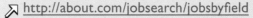 http://about.com/jobsearch/jobfairs

Chapter 9

Jobs Listed by Location

How to Find Geographic Job Sites

There are several reasons why a job seeker might be looking for work in a certain town or city. Sometimes job seekers relocate because the perfect job happens to be located somewhere else. There can be a need to move for family reasons. In other cases, you might simply want a change in climate. The type of jobs that you want may not be available where you currently reside or you may want to stay where you are living and find a job in your hometown. In still other cases, you may simply want a change, for professional or personal reasons.

When any of these scenarios fits, it's time to consider how to find a job in the place where you want to be. First of all, though, consider how much geography comes into play, and take some time analyzing where it is you might want to live.

Bonnie is a good example of someone who moved because she wanted to spend the remainder of her working years in a warmer climate. She decided that Chicago, the windy city, was just that—

About.

▶ When you're interested in a summer job, internship, or short-term work assignment and need to find housing, there are Web sites that list sublets, student housing, and other short-term living options. The University of Berkeley has links to Web sites with housing at http://career.berkeley.edu/Internships/IntHousing.stm. You'll find housing in specific locations, like New York City and Washington, D.C., as well as nationwide listings.

too cold and windy for her to enjoy as she got older. She moved to Florida, because she felt that life on the beach was much easier. The weather was warm, she didn't need to worry about bundling up in a winter coat, and her housing costs were much less.

Another Floridian I talked to told me that he had known from the time he was young that he didn't want to live anywhere else in the world, so he made sure that his career was a local one. He spends his days captaining a sailing ketch on Tampa Bay, taking tourists on day cruises.

On the other end of the spectrum, Barbara, a visitor to my About.com site, moved to a small Vermont town so she could work in the ski industry. Another visitor to my site, Dave, a self-defined ski bum, moved to Colorado and worked a variety of resort jobs, including waiting tables, assisting at the front desk, and working the chairlift so he could make sure he had time on the slopes.

On the other hand, Peter, another visitor to my About.com site, wanted to stay near his family in his hometown. He targeted his job search after he was laid off, to focus on local jobs that were an easy commute from home.

As you can see, there are a variety of reasons for wanting a job in a specific city or town. There are a comparable number of ways to find jobs in just about any location. How you will search for a job depends on how flexible you are.

If your job requirements are open and you'll consider a variety of options, your search can be simple. Your job hunt will involve searching the job banks and the job sites that focus on a particular geographic area for jobs that you are qualified for.

When you want to find a specific type of job in a specific location, your job search will be more targeted, but it's easy to use the predefined locations that are set in most of the major job sites and job search engines, along with keywords to find job listings.

Simply select the location in the search box and use either the list of types of jobs or keywords to search for jobs in your field of interest.

The willingness of employers to accept out-of-town candidates can vary. Some companies recruit on a national basis. They are willing to consider any qualified candidate for the job, regardless of where the person lives. They may, or may not, be willing to pay interviewing or relocation expenses, but they will consider your resume if you have the qualifications they are seeking.

Considering all applicants who apply is becoming more prevalent as Internet hiring increases and geographic boundaries dissolve. A recent study by the Direct Employers Association of leading U.S. companies reports that Internet sources produced 51 percent of all hires in 2005. When candidates apply online they could be anywhere. The thinking is that it doesn't matter where the candidate lives, as long as he is available to interview upon request.

However, some employers prefer to hire local candidates. The job posting may specify that relocation expenses will not be paid or the help-wanted ad may say to apply in person in order to limit the number of applicants.

Some postings are clear as to which candidates will be considered for employment, saying, "Local candidates are given preference" or "Local Candidates *only*."

Employers may opt to post jobs only on their company Web site or on local job sites, again to limit the applicant pool as much as possible to candidates who live nearby. The goal for many hiring managers isn't to get the most applicants. Instead, they are hoping to get a reasonable number of good, qualified candidates.

When applying for these types of jobs, it's important to convince the employer that you are qualified, interested, and flexible enough to interview and relocate in a timely manner if you are offered the job.

Target your resume and cover letters. As I said, some employers aren't interested in hiring candidates from out of town. Unless they are looking for candidates for jobs that are high level or hard to fill, some employers are reluctant to consider interviewing candidates who live out of the area or are unwilling to cover relocation costs. It isn't just the travel or moving expenses that are the issue. The logistics of arranging interviews in a timely manner when the candidate isn't local is also a concern.

A way to overcome these challenges is to think local when writing your resume and cover letters. Do you have family or friends that you can stay with in the new location while interviewing? If so, consider using that address on your resume and your cover letters. Be sure to include your full phone number with area code so the company doesn't have to try to track you down.

Use your cover letter as a way to let the company know that you are planning to relocate and will be available to interview at their convenience. It's important to clarify the fact that you are very interested in the position despite the fact that you may live hundreds of miles away. Otherwise, your application materials may end up in the "no" pile.

Some employers classify applicants by location. The applicants that are local will be considered before applicants from out of town. In these cases, hiring managers only consider applicants who are out of the area if they can't find enough local candidates.

That's why it's important to make a compelling case for considering you in your cover letter. You will want to overcome the hiring manager's objections and sell her on considering your candidacy for employment. Start your cover letter with a paragraph stating

WHAT'S HOT

▶ For those of us who like to stay home, we're not alone. More and more people are opting not to move when their spouse gets a new job in a new city. Instead, the relocating spouse gets an apartment or long-term-stay hotel room and commutes. When you're not sure about whether the new job is going to work, it's a good way to test it out without making a permanent commitment.

why you are interested in this job and this location, and target your cover letter to match the job requirements for the position for which you are applying.

Also make sure that your resume is targeted specifically to each job. This is important all the time, but it is even more important when applying for jobs in a different geographic area, because you have an additional hurdle to overcome (not living there) when making a pitch for the job.

Here's a resume and cover letter relocation checklist:

- ○ Always include your area code on your resume
- ○ List both your home phone and cell phone numbers
- ○ Include your e-mail address
- ○ Use a local address, when possible
- ○ Explain why you are relocating
- ○ Mention that you are available to interview at the employer's convenience

Remember to target your resume and your cover letters toward the jobs for which you are applying. It's especially important when you are making a move to a new location, because you will want your resume and cover letter to impress the employer more than the local candidate's application materials.

State, Local, and Regional Job Banks

There are many job sites that list local job postings. The quickest way to find local job listings is to start with the job search engines. Start by searching by the city and state where you are interested in working. Be specific and list the exact location, because you can always expand your search later on. Use keywords to search for the types of jobs you are interested in, again being specific, at first.

ELSEWHERE ON THE WEB

▶ Did you know that unemployment benefits might be available if you are relocating because your spouse has accepted a job in a new city? It's called a "following spouse benefit," and if it applies to you, check with the unemployment office (www.workforcesecurity.doleta.gov/map.asp) in your current state and your new state to determine what, if any, benefits you are eligible for.

The next step is to visit the job banks that focus on a specific geographic area. Like the niche job sites that list jobs in a specific career field, there are thousands of sites that list local jobs in a certain city, state, or region. This is important because the search engines may not find these smaller job banks; that is, the search engines may not pull listings from these smaller sites. In some cases there will be listings from these job bank sites, while in others there won't—so it's important not to count on it and to search the smaller sites directly.

How do you find local job sites? There are job sites, like my About.com site, that list the top sites for most locations. You will typically find a list of sites that list or find jobs on a nationwide basis (like the job banks and job search engines), as well as lists of regional, state, and local sites.

The volume of sites for any particular location depends on the job market and the population. As you might expect, there are many sites that list New York and California jobs, while there are fewer sites that cover the less populated areas of the country.

It's important to remember to explore all the local job site resources. Wherever you live there will be sites you can use that only list local positions. These sites should be integrated into your job search, because some employers won't list anywhere else.

There is less competition from job seekers on these local sites, so your chances of having your resume screened and getting selected for an interview are higher. That's why it's important to incorporate small, local job sites into your job search. You don't want to miss out on a job that you may have a good chance of getting because there is a limited pool of applicants.

The local sites are also good tools to use to get a snapshot of what jobs are available in a particular job market. The jobs that are "hot" and in need of workers in one part of the country may have an oversupply of workers in another. In addition, there are parts of the country that have more of certain industries than others.

I've seen hiring bonuses and very high salaries offered for jobs in some markets that pay much, much less in a different market because there are many more applicants who are in need of work.

To get a picture of what the hiring market is like in the location where you want to work, use Indeed's job trends at www.indeed.com/jobtrends. Enter the type of job and the location you want to know about in the search box, then click on Create Graph to view the percentage of jobs that contain your search term.

Do make sure that you are covering all the bases when conducting a local job search. This checklist will help you ensure that you have covered all the sources of local job listings:

- Job banks: search by location and keyword
- Job search engines: search by city, state, and keyword
- State, local, and regional job sites
- Help-wanted ads
- Association and chambers of commerce sites

For example, CapitalAreaHelpWanted.com only lists jobs in close proximity to Albany, New York. If you're interested in working in or around New York's capital city, it's a good resource to use. If you're interested in refining your search even further, there are sites, like the local chamber of commerce site, that only list jobs in Saratoga Springs, New York, which is just north of Albany.

You will find a similar pattern of job sites for every U.S. state. NationJob (www.nationjob.com/texas) lists jobs throughout the state of Texas, while HoustonEmployment.com focuses on employment opportunities in Houston and the immediate vicinity.

ELSEWHERE ON THE WEB

▶ Moving can be a stressful experience, even for people who relocate often. Moving.com has some tools to help you organize and plan your move. You can get moving quotes, set up a customized to-do list, and sign up for e-mail alerts with helpful hints to remind you what you need to do before, during, and after the move. With proper planning, your move should run smoothly.

So, check the sites that list job sites for each state, then use the sites that are most relevant to where you want to look for job opportunities.

Some top sites with jobs listed by location include:

- **America's Job Bank:** www.ajb.org
- **Craigslist:** www.craigslist.org
- **Job-Hunt Job Search Resources by State:** www.job-hunt.org
- **Local Careers:** www.localcareers.com
- **Oodle:** www.oodle.com
- **The Riley Guide Location-Specific Sites:** www.rileyguide .com/jobs.html#loc

As with the niche jobs sites, the geographic job site market is fast and furious. New sites are being added frequently. So, if you're not finding what you're looking for, search Google using the specific geographic location and type of job you are interested in as keywords. You may find some additional job listings that way.

Associations and Chambers of Commerce

Using professional associations and local chambers of commerce sites are another good option for finding local jobs.

There are professional associations in just about every location for every industry. If you belong to an association, and even sometimes if you're not a member, you can get contacts to network with and may also be able to access job listings. Search the ASAE Gateway to Associations online at www.asaenet.org to find associations in a lengthy list of categories in many locations.

Once you have found associations in your career field and location of interest, check the Web site to see if they have job postings. Also check to see if they have networking events you can attend.

Some events may be open to nonmembers, and if you have to join to participate, the fee may be worth the investment.

Chambers of commerce often post job listings for member companies. They are an excellent source of local job listings, and the jobs are typically available to anyone who visits the chamber Web site.

I know several people who have obtained employment through our local chamber of commerce site. In addition, the hiring process for these job seekers was really fast. They applied online and were contacted for employment within a day or so. Because both the candidates and the jobs were local, there was no delay in scheduling interviews or starting employment.

You can find chambers of commerce in your area by using the map at the U.S. Chamber of Commerce Web site (www.uschamber.com). You'll usually find a chamber for the entire state, as well as chambers for most mid-sized to larger towns and cities. Not all chambers of commerce list jobs on the Web sites, but on those that do you'll find a good selection of local job openings.

International chambers of commerce can be helpful if you are interested in working abroad. Check out the directory at www.worldchambers.com. There is a directory of chambers of commerce that you can search, information on international companies, and other information available for those interested in international business.

Association and chambers of commerce sites are also a good source to find jobs with smaller companies. New and small companies may not necessarily be recruiting aggressively, but they do hire a lot of workers.

In fact, small companies hire many more employees than larger organizations do. According to the U.S. Small Business Administration, small businesses represent more than 99.7 percent of all

WHAT'S HOT

▶ Rather than taking a job wherever it may be, more and more job hunters are looking for employment in places where they would like to live. They are evaluating locations and the pros and cons of living in a certain city, then looking for jobs in places where they want to be. CNNMoney has a popular list of the 100 best places to live at www.money.cnn.com/best/bplive.

employers, employ more than half of all private sector employees, pay 45 percent of the total U.S. private payroll, and have generated 60 to 80 percent of new jobs annually over the last decade.

Many, if not most, local employers are small companies, so investigating opportunities at these companies is a good option. The article "Think Small and Diversify Your Job Search" on my About.com Job Searching site (http://about.com/jobsearch/small companies) will help you find the right smaller companies to target. It also discusses the pros and cons of working at a small company, as well as why tenure at a small company can be a good rung on your career ladder.

International Job Sites

When you want to work abroad, your job search is a bit more complicated. You not only have to find jobs to apply to, but you also have to convince an employer to consider your long-distance job application, obtain the appropriate visa, and complete the masses of paperwork that you will need to fill out in order to work in a foreign country.

When you are interested in working abroad, start your job search by using the sites that list international jobs. Also, search the major job banks, because many of them have international job openings as well as U.S. jobs.

Here are some top sites for international job listings and advice:

- About.com International Job Listings: http://about.com/job search/internationaljobs
- Escape Artist: www.escapeartist.com
- Monster Work Abroad: http://workabroad.monster.com
- The Riley Guide International Job Opportunities: www. rileyguide.com/internat.html

▶ Your alumni connection, if you're a college graduate, is a great way to get relocation help. Most colleges have alumni clubs in various cities around the country. These clubs usually have regular networking events, which are a great way to make connections. Most colleges also have resources available to help you connect online with alumni who can help with your job search and give advice and assistance about moving to their location.

Keep in mind that your application materials, including your resume and letters, will be different when applying for jobs at overseas companies. The United States has strict legal guidelines on what information job seekers can, and cannot, be asked to provide. There's a lengthy list of information that is considered discriminatory which employers are prohibited from requesting.

The international rules vary significantly and you may be surprised at some of the information you will need to provide.

You may need a curriculum vitae (CV) instead of a resume when applying for overseas employment. When seeking employment in Europe, the Middle East, Africa, or Asia, you will be expected to provide a CV instead of a resume. A curriculum vitae is similar to but more extensive than a resume. It includes a summary of your educational background as well as teaching and research experience, publications, presentations, awards, honors, affiliations, and other details.

Overseas employers often expect to see personal information listed on a CV that would not be included on an American resume. The information includes date of birth, nationality, place of birth, and even marital status and number of children. In addition, a CV is longer (two or more pages) than a resume and includes more detailed information on your background and skills.

The formatting and style of CVs varies from country to country, so before you apply make sure that you know what's appropriate for the specific country that interests you.

Eurograd.com (www.eurograduate.com/plan2.php) has advice on writing CVs and preparing for interviews that is specific to each of the twenty-three countries the site covers. There is also information about specific careers. This Web site is a good source for information on preparing targeted applications for jobs in your country of interest.

ASK YOUR GUIDE

I travel frequently for business and I'm not sure how to job search on the road.

▶ I've found that what works best for me is to bring everything I need with me when I'm traveling. When all the programs, files, and Web sites you need are on your laptop and when the phone numbers you need are on your cell phone, you can job search from anywhere. It's like bringing a mobile office on the road with you.

Determining when to use a CV instead of a resume, and what should be included on it, can be complicated, so use these resources from my About.com site to prepare your curriculum vitae:

- How to Write a CV: http://about.com/jobsearch/writecv
- Curriculum Vitae Samples: http://about.com/jobsearch/samplecv
- Curriculum Vitae Resources: http://about.com/jobsearch/cvresources

Another thing to keep in mind when conducting an international job search is the time difference. Use e-mail as often as you can. When calling be cognizant of the time differential—it may be the middle of the night where you are calling. Timeanddate.com has a world clock you can use to make sure that you're calling during business hours.

Volunteering is a very good way to gain international experience. Another option for those who want to work abroad is international volunteer programs. Peace Corps (www.peacecorps.gov) volunteers work in 137 countries around the world on issues including information technology, education, and environmental preservation. You have to be eighteen to volunteer, but there is no upper age limit. In fact, the oldest volunteer to date was eighty-six when she volunteered!

There are a variety of other volunteer programs, short-term and long-term, available throughout the world. I have a list on my About.com site at http://about.com/jobsearch/volunteer.

Alternatives for students, and sometimes recent graduates, include work/study programs. There are organizations like BUNAC (www.bunac.org.uk) and the Council on International Educational

▶ Anyone job searching long distance needs a cell phone with a plan that includes nationwide (or international) calling, as well as a phone that gets service wherever you may be. The About.com Cell Phones site has a quiz you can take that will help you find your perfect phone. Check it out at http://about.com/cellphones/buyers guides. The quiz will step you through the process of finding a phone that will work effectively for you.

Exchange International (www.ciee.org) that run work and travel programs for students. These programs will assist with job placement, housing, and paperwork.

Newspapers

Newspapers are a good way to find job prospects, in more ways than one. In addition to listing jobs in the help-wanted section of the classifieds, you'll also find information in the business section on companies that may make a good next employer for you.

CareerBuilder (www.careerbuilder.com) is affiliated with over ninety Gannett newspapers and has a presence in over 200 local job markets. You can find job listings by going directly to Career-Builder or to the Web site for your local newspaper. When you click on Jobs, either in its own section or in the classified sections, you will be able to search for help-wanted ads by location, keyword, and type of position.

When using newspapers you will want to target your search very specifically (by town or city), because all the listings in your search results will be jobs in your local community or the vicinity. So, focus your job search, at first, on the specific types of jobs you want to find. Start as close to home as possible, then expand your search by radius (X number of miles from the town) to generate more listings.

Local business newspapers are a valuable source of information. In addition to your local newspaper, if there is a weekly business journal that covers your area, read it.

The one in my town, for example, has articles and information on new and growing businesses. There's information on what is happening in the local job market, as well as lists of the top companies in the area, categorized by career field. So, for example, I

TOOLS YOU NEED

▶ When you're interviewing in a location you're not familiar with make sure you map your directions. Mapquest (www.mapquest.com) and Yahoo! Maps (http://maps .yahoo.com) are excellent resources for getting directions and for mapping the location where you need to go. Be sure you do a trial run and visit your interview location ahead of time so you know exactly where you're going. That way, you'll be sure not to be late for your interview.

can review the top health care employers or the top banks in my region. The lists include contact information, so I can research the companies to see if they post jobs online.

There are many Web sites you can use to find local business information. The following sites have information on online newspapers and on local business information and news:

- **AllBusiness.com:** business directory
- **Biznews.com:** local business news
- **CareerBuilder.com:** local job postings
- **Online Newspapers:** U.S. and international newspapers (http://about.com/jobsearch/newspapers)

Some of the research you conduct won't bring you directly to job listings, but it will help you find companies that may be hiring. If they don't have listings on the company job sites, and some may not, you can contact the company directly to inquire about possible job openings.

Relocation Advice

Relocating isn't always easy. When I was a child, my parents moved to the United States from England because of my dad's job. He wanted to be part of the growing aerospace industry in the United States, and he received a job offer that was too good to pass up.

I remember how hard it was for our family to leave our relatives, to meet new friends, to attend new schools, and to create a new life in a new community. I have nephews and nieces who relocated much more often than that. My brother-in-law was in the military for over twenty years and he and his family spent many years moving from military base to military base.

TOOLS YOU NEED

▶ When you have been offered a job in a location, About.com's Salary Calculators (http://about.salary .com) will help you decide if you can afford to get by on your new paycheck. There's a salary calculator to help you determine if your job offer is reasonable compared to other positions in the same industry and location. There's also a cost of living calculator to help you evaluate whether you can afford to relocate.

Regardless of how often you move, it's good to plan in advance to both ensure the move goes smoothly and to make sure that you are making the right move, both for yourself and for your family. My father, for example, relocated six months before the rest of the family, so everything was set when we arrived.

A sales manager who had been recruited by a company I worked for did the same thing. In Jeremy's case, it was a very wise move, because the job didn't work out. Jeremy was recruited from a large national company to grow our regional company to the next level.

The job we hired him for wasn't a step down, but the company culture was very different. He moved from a company with thousands of employees to one with about 100. The location (upstate New York) was very different from Boston, where he had lived before.

Jeremy missed city life and he missed working for a large corporation. He ended up returning to his prior job. He had the foresight not to sell his house and relocate his family until he was sure that the new job was going to work out. When he knew that it wasn't, he was in a good position to undo a career change that didn't work out. He was also lucky that his previous employer valued his services enough to rehire him.

There are other ways to make sure that the decisions you make to relocate make sense. Spend time visiting the new city before you take a job. Research the company you will be working for very carefully to be sure it is a good fit, both personally and professionally.

Plan ahead when you have to move. When you need to move sooner rather than later, be open-minded and flexible about the jobs you are willing to take. Consider a temporary job as a

ASK YOUR GUIDE

How do I find out more about the cities where I'm interested in relocating?

▶ Lots of visitors to my About.com Job Searching site ask me about moving and how they can find out more about local communities. I always point them toward the About.com local sites, where they can find everything they need to know. Whether you are interested in Long Island or Seattle, there are sites that can help. Check out the list at http://about.com/citiestowns.

means to get established (and get a paycheck) in a new community. It's easier to find a local job when you are already in the new location, so you may want to broaden your job options in order to make the move happen in a timely manner.

Don't move on the spur of the moment. Take the time to learn about the community, the job market, housing, transportation, salaries, cost-of-living, and the other issues that factor into your job search and your decision to relocate.

Here's a list of what to consider before you make a final decision on moving:

- Do you have a job offer? If not, what are the prospects for employment?
- Can you afford to take the position? Have you checked a cost of living calculator?
- What is the availability of housing? How quickly can you arrange housing?
- How about transportation to and from work?
- Have you checked on schools if you have a family?
- Have you investigated employment (or unemployment benefits) for your spouse?
- Is the community a place where you would enjoy living?

All these factors are important. In fact, sometimes they can be more important than the job itself. If you're not happy where you live, if you have to struggle to pay the bills each month, if the school system is awful, or if the commute to work is a pain, the job may not be worth taking.

Here's an example why factors other than the job itself can be important. One of my clients, George, took what seemed like an ideal job after graduation from college. He was familiar with the area where he was moving. Even though the cost of living was high, he found an apartment with several friends from college.

There wasn't much of a local community, but there were plenty of amenities at work, like a health club and a spa. What ended up being the problem was that this job was in a major suburban area and commuting to work (even though George lived close by) was a big time waster. Getting in and out of the region to travel on business or to visit his girlfriend or family was a hassle.

On top of this, the job was much more stressful than he anticipated. When you add all those factors together, it didn't end up being a good situation for George. As a result, a second relocation, this time back to his hometown, was in order.

He accepted a contract job that got him where he wanted to be working, even though it wasn't a permanent position. However, the contract was converted to permanent employment after ninety days, and he was set, at least for this stage of his career.

Even when you do everything right, relocation doesn't always work out. That's why it's important not to burn your bridges and to stay in contact with prior employers, with networking connections, and with those who can help with your job search. Just in case you need to start over sooner than you expected.

ELSEWHERE ON THE WEB

▶ Interested in a trouble-free move? Check out the About.com Guide to Home Buying's advice on moving and relocation at http://about.com/homebuying/relocation. There's information on what you must do before you sell your house, suggestions on how to buy a home, advice on how to plan a move, and tips on how to successfully relocate across town or across the country.

Get Linked

Here are some links to more advice on finding a job in the location where you want to live from my **ABOUT**.com *site.*

LOCAL JOB LISTINGS

Here you will find local job listings and employment resources, as well as local job search help and advice.

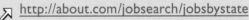 http://about.com/jobsearch/jobsbystate

COMPANY RESEARCH

Use these resources to help you research the company before you accept employment out of town. That way you can ensure that your move is a good one.

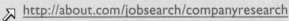 http://about.com/jobsearch/companyresearch

RELOCATION RESOURCES

There are ways to get ready to relocate and to have a job waiting for you when you arrive. Here are tips and suggestions on how to relocate for a new job.

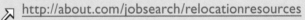 http://about.com/jobsearch/relocationresources

Chapter 10

Job Search Networking

Traditional Networking

Even though online job searching is the way many people are hired, networking is still one of the most important ways job seekers find employment. There are some estimates that say as many as 60 to 80 percent of all jobs are found through networking. I'm not sure if the numbers are quite that high, but a significant number of job seekers do find jobs by networking. Sometimes, it's jobs that have never been advertised. When the job isn't advertised that can mean there's less competition from other candidates, so you may have a better chance of getting the position.

Job search networking means using contacts, personal or business, to help you enhance your career or find a new job. Networking is connecting with people you know who may be able to help you with your job search. It's also asking those people if they know someone else who can also assist.

Networking can help you:

- Find job listings
- Get referrals for jobs
- Get references for jobs
- Gain knowledge about a job, a company, or an industry

There are two main types of **career networking**: online and offline networking. There is the traditional form of networking, where the contacts you make are personal ones. There's also online networking, where job seekers and career changers can use e-mail, instant message, and discussion forums to network.

Both types of networking are very valuable job search tools and both can help you find jobs. Networking is especially important because it can help you find unadvertised jobs, get your resume looked at, assist you in obtaining an interview, and even help you get a job offer.

With online networking there are several types of Web sites you can use to assist with making contacts. You can incorporate each of these types of sites into your job search.

The various types of networking sites include:

- Business-networking sites
- Career and job search networking sites
- Social networking sites

Here's an example of very basic personal networking. I happened to be chatting with my vet (her child goes to school with mine) at a school function. She mentioned that she was looking for someone to work in her office. I told her that my niece was job searching. She called my niece in for an interview and hired her on

▶ A contact manager is an essential networking tool. Every job seeker needs software to keep track of career contacts. Your e-mail program may have a built-in contact manager or address book you can use. I use Eudora, for example, and my address book allows me to list home and business contact information, as well as notes regarding my communications with my contacts.

the spot. All it took was a brief conversation in a school gym to get an employer to look at my niece's resume.

Online networking works too. I am always aware of the employers that I know who might be hiring and which of my clients might be a good match for the company. I've sent several candidates to one company that is in the midst of a growth spurt. The last time, all it took was an e-mail to the vice president of technology mentioning that I knew someone who would be a good candidate. I forwarded the candidate's resume and he was offered a contract job, which later turned into full-time employment.

Networking can be formal or informal. Formal networking events include professional association or chamber of commerce mixers, seminars and conferences that include a networking component, and service-oriented organization (like the Rotary) activities. At some of these events the program includes networking as a scheduled activity. At others, it's less planned and organized but still effective.

Formal networking events can include, for example, weekly chamber of commerce breakfasts, after-work mixers, or association gatherings where members from a specific industry or type of job get together. For example, a local association of human resources personnel meets regularly to share information on new labor laws and policies, as well as to network with other members.

Informal networking can happen at any time and any place. An acquaintance of mine recently hired a person who happened to be seated next to him on an airplane. They were both in the aerospace industry and his fellow traveler was looking for a new job. They exchanged business cards. The gentleman then sent my acquaintance his resume. It was passed along to human resources and the company had a new hire shortly thereafter.

ASK YOUR GUIDE

Is it appropriate to network at parties and other social events?

▶ It's appropriate to network on most occasions, as long as you're discreet. You don't need to let all the attendees know that you desperately need a job, but it's fine to mention in conversation that you're job searching. I wouldn't ask outright for a job, but I would ask for advice and assistance.

I've known people who have found jobs by networking at birthday parties and holiday parties. One job seeker I know, Cicely, who was interested in book publishing, made a great connection with a senior editor at a large New York City book publisher during a children's birthday party. She mentioned her goals, in passing, to the editor, who thought she would be a good candidate for employment.

In another case, I helped an assistant at my dentist's office get a part-time job at a local horse farm. She had mentioned to me that she was looking for a weekend job, and I knew of an opening. So, as you can see, networking can take place anytime.

As long as you're not too obnoxious about how you network, you can network anywhere. It is important, though, not to overdo it. I recommend being subtle rather than broadcasting your hopes and dreams to a roomful of people.

I always recommend asking for assistance rather than asking bluntly for a job or help getting a job. People are more likely to help, I believe, if they don't feel obligated to provide assistance and don't feel pressure to do something for you.

In order to network effectively, your communication skills must be top-notch. You want to make a good, positive impression each and every time you talk to a contact. The following are tips for effective networking:

- **Be professional:** Make sure your e-mail address, instant-messaging screen name, and voice mail sound professional.
- **Identify yourself:** Explain who you are and why you are contacting the person.
- **Perfection matters:** When writing or e-mailing your contacts, proofread everything you send.
- **Ask for advice:** Request advice; don't ask for a job.

- **Manners matter:** Send a thank-you note to every contact person who helps you.
- **Be brave:** Don't be hesitant to mention that you're job seeking.
- **Watch the clock:** When contacting people at home, don't call too late (or too early).

Business Networking

Business networking is networking with a purpose. Rather than being an offshoot of personal communications and relationships, it's designed to focus on business connections. This is the nuts and bolts of networking. You're not asking for help as an aside, you're using connections (and they are using you) who know how to help and who are ready and willing to assist. You are also making yourself available to contacts who may need your help.

Networking is a two-way street, and that's important to remember. You can't network effectively or successfully without being willing to provide assistance to your networking contacts. The more people you help, the more likely you will be to get help in return.

Business-networking connections aren't just for job searching. They are designed to help with a variety of business-related endeavors. Business networking can help a start-up company connect to investors who can provide capital and assist a company in finding customers or business partners. When it comes to careers, networking can help a company find employees or help a job seeker find a job.

The premise behind how business networking works is quite simple. It's the "six degrees of separation" theory, which says that each person in the world is connected to every other person through associations that include no more than five people in between the first person and the last.

TOOLS YOU NEED

▶ Time moves so fast that it can be hard to keep track of when to connect with people in your network. An online calendar will help you stay connected and remind you when you need to get in touch. Yahoo! Calendar (http://calendar.yahoo.com) is a free online tool that you can use to remember important dates. You can set up automatic reminders to notify you that it's time to e-mail or call contacts.

Networking works then, because everyone knows someone who can help. If you're seeking employment at a specific company, you should, in theory, be able to find a connection you can use to help you get a foot in the door. Or, if you are trying to grow a business you should be able to find connections that can assist with marketing, with expanding a customer base, and with finding employees. On the flip side, when you are affiliated with a busi-ness-networking site, you could be the prospective employee the company is actively recruiting.

That's part of the power of networking. You're using it to find contacts, and other people are networking to find you—that is, a good, qualified candidate for employment. The more you network, the more contacts you make, and the greater chance you have of making connections that can help jump-start your career or job search.

Online networking, on some levels, is like online dating, which has been highly successful. You meet (virtually) people with simi-lar interests and then you get together, either online or offline, or both. Some of the dating sites advertise how many weddings have taken place because of the services they provide. Similar suc-cesses, from a business perspective, are reported by business and job search networking sites.

Some online networking sites require an invitation to join; oth-ers let you sign up without a recommendation. Some charge a fee for some services, while others are free. So, before you join, research what the site offers and how it can help you. If you need a referral, ask around. I bet you know someone who already belongs who can refer you.

The following is a list of business-networking sites:

- **Buzzoodle:** www.buzzoodle.com
- **Company of Friends:** www.fastcompany.com/cof

- LinkedIn: www.linkedin.com
- OpenBC: www.openbc.com
- Ryze: www.ryze.com

I was invited to join LinkedIn by a colleague, so I decided to give it a try. My main reason was to learn how to use it and to understand how it could help job seekers. After I joined, I was pleasantly surprised to receive a message from a voice from the past. Scott, who had written a guest article on Alaskan fishing jobs for my About.com site years ago, had found me on LinkedIn and contacted me to let me know about what he was doing now.

It was great to learn how his career had progressed and to hear all about what he was doing. I've connected with other people, as well, who have helped me with my career and vice versa.

Once I registered with LinkedIn, I had the choice of setting up a personal, business, or pro account. The personal account is free. The other accounts offer wider access to other users and additional services for a monthly fee.

I can find contacts on LinkedIn by using my personal account to search by industry, keyword, or name. I can also search for references for a particular person or company. This would be very useful if I were interested in working for a specific company and wanted to find out more about it.

There's also a job search section of LinkedIn that I can use to look for job openings. When I find a job I'm interested in, I can look for connections at that company who can help with my application. Employers can also find me via my LinkedIn profile.

As you can see, sites like LinkedIn do more than just generate a list of networking contacts.

I'm not sure whether I would pay for an account at a business-networking site. I think I would be more likely to if I were hiring or networking on a regular basis and wanted to outreach to contacts

ELSEWHERE ON THE WEB

▶ CareerJournal has an excellent article on how to expand your connections by using online networking. It's available at www.career journal.com/jobhunting/using net/20040121-gunn.html. It has good information on how virtual networking works, how it can help your career, and how to mix online and offline connections. There's also insight into how you can turn an online connection into a viable opportunity.

more frequently and more often. For now, the personal account works just fine for what I need.

Job Search Networking

Job search networking is a little different than business networking. It's focused networking to find employment. When you use a job search networking site, you target your networking efforts just like you focused your search when looking for job listings. Rather than focusing on business connections, it's specifically focused on your career and your search for employment. Job search networking involves networking specifically to get help finding a job.

The components of job search networking include using your network to find jobs that aren't listed, networking to get a recommendation for a job, as well as using your network to gain inside information so you can ace the interview and, hopefully, get a job offer.

There are numerous Web sites and discussion forums that focus specifically on job search networking. They include contacts and information on careers, job opportunities, and companies.

Here are some job search networking sites:

- Jobster: www.jobster.com
- Meetup Work and Careers: www.meetup.com
- Monster Networking: www.monster.com
- Vault Message Boards: www.vault.com
- WetFeet Discussion Boards: www.wetfeet.com/discuss/home.asp

There are several steps involved in job search networking online. Depending on the site you are using, how you create a profile and how you network may vary slightly, but the concept

ELSEWHERE ON THE WEB

▶ For tips on virtual networking, visit the Virtual Handshake Web site. You'll find suggestions on how to use networking and the Internet to enhance your job search, as well as to find business contacts and connections with people who can help you. There's also a blog with the latest networking news and advice. Check it out at www.thevirtualhand shake.com.

is the same regardless of what type of site, and which specific sites, you use for networking.

What you are going to do is create a profile that includes business, and sometimes personal, information. You will then be using this profile to network with people who can help with your job search. Those people could be recruiters or hiring managers or contacts at a company or in an industry that interests you.

When you log in to Monster, for example, you will be able to create a profile to use for networking. First of all, you will need to be registered with Monster. Once you log in, click on Networking Profile, then enter the information you want to include.

Keep in mind that you can make your profile public or private. If it's public, any other member can view it. Making your profile public isn't necessarily a good idea, especially if you are employed and job seeking. You don't want your boss to find it! Of course, you can set up a public profile if privacy isn't a concern. If you're not pleased with the contacts you get, you can make your profile private at any time.

Profile options typically include uploading a picture, writing a personal description to include, and listing the information (skills, experience, certifications, etc.) from your resume. As well as your professional information, you can also include your interests. The thought is that you can use your interests as a common denominator when seeking contacts.

One of my brothers, for example, is a competitive runner. He's used the contacts he's made while running to enhance his career on several occasions. An acquaintance of mine is a member of local yacht club. Other members, knowing of his skills and success in his field, have actively recruited him. Mentioning your interests in your networking profile can be an additional way to find contacts that can help. Most people are thrilled to talk about their hobbies and

ASK YOUR GUIDE

I'm not sure about networking online. Does it really work?

▶ It sure does. Let me give you an example of how connections can help with your job search. I received an e-mail from a visitor to my About.com site who had a question on revamping his resume. I noticed that he was an aviation writer and I knew someone who needed a writer for a book project. I connected them and within a few e-mails the writer had a new project.

activities with someone who understands them and are often very willing to offer assistance to those with similar interests.

There's also an option to forward your profile via e-mail to a friend or networking contact. This can be a timesaver, because you just need to click Send to e-mail your profile. That's much easier than having to create a new e-mail message to send every time you want to make a connection.

When you search for contacts on Monster, you can search using a variety of criteria. Search options include keyword, skills, location, school, company, and people. As you can see, there are many ways you can search for people to help with your job search.

You'll find different contacts on different sites, so it's worth using at least two or three sites for networking. Not everyone uses the same Web sites, so it makes sense to use several. The more resources you use, the broader contact base you'll establish.

Company alumni networks can be a useful resource. There are Web sites that contain alumni networks for specific companies. A company alumni network is similar to a college alumni network. In the case of a college, alumni are people who attended the institution. With company networks, alumni include ex-employees and retirees.

Apple, Bell Labs, and Fidelity, to name a few, have alumni networking sites. These sites can help with job search networking, insider information, and job listings. Some are sponsored by the company (like Fidelity's alumni Web site), and others are sponsored by ex-employees or even current employees.

Job-Hunt has a list of company alumni sites at http://job-hunt .org/employer_alumni_networking.shtml. If you're an alumnus of the company or if you are interested in a job working at one of the companies that have alumni Web sites, take a look to see how they can assist with your job search.

Social Networking Sites

The reason for using social networking sites is that your friends can help with your job search too. You never know who might be able to help you. Friends and acquaintances (even virtual ones) may be able to provide job search assistance.

I was able to provide a reference for someone who I had worked with years ago. I remembered her qualifications and abilities, and the company she was going to work for was glad to get a good reference for her. We had stayed in touch, as friends, so I had kept up with her career transitions over the years and was still a valuable reference.

Some sites, like Meetup.com, are open to anyone who wants to join. Other sites, like Facebook.com, require that you attend a certain school or are affiliated with other members. Requirements vary, so check to see what the membership criteria is and check to see what the site offers that may be useful to your job search.

The following is a list of social networking sites:

- Facebook.com
- Friendster.com
- Meetup.com
- MySpace.com
- Tribe.com
- Yahoo!360 (http://360.yahoo.com)

When you post personal information on these sites, be careful about what you write. Also be careful about posting pictures and providing details on your personal life, especially if you are using these contacts to help with your career.

Consider the case of a young lady I know. She posted information on a social networking site about where she lived, what school she went to, and what she did for fun. She also wrote about

▶ Networking your way to a new job is high on the list of many job seekers daily activities. About.com's Human Resources Guide, Susan Heathfield, has information on how to create a pool of contacts from which you can generate leads, referrals, advice, and information for your job search. You can read it at http://about.com/human resources/networking.

stealing, drinking, and not getting along with her parents. Unfortunately, or perhaps fortunately, her parents came across her profile. It could have been worse. From a career perspective, the person who found her information could have been a prospective employer. More importantly, from a safety perspective, she had divulged more personal information than was appropriate under any circumstances.

I've heard about cases where college alumni who have Facebook accounts have read some students profiles that didn't impress them in the least. One college alumnus was a recent graduate who was recruiting for his employer. He used Facebook to check out the applicants. Some of what he read made such a bad impression that the students knocked themselves out of contention for a job opportunity.

I've also read about colleges finding out about violations of the school honor code by reading Facebook profiles. They have sanctioned students because of what they read on Facebook.

Even though what you do in your personal life shouldn't impact your professional one, when someone reads something they would rather have not known about you, it's hard not to consider it when evaluating what type of employee you would make.

Use your alumni network. Many colleges and universities have alumni networks that are specifically focused on career networking. When a college has a career network, career advisors typically offer informational interviews to students, they provide job and internship listings to the school, and participate in on-campus and off-site recruiting and networking programs. Career advisors can also help provide insider information about their company and can help promote candidates from their schools to hiring managers.

If you're a college graduate, check with your career services office to see how they can assist and what career networking services they provide. You should be able discover more about your career field(s) of interest and find out about employment opportunities at their company or in their industry from your alumni connections.

There are school networking sites that are run by colleges and there are also independent sites you can use to make connections. All levels of education, including high school, are represented by these sites. The high school I attended doesn't even exist anymore, but there are still close to 400 alumni registered on one of the school networking sites.

Check out the following school alumni networking sites:

- Alumni.net
- Classmates.com
- Your college alumni Web site

How to Create a Career Network

You should start creating your network on your first day of work at your first job. My first job, more than a few years ago, was in a small grocery store near my home. Even though the store has changed hands, some of the employees are still there. I stop in whenever I'm in town to say hello. Do I need them in my network? Maybe not, but it can't hurt to stay connected, because you never know when your network can help.

The way to build a network is, first of all, to remember. Remember who you have worked with over the years, and keep track of where they are, as best you can. The next step is to stay in touch. Staying in touch can be as simple as sending a brief e-mail message on occasion. It can mean remembering to send a birthday card or a thank-you note to a contact person who has helped you.

Online networking can be more involved than that. I have online business relationships (and friendships) with people I have never met in person. I hope to meet some of them sometime. I

TOOLS YOU NEED

▶ Using connections from your past to help you in the present can be an excellent networking tool. Sites like Classmates.com let you connect (or reconnect) with high school, college, military, and career/work friends and acquaintances. You can also post on message boards and find out about reunions.

probably will never meet others because of where they are located and because we won't have an opportunity to connect in person. In both cases, whether I have met the person or not, I still consider them part of my network. I've helped them and they have helped me—on numerous occasions.

Build your network. Build your network one person at a time. Add the contacts to your contact planner. Stay in touch with your contacts on a regular basis.

Once you've built your network, expand it as your career grows. You will meet new people almost every day that should be included in your network. Add them to your contact manager and utilize them when you need assistance.

Another word of advice is to never feel too important or believe that you have achieved more or moved further up the career ladder than someone else and don't need them anymore. Include everyone you can in your network, regardless of their status in life and in their career.

One of the reasons that my network has been so beneficial to me is that it's inclusive. I've always felt that it was important to consider everyone I've met over the years as valuable, whether it is the person who has helped my mom around the house for the last thirty years or the people who deliver my packages or who pack my groceries.

People remember when you're nice to them and will want to help you, sometimes when you least expect it. Even more importantly, your network can be there whenever you need it.

When my dad was ill, my mom's coworkers and colleagues from thirty years of work as a legal secretary helped our family tremendously. They brought food, they sent flowers, they offered to drive my dad to doctor's appointments, and they offered assistance with legal issues. It wasn't career-related help, but the assistance my mom provided during her career, like notarizing signatures or expediting house closings, came back in multiples when it was needed.

As you can see, networking works both ways, so consider what you can do for your network as well as what your network can do for you. I guarantee that the time you spend will be well worth the help you get when you need it.

How to Use Your Network

More than 80 percent of job seekers say that networking has helped with their job search.

Networking may not have directly found them a new job, but it certainly helped. Career networking can provide job seekers with information on what the job market is like in a city where they would like to live or provide information on what the prospects are like for employment at a company or in an industry of interest. Your network can help you with your resume, provide a reference for you, or send you job leads.

Your networking contacts can be made online or in person. In some cases, you may rarely, or even never, personally meet your networking contacts. Other contacts may be friends you socialize with, colleagues from work, or business acquaintances that you spend time with offline.

Regardless of whether your networking is personal or virtual, your communications need to be professional, polished, and perfect. Regardless of how you met your contact (and even if it was at a club or party), when you're communicating about career-related matters you need to write and act as a job seeker, not a friend.

All your correspondence needs to be perfect. Your letters, your e-mail, and even your instant messages need to be polite and error free. Spell check, check your grammar, and check for typos. When instant messaging, keep your messages brief because it's easier to look them over to check for mistakes when they are short.

ELSEWHERE ON THE WEB

▶ WetFeet.com has good advice on how every job seeker can network like a professional. There's information on how to talk to strangers, how to find a mentor, how to network like an expert, how to stay networked, and how to (painlessly) work a room. Check it out at www.wetfeet.com/advice/networking.asp. It's well worth reading if you're ready to network or even just thinking about it.

When meeting networking contacts in person, it's important to dress professionally in business attire. Business attire means a conservative suit and shoes and minimal accessories. The only exception would be if you were at a networking event or program where the dress was advertised as business casual or casual.

The reason for dressing professionally is because your networking is as much a part of your job search as going on interviews. You will want to accord the same level of professionalism and the same attention to your networking activities as to the other facets of your job search. Because, as is often the case, networking could be what gets you the job.

When building a network, quality is as important as quantity. Jason Goldberg, CEO of Jobster, says, "People often perceive networking as quantity vs. quality, boasting how many people are in their online networks, etc. At the end of the day, it is better to have three strong connections than to have 300 people you've met in passing. Networking within your groups can help establish stronger connections and ultimately help you learn about and get noticed for great opportunities."

As you can see, it's better to have a strong network than a big one. It's more important to have a solid base of contacts that you can count on to help you when you need it than to have masses of people in your network that you barely know. One reason is because if you have too many people in your network it's hard to effectively manage it and stay in touch.

You can stay in touch with your network by mail (holiday cards are always appropriate), e-mail, instant message, telephone, and in person. I try to have lunch or dinner every once in a while with my contacts who are close to home. With the people who are further away, I make sure that I e-mail or call on a regular basis, just to say hello.

Staying in touch doesn't have to be done daily or even weekly. Even when you're actively job seeking, sending a quick e-mail to update your contacts on your status is sufficient.

Just as quality is more important than quantity in the number of people in your network, quality is more important in the outreach you do. It's annoying to receive too frequent e-mails on the same topic. What's better, as far as I'm concerned, is to receive a nice note asking how I'm doing that includes a brief update on how my contact is doing.

Working your network works both ways. I'm more inclined to be helpful, and most people think similarly, when someone cares about me and inquires as to how I'm doing.

Review sample networking correspondence. If you're contacting people who you have been referred to and you're not sure what to say, take some time to review sample letters.

Here is a sample networking letter:

Dear Mr. Smith,

I was referred to you by Diana Heathstone from ABCD in Boston. She recommended you as an excellent source of information on the publishing industry.

My goal is to secure an entry-level position in publishing. I welcome your advice and insight on career opportunities in the publishing industry, on how to job search, and on how best to generate job leads.

Thank you in advance for any help and suggestions you can share. I look forward to hearing from you.

Sincerely,
Signature

TOOLS YOU NEED

▶ **When you have lots of contacts to manage and want to keep your phone and your computer address book synchronized, consider software like DataPilot that will synchronize your cell phone contacts and your phone's calendar. DataPilot synchronizes your cell phone contacts to Outlook, Outlook Express, and Palm OS and your calendar to Outlook.**

ELSEWHERE ON THE WEB

▶ When you need to improve your network, the article "Ten Steps to Dramatically Improve Your Network with Social Software" (http://about.com/entrepreneurs/improvenetwork) will help you find and make connections that can help with your job search. It discusses who participates in online networking and how networking can work for you.

There are additional samples of networking letters available on my About.com site at http://about.com/jobsearch/samples. If you're not sure what to say, take the time to review them before you write to a contact.

Networking correspondence can be sent by e-mail or by regular mail. Both are appropriate, but if you use e-mail you'll be able to network much faster than you will if you correspond by using paper.

However you network, it's important that you take the time to do it. It sometimes seems like it can be a hard thing to do, but it really isn't. Most people are ready, willing, and happy to help. If for some reason they're not able to assist, move on to the next person. Most people are also thrilled to talk about what they do for a living and how they got there. If you take the time to inquire, you will likely benefit from the help your networking contact will be glad to give you.

Get Linked

Here's more networking advice and information from my **ABOUT** *.com site. These will point you toward additional online resources that will help you use networking to enhance your job search.*

JOB SEARCH NETWORKING

Read more about the importance of career networking, how to develop contacts, and how career networking should be an integral part of your job search.

 http://about.com/jobsearch/networkingresources

SOCIAL NETWORKING

These career and social networking online resources have information on where to network online and how to use a social network to help you land a job.

 http://about.com/jobsearch/networkingarticles

HOW TO FIND THE IDEAL JOB USING SOCIAL NETWORKS

Social networking can help with a job search by promoting traditional networking and by building relationships by e-mail and interviewing. Here you'll find information on how to use a network in your job search.

 http://about.com/jobsearch/socialnetworking

Chapter 11

Getting Job Search Help

Career Counselors and Coaches

There are times when you may need a career counselor or career coach to help you with your job search. A career counselor can be especially useful when you're not sure what you want to do, when you're going through a career transition, like losing your job, or when you're changing careers.

Harold, a job seeker I know, definitely needed help. He had some learning disabilities, a not-so-great work history, and no idea what type of job to look for. He had gone to college and participated in several training programs, to no avail. He couldn't find a job he wanted and he couldn't keep the jobs he got. Even though it was a challenge, his career counselor was able to help him define his objectives and help him find a job he could do. He's been gainfully employed for several years now, thanks to the help of his counselor.

I can't afford to pay for job search help. What can I do?

▶ There are free and low-cost services available to job seekers. Most of the information you find online is free, and there is in-person assistance available from local organizations. It may take some time to find help, but it is available.

Career counselors help people define and clarify their goals. A career counselor can also administer tests to assess your interests and skills. These tests can then be matched to potential careers. A counselor can help you narrow down career options and help you find a career that matches your goals and objectives.

A career counselor can also help you create a career plan that you can implement to achieve your goals. Counselors can help with resume and cover letter creation, as well as teach you job search strategies. For people who have lost their job or are transitioning to a new career, a counselor can provide advice and support.

Penny Loretto, a career counselor in private practice at Career Choice (www.careerchoice.com), explains how career counseling can help: "Career counseling can assist clients with many aspects of the career-planning process and can help to clarify life/career goals." Penny goes on to say, "Many people simply fall into careers or enter a field based on the expectations of parents, friends, teachers, or other personal influences but have never actually made a career decision based on individual skills, interests, values, and personality traits." A career counselor can help clients make decisions based on their individual attributes and interests rather than on the expectations of others.

Mark is a good example of how counseling can help. Mark was forced to take early retirement from his corporate position and he wasn't sure what he wanted to do next. He was still relatively young and had many years of work ahead of him. He worked with a career counselor to explore career options and to analyze what options were available to him, given his background and skills. With the help of his counselor, he ended up in a totally different career from his first one and was thrilled to be starting over in a brand-new, exciting career, doing what he had only dreamed of the first time around.

A career counselor can help you find the job you have dreamed about. Michael Landes, author of *The Back Door Guide to Short-Term Job Adventures*, says, "Once you realize that your self-worth has nothing to do with your net worth, money will not be the only source of richness and fulfillment in your life." If you're not sure what path you want to take to find fulfillment, consider using a counselor to help point you in the right direction.

In order to be certified as a career counselor, an individual needs graduate level training and a specialization in career counseling. Career counselors with a master's degree or higher in counseling, and a certain amount of experience, are eligible for additional certifications.

Job seekers can also use career coaches to help achieve career and employment goals. A career coach isn't necessarily a certified career counselor, but she can help you with your job search by identifying career options, helping you select career choices, and assisting you with the job search process.

You will most likely want to find a career counselor or coach who you can meet with to discuss options, goals, and plans for your career. However, distance counseling is also available via phone, e-mail, or instant messaging. Some people need personal assistance along with the opportunity to review test results, options, and job search materials while meeting with your counselor.

Other clients find distance counseling more convenient, because they don't need to take the time to go to a meeting. They can expedite the process by conducting it online.

There are online resources you can use to find a certified career counselor. The National Career Development Association (www.ncda.org) provides consumer guidelines for selecting a counselor, addresses what a career counselor does, and explains counselor training and credentials.

The following are directories you can use to find a certified career counselor or a career coach:

- **Association of Career Professionals:** www.iacmp.org/experts.html
- **Career Coach Institute:** www.careercoachinstitute.com
- **CoachLink:** www.coachlink.net
- **Institute of Career Certification International:** www.careercertification.org/searchdb.asp
- **National Career Development Association:** www.ncda.org

Do not just sign an agreement with the first counselor you see on the list. You will need to do some research to make sure that the counselor will provide the services you need at a price you can afford. There isn't a standard list of services offered. Career counseling will vary from counselor to counselor. Fees can vary too. Very carefully evaluate what the counselor is offering and decide whether the services meet your needs.

In fact, it makes sense to talk to several counselors before you make a final determination on which one you want to use. In addition to services varying, personalities are different as well. You will want to make sure that the counselor's personality meshes well with yours. It's important to feel comfortable with the counselor and to have a good rapport with the person you select.

Before you select a career counselor:

- Ask what the counselor charges. Is it an hourly rate or a flat fee?
- Inquire as to what services are provided.
- Ask if some services are optional.
- Find out how much time the counselor will commit to spending with you.

- Check to see if the counselor can provide you with references from other clients.
- Make sure you are comfortable working with the counselor.

Fees vary widely depending on the counselor you select and the services you need. I've seen hourly rates as low as $50 an hour and as high as $200 an hour. There are also counselors who will offer you a package deal that includes unlimited help for a flat fee.

Before you decide on a counselor, evaluate what is included and what services you need. Also consider how much you can afford to spend and plan accordingly. Then decide whether, as career counselor Penny Loretto says, "A trained counselor can help you eliminate old irrational beliefs and personal obstacles that perhaps have not worked well for you in the past." If so, assistance from a career counselor is in order.

Career Services Offices

The first place college students or graduates should go for help is their career services office. Students should start using their career office early—as soon as their first year. It's never too early to start working with your career service office. It's never too late either. Most offices provide lifetime services to alumni.

Staff will work with constituents who have just started school and with alumni who have graduated twenty or thirty years ago. If you're affiliated with the school, and if they provide services to alumni, they will be happy to assist.

Your career office can help you choose a major or find an internship. The staff can help you write a resume and help you find jobs to apply to. Most colleges offer career and graduate school advising and offer career inventories and assessments so students can begin to explore career options.

TOOLS YOU NEED

▸ There are a variety of job search tools available in the About.com Salary Center at http://about.salary.com. You can compare your current position with your dream job (or any job), see how your salary measures up, and how much a new job is worth. You can also determine the cost of living in a new location if you're considering relocating.

▶ The article on how to find job search help on my About. com site is always popular. It lists the type of help available to job seekers and provides advice on where and how to get job search help. There's advice on where to get online help, as well as information on how to find local assistance. Check it out at http://about.com/jobsearch/ help.

There may be campus job fairs you can attend, as well as seminars, informational programs, and networking events. The career services staff may be able to conduct a mock interview so you can enhance your interviewing skills. There's also help available for graduate school planning and with managing your references.

In some cases, online career assessments and evaluations are also available via your career services office. Check on what proprietary resources the office has that are only available to students and alumni from your college. Available resources may include targeted job listings, a career network of alumni who are willing to assist with a job search, and specialized career exploration and research software and tools.

Alumni career networks are invaluable. Career advisors can help you find out about the jobs they have and the career field they are in, give you insight into the company they work for, and can help you if you're relocating to a new area.

Some schools have special affiliations with vendors of career research products like Vault and CareerSearch. If your school participates, you will be able to explore in-depth career resources and find and research employers in a large variety of career fields. There are also a variety of newsletters and Web sites that your school may subscribe to. Inquire as to what resources are available and ask how you can obtain access to them.

For alumni who live out of town, the career office may also be able to refer you to a college in your area where you can get local assistance. The career center staff can let you know if there are any colleges in your area that allow nonaffiliates to access their career resources and job listings.

Many colleges and universities offer free career services for alumni. Other schools may offer limited services for alumni or services at very reasonable rates. If your college does charge, you'll find the rates are much less expensive than those of private career counseling services.

Some colleges offer long-distance assistance—by telephone, e-mail, or even instant messaging. Telephone appointments with the career development staff at your alma mater may be available for career advising sessions on job searching and interviewing. You may also be able to have your resume and cover letters reviewed.

If you're abroad or unable to call because of work or time constraints, you may be able to get assistance via e-mail or instant message. In addition, instant-messaging services may be available for answers to quick career-related questions.

There are also ways you can help your career center when you're in a position to do so. Options for alumni to help typically include:

- Join your alumni career network
- Participate in campus career programs
- Participate in college-recruiting programs
- Invite students to job shadow
- List jobs and internships

When you offer to assist your career center, you'll also be helping yourself in the long run. The more resources your career services office has, the more able they will be to meet the needs of their student and alumni constituents.

Your career center should provide information online on services and resources. The easiest way to find out what help is available from your college or university is to visit the career services Web site. It should detail the services available to both students and alumni.

ELSEWHERE ON THE WEB

▶ MonsterTrak's Major to Career Converter (www .monstertrak.monster.com/ mtcc) helps students and graduates review careers related to their major. It's really easy to generate a list of careers. Select your major, then click on results to get a list of career options that reflect your major, interests, personal style, values, and skills. You can also search for job openings in the list of potential jobs that you generate.

▶ Do you need help getting started job searching? My How to Speed Up Your Job Search class provides online resources and personal help to job seekers. This six-week online program offers advice, discussion, and assistance with every stage of job searching. Participants will be able to ask questions and receive help with their job search. Sign up online at http://about.com/jobsearch/classes.

Many employers actively recruit candidates from their college. I spoke to a human resources manager who listed jobs with her alma mater before she listed them anywhere else. She knew the school candidates were strong and it was less expensive to recruit at the college, where she could post jobs free, than it was to post elsewhere online.

Other companies regularly use recent graduates to recruit on campus. They know the employee has a connection with the college and they can network with current students. Alumni employees can be a good source to recommend candidates for employment, because they know both the school culture and the company culture and can help determine when there's a good match.

On most college Web sites, the career center should be linked from both the Students and Alumni sections.

Another option is to search Google using the name of your college and the keyword *career services* or *career center* to find the Web site quickly. Or, you can use the following sites, which have a list of career services offices, to find your school's career center Web site:

- NACE—College Career Center Web Pages: www.jobWeb.com/Career_Development/collegeres.htm
- The University of Texas at Austin—U.S. Universities: www.utexas.edu/world/univ/alpha

Once you've reached your college's Web site, check to see what services are available and review how you can access them. Then contact your career office to schedule an appointment to get job search assistance and passwords for the online job postings and career resources available to students and alumni.

One-Stop Center Resources

CareerOneStop Centers are sponsored by the U.S. Department of Labor. These are centers that you can visit to get personal assistance with job searching. Trained counselors provide clients with career advice and help, as well as job hunt assistance. There are also special programs available for job seekers with disabilities, veterans, and displaced workers.

CareerOneStop Center services include:

- Job loss help
- Job search help
- Career planning
- Career workshops
- Training or retraining

Some CareerOneStop Centers provide equipment you can use to job search, including computers and printers. Others provide help with accessing education resources and applying for jobs and interviewing.

Not all services are offered at all centers, so use the CareerOneStop Center search tools to find a center that can help with what you need. America's Service Locator (www.servicelocator.org) is searchable by location (within twenty-five, fifty, or more miles from a zip code or city), by service offered, and by keyword.

The search will generate a list of centers that match your search criteria. You can click on a link to access the OneStop Center's Web site and view a map and get directions to the facility you choose.

Before you visit a site, call to double-check what services are available and which services you are eligible for. It's a good idea to schedule an appointment in advance so the staff can give you an appropriate amount of time and attention when you arrive.

ELSEWHERE ON THE WEB

▶ The United States Department of Labor has a special program available to assist veterans with employment. Information on employment for veterans is available online at www.hirevetsfirst.gov. In addition to resources for veterans seeking work, there is information for employers on recruiting and hiring veterans. There's also a schedule of local job career and job fairs and advice on resume writing.

Under the broad umbrella of CareerOneStop, there are several Web sites that help students and job seekers, as well as employers and career professionals, find employment information, as well as career resources.

There are a variety of CareerOneStop resources available:

- **CareerOneStop:** www.careeronestop.org
- **CareerInfoNet:** www.careerinfonet.org/acinet
- **America's Job Bank:** www.ajb.org
- **America's Service Locator:** www.servicelocator.org

Employers and career professionals can use CareerOneStop resources to research the labor market, to get career news and updates, and to post jobs and review resumes from candidates for employment. Job seekers can use the resources to evaluate their skills, to post their resume, to find job postings, to find out about training opportunities, and to apply online for jobs.

For those who need help navigating the resources, there is a CareerOneStop Coach that will help you research salaries, research occupational information, and look for a job. It will step you through the process of finding what you need to know and help you find job listings. You can access the OneStop Coach at: www.onestopcoach.org.

Help for job seekers is available by phone as well as online. Job seekers can find out about services, including assistance for laid-off workers, training, and access to service locations on the Web at www.servicelocator.org or by calling (toll free) 1-877-US2-JOBS or 1-877-872-5627. There's help available when you need to find jobs on America's Job Bank at (toll free) 1-800-833-3000.

When you call, you can also find out about local services that are available and how you can access them.

I first used a OneStop Center (though I'm not sure that's what it was called then) years ago when I was seeking my first job after college. I had moved to a new city and wasn't sure about what types of positions I was qualified for or clear on the best way to apply for jobs.

The staff helped me with my resume, found jobs for me to apply for, and actually scheduled interviews for me. I was hired by one of the first companies I applied to. I used the services again after being laid off from another job. The staff was helpful and concerned about how they could help me. I know other job seekers who have had similar positive results.

Job clubs can help with your job search. Your local library or continuing-education center may be another place where you can get low-cost or free assistance with your job search. There are also nonprofit groups that provide career services to job seekers. Some offer classes and seminars, while others offer more in-depth job search assistance.

One of my colleagues ran a job club at our local library for several years. She helped the members with writing their resumes, taught them how to look for employment, and worked with them to improve and enhance their job hunt skills. The club met one evening a week in a library conference room and the members were able to use the library's computers and other resources to conduct their job search.

There are also job clubs that aren't affiliated with a particular organization that can help you with your job search. These are local groups where job seekers with a similar background or goals get together to help one another find employment.

For example, there are 40-plus job clubs, senior job clubs, and job search groups for all types of job seekers. Work Ministry has

ELSEWHERE ON THE WEB

▶ The *New York Times* has career resources you can use to help with your job search. There's a calendar of career fairs, online interviewing advice, employer research tools, and information on starting your own business. You can also complete a job skills interview and make it available to prospective employers. Check it out at www.nytimes.com/marketing/jobmarket/career-resources.

a searchable database of faith-based and community job support groups at www.workministry.com/job_support_groups.shtml.

Besides providing networking assistance and advice, other job club members can provide support and a willing ear to listen to your job search trials, tribulations, hopes, and successes. Other job club members are in exactly the same situation you are, and it's always good to have someone in similar circumstances who you can talk to in order to get advice and support. Also, they are there because they want to be—they have the same objectives that you do and will be glad to help.

Job Search Sites

Job seekers who are self-directed and motivated can job search online without the help of a counselor or coach. In fact, most of us can job search on our own, as long as we are focused and dedicated. You will need to commit time and energy to the process, but if you do you'll be able to find a job without much trouble.

I have spoken to many visitors to my About.com site who have found a job on their own by searching online. They have taken the time to use the resources that are available on the Web to effectively job search.

Job search sites can help you plan and conduct a job search by helping you:

- Get ready for a job search
- Research careers and occupations
- Write resumes, cover letters, and curriculum vitae
- Prepare job applications
- Learn how to job search
- Find job listings
- Apply for jobs

Job searching is more of a process than an event. Most job search sites provide information on every component of job searching and will step you through the process. Or, if you only need help with one facet of job search, you can go directly to the resources you need. You can find all the job search help you need online with just a click or two of your mouse.

For example, Molly, a visitor to my About.com site, needed help with how to handle thank-you letters after a second interview. I was able to direct her toward some advice on the best way to say thank you for a second time.

Craig, another site visitor, wrote to me because he was concerned about background checks. He discovered that he had an outstanding warrant (that he wasn't aware of) and wasn't sure how to handle it with the company with whom he had just interviewed.

You may need a little job searching help or a lot, but either way it's available online. There are sites that will assist you with every phase of your job search and help you prepare your application materials.

Top job search sites include:

- **About.com Job Searching:** http://jobsearch.about.com
- **America's CareerInfoNet:** www.careerinfonet.org
- **JobStar:** www.jobstar.org/index.php
- **O*NET OnLine:** http://online.onetcenter.org
- **The Riley Guide:** www.rileyguide.com

Regardless of where you are getting job search help, you need to dedicate time to job hunting. When you are unemployed, your job search should become your job. You should plan on spending at least thirty-five to forty hours a week job searching. If you're

ASK YOUR GUIDE

There's a lot of information on job searching available, but where do I start?

▶ There's a wealth of information online and it certainly can be confusing to read through it all and figure out what's relevant to your job search. To make it easier, I recommend visitors to my About.com site start with my OneStop Job Search Center (http://about.com/jobsearch/onestopjob). It covers all the job search basics, and it clearly and simply steps you through the process of finding a new job.

▶ The Occupational Out-look Handbook is an excellent resource for those who want to find out more about specific occupations. There's information on what the job market is like for each listed occupation as well as expected earnings, working conditions, and job prospects. There are also job search tips and information on the labor market in each state. It's available at www.bls.gov/oco.

working, plan on allocating at least ten to fifteen hours a week to job search activities.

I know that sounds like a lot of time and a lot of work. It is, but in order to job search effectively you need to commit to it, and even though there are ways to expedite your hunt for employment, it can take time.

As an aside, if you're unemployed, make sure that you are collecting unemployment benefits if you are eligible for them. I know people who don't apply for unemployment because they think it's taking a handout. It's not. You paid for those unemployment benefits while you were working—they are funded by the government and you pay taxes.

When you're not sure about eligibility, check with your state unemployment office. You can apply for unemployment online or over the phone. I have an overview of unemployment benefits and eligibility requirements on my About.com site at http://about.com/jobsearch/unemployment.

Jason, a visitor to my About.com site, e-mailed me to ask about unemployment. He wasn't sure whether or not he was eligible. I suggested that he visit his state unemployment office Web site to find out. He applied online and received a check shortly thereafter.

When job searching on your own, it's important to be organized. In order to successfully dedicate the time to your job search, it can help to set a schedule. You may spend a couple of hours each morning making phone calls and networking, and a few hours looking for new job listings and targeting your resume and cover letter so you can apply to the jobs you find.

The part I most dislike about job searching is phone calls, so I usually try to do them first and get them out of the way. It's also a good way to reach hiring mangers and employers before they get into the busiest part of their workday.

You will also need to spend time following up on jobs you have applied to and researching the companies where you would like to work.

The following is a list of the job search activities you will need to conduct:

- ○ Research career options
- ○ Research jobs and companies
- ○ Write a resume and cover letter
- ○ Find job listings
- ○ Follow up on job applications
- ○ Network

Once you start getting phone calls to schedule interviews, you will be able to find interview advice and tips on the Web. You'll also be able to learn about appropriate and inappropriate interview attire. There's information on how to follow up after an interview, what to write in your thank-you notes, and how to research salaries and analyze job offers.

All the information you need, and then some, is available online. If you need help with it, you can find it on the Web.

There are also sites where you can get assistance with career planning and career transitions. Some sites focus on career planning and career change rather than on how to find a job. These sites are an excellent resource for people who aren't sure what they want to do or are interested in making a career change. They offer career advice, career-planning tips and techniques, and general information on careers and the world of work.

TOOLS YOU NEED

▶ A good-quality leather briefcase always makes an excellent impression on prospective employers. It also helps you keep all your job search equipment, like your resume, your cell phone, your references, and your notepads and pens, organized when you're interviewing. You don't have to spend a fortune, but I suggest investing in a nice leather briefcase to add that professional touch to your appearance. I have a list of my favorite briefcases on my About.com site at http://about.com/jobsearch/briefcase.

The following is a list of career sites that are well worth visiting:

- **About.com Careers:** http://about.com/careers
- **About.com Career Planning:** http://careerplanning.about.com
- **CollegeBoard's Majors and Careers section:** www
  .collegeboard.com/csearch/majors_careers
- **Princeton Review Career Research and Planning:** www
  .princetonreview.com/cte

Discussion Forums

When you have a job search question or want input from career professionals and/or other job seekers, discussion forums are a good resource to use. Discussion forums are a venue to post questions or comments and to get answers and insights.

At most forums, like my Job Searching Forum, you will need to complete a quick registration form to post a message. You can read messages without registration, but registration is required to join.

Once you have joined the forum you can ask and answer job search questions, read comments, or add your input to the topic being discussed. You can also start a new discussion, which is usually called *a thread*.

Forums are an excellent source of information on finding jobs. You will find posts from other job seekers, from career experts, and from employers. Some sites allow you to post a "Job Wanted" listing, and you can also find help-wanted listings posted by recruiters or hiring managers.

Here are several top career and job search discussion forums:

- **About.com Career Planning Forum:** http://about.com/
  careerplanning/forum
- **About.com Job Searching Forum:** http://about.com/
  jobsearch/forum

- About.com Job Searching Technical Forum: http://about.com/jobsearchtech/forum
- Jobseekers Advice: www.jobseekersadvice.com
- Monster's Career Advice Discussion Forum: http://discussion.monster.com/messageboards

When you post a comment or start a discussion, you can indicate that you would like to receive a notification via e-mail when someone posts a response. That way, you won't have to spend too much time on the forum, but you will know when someone has answered your question or written a comment about one of your posts.

The other reason discussion forums are a worthwhile inclusion in your job search tool kit is because they can help you make connections that can assist you with your job search. Active forums are often frequented by regular visitors. These can be career experts willing to give advice in exchange for some traffic to their Web site, employers and recruiters who are seeking candidates for employment, and other job seekers looking for help.

They can all help you, one way or another, and the broader your search for employment the more likely you are to be successful.

TOOLS YOU NEED

▶ It's very important to have a job search system in place before you start looking for a new job. New jobs are posted around the clock, and you need to stay on top of the new listings so you can beat the crowd and be among the first to apply. It is best to use your computer to help manage your search. Take a look at How to Start a Job Search System at http://about.com/jobsearch/searchsystem.

Get Linked

Here's more job search help and advice from my **ABOUT**.com *site. These will provide you with resources you can utilize to get job search help.*

JOB SEARCH HELP

Here you'll find advice on how to find a job including writing job search correspondence, where to find job postings, where to get help, and all the resources you need for a successful job search.

 http://about.com/jobsearch/jobsearchresource

CAREER ADVICE

This resource offers help with your job search, including career change information, career educational opportunities, career options, career tests and quizzes, and career advice.

 http://about.com/jobsearch/careerchange

JOB LOSS

Whether you have resigned or have been laid off or fired, here is how to handle a job loss, including information on what to do if you are fired, how to resign, and how to move on to the next opportunity.

 http://about.com/jobsearch/jobloss

Chapter 12

Interviewing and References

Types of Interviews

There are several types of interviews that you may have to participate in to get hired for a new job. An interview could be as brief as a few minutes of questions about your background, or you could spend days interviewing at a company with employees and management from a variety of levels and departments. How you will be interviewed depends on the job, the company, and how much the company invests (both money and time) in screening and hiring candidates.

The depth of the interviewing process also depends on the quantity and quality of the candidate pool. If the candidates are very competitive, it will be hard to choose the best person for the job. As a result, there may be more layers added to the interview process.

One human resources manager I spoke to told me that she screens the top candidates for each position, even entry-level jobs, on the phone. Those who make it past the first interview are

I'm petrified when I interview. What can I do?

▶ A lot of visitors to my About.com site say that they get very nervous when interviewing. Many people do, even those who have interviewed often. It's tough to be on the hot seat and have to answer questions about yourself. The best thing you can do is to practice until you are comfortable answering questions. During the interview, stay as calm as you can and take some time, if you need it, to think over your answers before you respond.

scheduled for a company visit. They have dinner with representatives from the department in which they will be working, then spend the next day interviewing.

Interviews at this company are a combination of individual interviews and group interviews. Candidates are expected to sit in on presentations and contribute to the discussion. After a full day of interviewing, the best candidates will be brought back one more time for a final round of interviews. These types of extensive interviews are a way to determine how the candidate handles stress as well as a means of fully evaluating the applicant.

Typical types of interviews include:

- Behavioral interview
- Dining interview
- Group interview
- Hiring interview
- Second interview
- Screening interview

A screening interview is the quickest and most straightforward type of interview. It can take place in person or on the telephone. A screening interview is conducted in order to determine if the applicant has the qualifications necessary to do the job.

After the candidates have been screened, some of them will be invited to participate in a hiring interview, where they are actually being considered for the job. How you will be interviewed depends on the company. You may be interviewed on a one-on-one basis by a hiring manager or by the person who will be your boss if you're offered the job. You could also be interviewed by employees from the department in which you will be working.

You may be interviewed by a group of interviewers. A group interview takes place when a candidate is interviewed by more than one interviewer at the same time. Alternately, a group interview can mean that you and other candidates are being interviewed together at the same time.

Sometimes you will be invited to enjoy a meal with your prospective employer. You may be invited to dine with staff, with management, or with a combination of both. A dining interview is a good way to see how you interact in a more relaxed setting. It's also a good way to ensure that you have the social skills necessary for the job. Do brush up on your manners before you go. That's likely one of things that the employer will evaluate.

I suggest ordering conservatively from the menu (just like I recommend conservative interview attire). One candidate we invited to dinner ordered surf and turf (the most expensive item on the menu), an expensive bottle of wine, and not one, but two desserts. I'm not sure who he was trying to impress, but it couldn't have been us. We would have been more impressed if he had ordered a more reasonable entrée, like the rest of the diners did. Refraining from alcohol while interviewing makes good sense too.

After the initial round of interviews, the top candidates are typically called back for a second interview. This may be even more extensive and time-consuming. If the company's hiring practices are sound, they will want to be very sure that they are hiring the right person for the job. It's a good investment to spend time and money prior to hiring someone to make sure you have made a wise decision, rather than having to deal with hiring the wrong person after the fact. That's one reason why the hiring process can seem cumbersome and complicated. It can sometimes be a lengthy process.

Regardless of how many people you interview with, it's always important to send each and every one of them a thank-you note. Take the time to thank them for the interview and to reiterate your interest in the position.

WHAT'S HOT

▶ "Meals, Manners, and Interviews" is an article that is always of interest to the visitors at my About.com site. It discusses why employers invite job applicants to dine, what will happen during the meal, and provides tips on what to do, and what not to do, while having a meal with a prospective employer. There's detailed advice on what to order from the menu and how to survive an interview while dining. Check it out at http://about.com/jobsearch/interviewdining.

Interview Attire

It's important to dress professionally when interviewing. As I define it, professionally means conservatively. There are several reasons why I think that way. First of all, you're not going to know what the company dress code is until you interview, and the last thing you want to do is make a bad impression by not being appropriately dressed.

Also, what might be considered fashionable may not be appropriate attire for an interview. I remember one young lady who interviewed for a customer service position at my company. She wore a suit, but the blouse she wore underneath was very low-cut and the skirt was very tight and very short—so short, in fact, that sitting down was an issue. Some of the employees thought she looked hot, but management didn't quite see it that way.

About.com's Human Resources Guide, Susan Heathfield, explained how one applicant knocked herself out of the contention for a human resources assistant job at her company: "My favorite candidate, on paper, showed up for her interview dressed in low-rider, casual pants with a top that barely met the edge of the pants and didn't meet the pants whenever she moved." Susan wondered what the applicant was thinking. Maybe she wasn't thinking at all about what was appropriate, but she should have been.

In both cases, the candidates were knocked out of contention. Why? Not just because of how they dressed, but because there were candidates with the equivalent skills and experience who did know how to dress to impress the interviewer. All things being equal, wearing the proper attire worked in favor of the other candidates.

The following is a list of what you should wear to interview:

Women's Interview Attire
- Conservative suit (solid color) with a coordinated blouse
- Moderate closed-toe shoes and pantyhose
- Neat, professional hairstyle, carefully manicured nails

- Limited jewelry
- Don't overdo the makeup or perfume
- Briefcase or portfolio

Men should also dress conservatively, making sure that their tie and shirt match their jacket.

Men's Interview Attire
- Conservative suit in a solid color with a long-sleeved shirt and coordinated tie
- Professional shoes with dark socks
- Neat hairstyle, neatly trimmed facial hair, if applicable
- Trimmed fingernails
- Don't overdo the cologne or after-shave
- Portfolio or briefcase

There are also some things that you definitely should not wear on an interview. The following are items that definitely make a bad impression!

- Old scuffed shoes
- Open-toe shoes or backless shoes
- Sneakers
- Jeans or shorts
- Bare legs
- Short skirts
- Sunglasses

Not overdoing the perfume or the cologne is important. I once worked for a manager who wouldn't hire anyone he could smell before they walked in the room! If they had too much perfume on he didn't hire them. It was simple as that.

TOOLS YOU NEED

▶ If you were to invest in only one item to ensure interviewing success, it should be a good-quality suit. The first impression is always the one that counts, and the hiring manager is immediately going to notice how you are dressed. When you are dressed professionally, in a classically stylish suit, you will be sure to impress the interviewer.

There's another reason why your image must be professional, and why it makes a difference to your prospective employer. When I was involved in hiring, my first impression of candidates, before they even spoke more than a few sentences, was a good indicator of whether we would hire them or not. I'm not quite sure why that was the case, but our company president said that I was always right. In most cases, if I didn't think the candidate was a good choice, he or she usually didn't work out.

Dressing appropriately, speaking correctly (proper English, not slang), and acting politely to everyone they met with, including our receptionist, were all factors that contributed to that first impression candidates made on me. These are all factors that are absolutely under your control, which you can use to make an impression that lasts throughout the interview and after.

Interview Practice and Preparation

The old saying that "practice makes perfect" is appropriate when it comes to interviewing. If it doesn't make you perfect, it will, at least, help you interview effectively. Don't start getting ready late the night before the interview. Take time in advance to prepare for your interview.

If you have a family member or friend who will spend some time helping you, ask them to ask you some typical interview questions. The more you practice answering, the more comfortable you will be with your responses. If you can, videotape your practice interview so you can watch what you look and sound like. You'll be able to see what you need to improve. Then do it again. Keep practicing until you're comfortable with your responses and comfortable watching yourself interview.

Check your nonverbal communications as well as your verbal responses. Be sure you're not fidgeting or twitching or disconnected—pay attention. Employers notice these nonverbal responses, so be cognizant of the demeanor you portray and try to stay calm and quiet while waiting for the interview and during it. Your goal is for your entire package, your image, to be perfect.

There are some things that you shouldn't plan on bringing with you to the interview. If you're a smoker, leave the cigarettes at home or in your car. Make sure you use a breath mint before you enter the building. Don't chew gum or munch on candy either. Leave your iPod at home. The same goes for coffee and soda. Don't walk into the interview carrying a cup of coffee, however much you might think you need it. There have been interviewees who have done some or all of the above and have jeopardized their chance of getting the job.

Here's an interview checklist to review:

○ Review job posting
○ Research the company
○ Review interview questions
○ Generate a list of questions to ask
○ Review your resume
○ Itemize the qualifications you have for the job
○ Map directions to the interview location
○ Get your interview clothes ready (the evening before)
○ Pack your portfolio with your resume, a notepad, and a pen
○ Double-check the name of your interviewer so you know with whom you are meeting

Reviewing your resume sounds a little odd, doesn't it? Believe it or not, I've interviewed job applicants whose answers didn't match what was on their resume. They either didn't remember what years they had worked at which job or they were fuzzy on the details of what they had done at their previous jobs. So, do make

ELSEWHERE ON THE WEB

▶ It can be helpful to view interview videos so you can get a sense of what interviewing is actually like and so you can learn how to effectively interview. CollegeGrad.com has several interviewing videos available on their Web site, including *Preparing for Your Interview, How to Interview Successfully with Anyone,* and *Dress for Interview Success.* Check them out at www.collegegrad.com/video/collegegrad.shtml.

sure you know what you put on your resume and make sure your answers match.

Researching the company is important too. It's important for a couple of reasons. First of all, one of the questions you may be asked is "What do you know about this company?" and you need to be able to provide an informative answer. Secondly, you want to know as much about the company because you need to decide if you want to work there. Visit the company's Web site (the easiest way to find it is to search for the company name on Google), and look at every single section. Read the company mission statement and goals for the future. Learn what the company does and how they do it. Understand the products or services the company sells and how they market them. Review senior management bios as well as the information about the company and benefits that is available in the Careers section of the company Web site. The more you know, the more effectively you will be able to interview.

Professional communications are also important during the interview. That means all communications from the time you arrive at the interview until you leave. Arrive on time for the interview. On time means a few minutes early. You may need to complete an application, and you don't want to be rushing into the lobby of the building at the last minute. If you aren't sure where the office is located, do a trial run the day before so you know exactly where you are going, where you can park, and how long it is going to take you to get there. Give yourself a little extra time so you have a cushion just in case you're delayed.

If you're nervous (and that can happen to anyone, even those who interview a lot!), visit the restroom, wash and dry your hands so your palms aren't sweaty, and get a drink of water. If sweating is an issue, keep a tissue in your pocket so you can dry your hands discreetly before you shake hands with anyone.

Next, consider manners, because they do matter. Remember that teacher who used to tell you to sit up straight and pay attention? Well, that's exactly what you need to do during the interview. Don't slouch or recline in your chair. Listen attentively to the interviewer and don't interrupt.

Do take time, if you need to, to consider your response so your answer is complete. Don't talk too much. I have interviewed some candidates who talked way too much. They were trying so hard to sell me on hiring them that they didn't listen to a word I said. Rambling on and on didn't make a good impression on me and isn't going to make a good impression on any interviewer.

Sometimes unavoidable things can happen, even when we do our best to prepare. Andrew, a visitor to my About.com site, wrote to me because he injured his knee a few hours before an important interview. He was able to make it to the interview, with his knee wrapped, but he felt ill and didn't feel like he had done the best he could during the interview. He was able to salvage the interview by e-mailing his contact as soon as he got home and explaining the circumstances. He also asked if there was any other information he could provide, which led to a dialogue with the hiring manager and a second chance to get the job.

Interview Questions and Answers

It's important to review the types of interview questions that you will be asked. Answer the questions yourself, so you know what you are going to say when you're asked. Make a list of questions and your answers so you can review them prior to interviewing. It will preclude fumbling around for words during the interview and feeling like you're on the spot.

Here are some common interview questions that you might be asked:

- What were your job responsibilities?
- Describe a typical day at your job.
- What were your expectations for the job and to what extent were they met?
- How much did you earn?
- Which was most/least rewarding?
- What was the biggest accomplishment in this job?
- What could you have done better?
- Why are you leaving/did you leave your job?

After you have been asked about yourself, the next set of questions will typically be about how you do your job and how you deal with situations that arise during work, such as the following:

- Tell me about the challenges and problems you dealt with. How did you handle them?
- How do you handle stress?
- Describe a difficult work project and how you overcame the problems.
- Do you prefer working on a team or independently?
- How do you measure success?
- You will also be asked specific questions about your experience and credentials.

Next, you will be asked about the job you are applying for and why you are qualified for it:

- Why are you interested in this job?
- What experience do you have?

- Why are you the best person for the job?
- Explain to me why you want the job.
- What do you know about this company and the job?
- Why would you want to work for this company?
- If you could describe your ideal position, what would it be?
- Can I answer any questions about the job or company for you?
- You will also be asked questions about your skills and how they relate to the job.
- When could you start if we offered you the job?

Finally, you will need to be able to discuss your goals and where you expect your career to be in a few years or even longer:

- What are your goals for the future?
- How do you plan to achieve those goals?
- How does this company fit with your plans for the future?
- What are your salary requirements?

Be careful how you answer every question and make sure your response is reasonable and appropriate. I once asked someone about his last position and he carefully took the time to explain to me that he hadn't worked in a while because of an injury he sustained in a boating accident. He then (literally) started unbuttoning his shirt to show me the injury. That was much more than I needed to know! Another job applicant told me she needed a minute to think of an answer, and then asked if she could borrow my phone to call a cab for the ride home. A third candidate, who was applying for a sales job, said that she hated prospecting and making cold calls. Obviously, she didn't get the job either. In all these cases, if the candidate had taken even a little time to prepare, they would have done much better in the interview process.

ELSEWHERE ON THE WEB

▶ The AARP has excellent advice on interviewing for older workers. There's an article titled "8 Interview Questions for Older Workers to Anticipate" (www.aarp.org/bulletin/yourlife/Articles/0905_sidebar_4.html) that discusses difficult interview questions that may be asked by a hiring manager. There is also a list of appropriate responses to each question that you can tailor to meet your circumstances.

Also prepare questions to ask the interviewer. Create a list of things you want to know about the job and the company. It's perfectly acceptable to ask questions. In fact, the employer will expect you to have questions to ask and will think less of you if you don't ask anything.

Ask about the job responsibilities, travel requirements, overtime, the company's management style, growth and advancement prospects, and when you might expect to start, if you were hired. If there is anything that you're not sure about or need more information on, now is the time to ask it. It's much better to ask all your questions when you have the opportunity than it is to have lingering concerns after you have left the interview.

There are also questions that the employer should not ask you. It is illegal, for example, to ask about age, citizenship, disability, gender, national origin, race, marital or family status. The questions the interviewer asks you should be related to the job and to your ability to do it. If you believe that you have been discriminated against there are options (including legal ones) for dealing with them.

If you have been asked questions that aren't appropriate, you can choose not to answer the question, answer the question anyway or provide a partial response, or you can try to change the subject and avoid the question. None of these is a perfect solution, especially when the question shouldn't have been asked in the first place, but you need to consider which response makes the best strategic sense and how much you want the job.

There are a variety of options available, including legal recourse, if you feel you have been discriminated against. The **U.S. Equal Employment Commission** (www.eeoc.gov) handles claims from workers who have been discriminated against by an employer, labor union, or employment agency either during the hiring process or on the job.

TOOLS YOU NEED

▶ Interviewing isn't always easy, especially when you haven't had a lot of experience doing it. If you need extra assistance there are books available that will help you with the process, including providing lists of frequently asked job interview questions, as well as interview advice, tips, and techniques. I have a list of the top interview books on my site at http://about.com/jobsearch/interviewbooks.

Behavioral Interviews

Behavioral interviews are based on the premise that your behavior in the past predicts your success in the future. Rather than asking typical interview questions like "Describe your weaknesses" you will be asked specific questions about your experience as it relates to the skills the employer is seeking. For example, you might be asked how you act when something (like an equipment failure or an interruption) happens while you are working.

Some sample behavioral interview questions include:

- Tell me about a goal you achieved and how you reached it.
- Give me an example of how you deal with problems.
- Give me an example of how you showed initiative.
- Have you done more than was required on the job, and if so, explain what you did.
- Have you had to overcome an obstacle at work? How did you do it?

As you can see, all these questions are about what you actually did in certain circumstances, rather than just about you and what you've done in your career. The interviewer is trying to get at how you will act on the job if you are hired. When answering these types of questions it's important to include specific examples from your work history in your response.

You don't know what type of interview you're going to have until it starts. It could be a traditional question-and-answer interview, a behavioral interview, or a combination of the two. So, the best way to prepare for a behavioral interview is to review possible scenarios from your work history to use in your answers. Compare your experiences to the qualifications the employer is seeking in the job posting. Write down a few possible answers of how you handled some work situations, in case you need them.

ELSEWHERE ON THE WEB

▶ Monster's Random Question Generator is a good way to practice for an interview, because you don't know what interview question you are going to be asked next. This interviewing tool will ask you some of the typical questions in random order, so you have the chance to think about your answers. Check it out at http://tools.monster.com/virtualinterviews/random.

ELSEWHERE ON THE WEB

▶ When you leave your job you may be asked to participate in an exit interview. About.com's Job Searching Technical Guide, Steven Niznik, explains what an employee exit interview is and the purpose of them for employers. The article also provides tips and advice on whether or not an employee should participate in an exit interview. Review the article online at http://about.com/jobsearchtech/exitinterview.

References

As part of the interview process, the company will probably want to check your references. Before you get a job offer, the company will want to verify that you have the credentials you have mentioned in your application materials and will want to confirm your dates of employment at your previous employer(s). The company may also want to talk to people who can verify and vouch for your skills and abilities.

It's always a good idea to have a list of references ready in advance. Bring the list with you to the interview. Here's a sample reference list format you can use to compile a list for yourself:

Employment References
- Your name
- Address
- City, state, zip
- Phone, cell phone
- E-mail

Reference List
- Name
- Job title
- Company
- Address
- City, state, zip
- Phone
- E-mail

Include three or four references on your list of references. For each reference, include full contact information, including an e-mail address, if you have it, so it's easy for the employer to get in touch with your references.

Don't include your references on your resume. Create a separate list that includes your contact information and your references. Use the same good-quality paper that you used to print your resume to print your reference list. Keep a few copies in your notepad holder or portfolio so you have the list ready to give to the interviewer when it's requested.

Give some thought to who to include on your list of references. Your reference list can include past supervisors and coworkers, business colleagues, customers, and vendors. In fact, your list can include anyone who will speak positively about your abilities and promote your candidacy to the reference checker.

On that note, you need to be sure that the reference giver is going to give you a good, strong endorsement. A negative or even a lukewarm reference isn't going to help you get the job. Talk to your references in advance to make sure that they are willing, and comfortable, giving you a reference.

I know an applicant who, when applying to a program where she needed a written reference, didn't check with the reference giver in advance. This very mediocre reference, in writing, hampered her chances of getting accepted. In other cases, when I've checked references, I've heard conflicting information about the candidate. I've even been told that the person wasn't a reliable employee. That's why it's really important to know ahead of time what your references are going to say about you.

You can ask hiring managers not to contact your current employer until they are very close to giving you a job offer. That can be important because your employer may not know that you're interviewing, and you don't want to jeopardize your current job until you have a new one lined up.

If you're seeking your first job or have been out of the work force for a while, you can use other types of references. If you've

ASK YOUR GUIDE

I was fired from my job. What can I say in an interview?

▶ That's always a tough question to answer, but career expert Joyce Lain Kennedy compiled some best answers and provided some advice for visitors to my About.com site. You can review her suggestions at http://about.com/jobsearch/whyfired. She also mentions how it's important to practice your answer in advance, keep it brief, and after you've answered, move on to why you're qualified for the job.

volunteered, considering asking the people you worked for or with if they would provide a reference for you. Teachers, professors, and even neighbors can make good references too.

A background check is a more extensive verification of your credentials. Depending on what the employer wants to know, a background investigation can include verifying your past employment, your Social Security number, and your educational background. It can also include a check of your credit, criminal records, medical history, and military records. However, when a background check is being conducted for employment purposes, the company must notify you in writing and get your written authorization before they can proceed.

It's important to note that the inquiries should be related to the job. For example, if you had an arrest on your record for embezzling money from a past employer, a company isn't going to want to hire you to handle money. In that case, a credit and criminal check would be acceptable.

There are also companies that will check your background for you, so you're not surprised by anything that comes up when an employer does the same. I received an e-mail from Craig, a frequent visitor to my About.com site. He was starting to interview and wanted to make sure that his record was accurate. The company that verified his background discovered a warrant for four or five different driving violations. It was a mistake and it took him awhile to clear his record, but he was able to let the employer know there was an issue in advance.

In addition, once you have been hired, you will need to provide information to prove that you are eligible to work in the United States. Employers are required to verify the identity and eligibility to work for all new employees who are hired. An **Employment Eligibility Verification Form** (I-9 Form) must be completed and

▶ There's a trend toward job seekers checking their own references or paying to have a background check conducted on themselves. The benefit is that you will know in advance if there is anything that might be a red flag to a prospective employer. If it's an error, you can clear it up, or if there's an issue you can determine how to address it, before the employer puts you on the spot and inquires about it.

kept on file by the employer. Employees are required to present documents (like a Social Security card, passport, birth certificate, driver's license and/or other documents) that confirm their ability to work in the United States.

Get Linked

*Check out the following resources from my **ABOUT**.com site for more advice and information on interviewing and references.*

INTERVIEWS

Here you'll find interview tips, interview questions and answers, interview preparation, interview thank-you letters and how to follow up after an interview.

 http://about.com/jobsearch/interviewresources

JOB INTERVIEW QUESTIONS AND ANSWERS

Reviewing these typical job interview questions will help you prepare your responses before you interview. There is also a list of sample questions to ask the interviewer.

 http://about.com/jobsearch/interviewqa

Shelton State Libraries
Shelton State Community College

Chapter 13

Evaluating Job Offers

Researching Salaries

Surveys report that over 90 percent of workers rank salary as the most important factor in deciding whether to accept a job offer. Salary is followed in most surveys by quality of life issues and benefits. As you can see, though, money matters most of all. It should—if you're worrying about how you're going to pay your bills, you're not going not to be a productive employee.

The other important factor in compensation is equity. Each and every one of us who is employed wants to feel like we are being paid at least a reasonable salary for the work we do. We all want to be valued and want to be paid a fair wage. When people believe that they are underpaid or otherwise short-changed, they aren't going to be happy at work and won't be the optimal employees that every company hopes to hire.

If you feel the job isn't offering what you expect, it's reasonable to turn it down and walk away from the job offer. If you're

What happens to the benefits provided by my current employer if I quit my job?

▶ That's a good question and one a lot of visitors to my About.com site ask. In fact, it's a question everyone should be able to answer before they resign from a job. Your Human Resources Department should have information available (and it may be online so you don't have to ask) on what benefits continue after you leave employment. Some benefits are mandated by law, and others are optional. More information on employee benefits is available at http://about.com/jobsearch/movingon.

not going to be happy, for whatever reason, it doesn't make much sense to take the job.

A visitor to my About.com site told me that he'd take a job just to try it out, then quit after a couple of weeks if it didn't work out. To me, it just wouldn't be worth the time, effort, and energy it would take to interview, to research the company, or even to do all the paperwork to get on the payroll if I didn't have a reasonable expectation that the job would be a good opportunity.

Before you can evaluate a job offer you need to know how much you are worth. You also need to know how much the job you have been offered is worth. You and your job aren't necessarily of equivalent value.

Your value is based on how much an employer is willing to pay to hire you. That might be more than the market rate for the position, because of special skills and experience you might have. It also could be less if, for example, you're changing careers and moving into a new field or if someone is taking a chance on hiring you for a position where you don't quite have the optimal experience.

I received an e-mail message from David, a visitor to my About.com site, who wasn't thrilled by the fact that companies wanted to know what his salary expectations were, without being willing to share what they were willing to pay. He said, "I've always disliked the employer asking me what my salary expectations are, particularly when they do not advertise their salary range. I've always felt that this is an unethical question to ask a job candidate, as it is very easy for the employer to short-change the candidate."

I agree that it can put a candidate in a tough position, but unfortunately that's the way the job offer process works. Unless you work for a union or a company that has a set salary structure with a specific rate for each job, salary is usually negotiable, at least to some extent.

Companies don't always ask for your salary range to short-change the candidate though. Sometimes they want to know how much you make to determine if they can afford you. What's difficult is that it's not always clear what to expect. You don't want to get short-changed and you want to get the top salary the employer is willing to pay.

Almost always, that is. Sometimes, there are other things that are more important than money. I know people who have willingly forgone a raise in order to get a couple of extra vacation days. I've also known people who have given up or not taken a job that would have required them to travel or work overtime.

What's important, though, is that they had a choice. The choice was theirs as to whether they took the job or gave up some money in their paycheck. That's the point that you want to get to when considering a job offer.

You will want to make sure that the entire compensation package—salary, benefits, and perks—is acceptable to you and that you can, hopefully, give a resounding "yes" to the hiring manager. When you feel positive about the offer, you will be eager and excited about starting your new job.

Salary isn't everything then, but it's definitely important. Workers want to be valued and want to be paid what they're worth. When you're not, there can be lingering resentment and hard feelings.

In one case I know of, a customer service manager at a local company discovered that a new hire was making thousands more dollars than she was. They both had a similar background and equivalent experience, but the latter person was able to negotiate a better deal. Unfortunately for the company, this arbitrary determination of compensation structure wasn't effective. The first manager was so upset that she quit.

ASK YOUR GUIDE

I'm really nervous about taking a new job. How do I know it will work out?

▶ There's no way to know for certain if a new job is a good career move. However, if you thoroughly research the job and the company, along with its staff and management, you'll have a strong chance of success. Once you have evaluated the job offer as best you can, and it feels like it's right, sometimes you just need to go for it!

All in all, salary needs to be fair. As About.com's Human Resources Guides Susan Heathfield (http://humanresources.about.com) says in an article for employers on salary negotiations, "Negotiation is not about winning—unless both parties win. If either party feels they have capitulated, not negotiated, both parties lose."

Conduct specific salary research. It's important to research salaries in your industry and geographic location. Keep in mind that what you find might not be 100 percent accurate (I've seen some salaries in online surveys that aren't), but they can give you a benchmark to use to determine what a reasonable salary is for the job you have been offered.

There are several Web sites you can use to research salary:

- About.com Salary Comparison and Calculator: http://about.salary.com
- Monster Salary Center: http://salary.monster.com
- *New York Times* Salary Calculator: http://salary.nytimes.com
- Salary.com Salary Wizard: www.salary.com

Try several salary calculators and compare results. I was interested in finding out how much a paralegal job would be worth in Huntingon, New York. I selected Legal as an industry and entered the zip code. Then I was able to select Paralegal I as a job title. Monster's Salary Wizard told me that the average salary for the position was about $45,000. As an added bonus I was able see related job openings and apply online for the jobs via Monster.

At Salary.com's Web site I could type in the job title (paralegal) and the zip code to search. Before you get results there's an option to sign up for several e-mail newsletters. Sign up if you're interested in receiving more salary information; otherwise click "not now," then "continue" to get results without signing up.

ELSEWHERE ON THE WEB

▶ The federal government regulates wages and benefits, and there are certain guidelines employers must follow. For example, there is a federal minimum wage, overtime pay regulations, and other legal protection for workers. If you have been discriminated against there is information on compliance and enforcement help available as well. Details are available on the Department of Labor Employment Standards Administration Web site at www.dol.gov/esa.

Salary.com's results include an option to calculate how much your net paycheck will be. You can enter your tax filing status and other deductions to generate your estimated net pay. This is really useful for planning a budget based on your new salary. You can also view job openings on CareerBuilder and Monster.

When you use these salary calculators, be sure to start by using the basic services; that way you won't need to pay for premium services and extra reports that you don't need.

Your results should give you a range for your position in the city where you are going to work. The results aren't etched in stone, so you may want to do some additional research or even talk to some recruiters in the area to make sure that your expectations aren't too high or too low.

Mary, for example, researched salaries for a vice president of marketing position in her city. It turns out that salaries reported by the calculators were much higher than she was currently making. She worried that she was underpaid, but she took the time to talk to a recruiter who told her that her salary was in line with the market conditions for her area.

Salary calculators are a helpful tool and that's exactly what they should be considered—something to help you gauge what you should be earning, rather than an exact predictor of your actual earning power. Once you've determined a salary amount that you hope to make, you can figure out what your net pay, after taxes and deductions, will be. There are paycheck calculators available where you can calculate your net pay. Try the following Web sites:

- PaycheckCity Calculators: www.paycheckcity.com
- Payroll-Taxes.com's Paycheck Calculators: www.payroll-taxes.com/calculators.htm
- Net to Gross Paycheck Calculator: www.dinkytown.net/java/PayrollGross.html

TOOLS YOU NEED

▸ When you have received a job offer that's borderline, you will need to calculate whether you can afford it. The About.com Financial Planning Guide has a Budget Worksheet you can complete to make sure that your finances are in order. It's an essential tool for anyone contemplating a salary that might not be enough to make ends meet. Print it out at http://about.com/financial plan/budget.

When you use these calculators you will be able to select your state, your tax filing status, and your optional deductions to get an estimate of what your net pay will be. There are different calculators you can use if you are a salary or an hourly employee and also calculators you can use to calculate 401(k) contributions.

The Net to Gross calculator is especially useful if you need to bring home a certain amount in your paycheck. You will able to see how much gross pay you will need and, therefore, be able to determine the minimum salary you can afford to accept.

Once you have taken some time to research salaries for your position and location, you will have information ready to use to negotiate a pay package with employers.

It's important to note that you don't have to wait until you have a job offer to start researching salaries. It can take time, so it's better to do it while you're job searching (or even before you start) so you're prepared in advance to negotiate.

Benefits and Perks

Benefits can be worth as much as 40 percent of your compensation package. With skyrocketing health insurance costs it's critically important to make sure the benefits that are provided by the company you are considering working for are sufficient.

Take Miriam, for example. She contacted me after she had accepted a job offer. The hourly rate was excellent; however, she hadn't asked about benefits and didn't realize until she had accepted the position that there weren't any benefits, other than those mandated by state law, like disability and unemployment.

That meant Miriam had to shop for and pay for health insurance coverage. The most reasonable policy she could find cost $300 a month so her paycheck was much less than expected. That's why it's important to ask about benefits before you take the job.

First of all, decide what benefits you need; then find out what benefits the employer pays for and which benefits you will have to contribute toward. Ask what your contributions will be so you know exactly what you will have to pay for if you accept the position.

Use the following checklist to identify the employee benefits that are important to you:

- ❍ Bonuses, stock options, profit sharing
- ❍ Child care
- ❍ Continuing-education benefits
- ❍ Insurance: health, life, dental
- ❍ Maternity/family leave
- ❍ Retirement plan
- ❍ Time off: sick days, holidays, vacation

There are Web sites you can use to evaluate how much benefits are worth in your total compensation package:

- ● HotJobs.com Salary and Benefits Wizard: http://salary.hotjobs.com
- ● Salary.com Benefits Calculator: www.salary.com/benefits/layoutscripts/bnfl_display.asp
- ● SalaryExpert Executive Compensation Calculator: www.salaryexpert.com

Analyze what benefits you need. Different benefits have different values, depending on who you are and what's important to you. If you have children, family health insurance will be high on your list of benefits. If you aren't married, you may want a health plan with domestic partner coverage that will insure your live-in

▶ When you accept a job offer you will need to complete a W-4 form to have federal income tax withheld from your paycheck. It's also a good idea to check your withholding allowances on an annual basis. The About.com Tax Planning site has information on how to fill out a W-4 form, along with advice on how to access and use the Internal Revenue Service withholding calculator. It's available online at http://about.com/taxes/W4.

partner. If you have a health condition or illness, you will need to make sure that the new company's plan covers pre-existing conditions.

What is most important is not so much the benefits that are offered, but whether those benefits are what you need. Will these benefits provide you with what you need, both short-term and in the future?

Perks can be a plus. There can be perks that you wouldn't expect to receive. Some companies offer on-site dry-cleaning services, others offer massage services. Google, for example, offers both dry-cleaning services and a coin-free laundry room. Workers at company headquarters have access to a company physician and to dental care.

Other companies have similar perks that can help both with your work and your life. On-site child care was of immeasurable value to me when my daughter was younger. I could visit her at lunchtime and knew she was well cared for when I was at work. I was also close by if I was needed. Having an on-site exercise facility is another excellent benefit that many employees appreciate.

Take a look at CNNMoney's list of Best Benefits (**http://money. cnn.com/magazines/fortune/bestcompanies/best_benefits**) to get an idea of the type of benefits that the country's best employers are offering. A sampling of some of the cool, and sometimes nontraditional, benefits offered include a paid month off before their due date for pregnant women at Eli Lily, lifetime membership at the company fitness center for S.C. Johnson retirees, and $4 onsite haircuts at Worthington Industries.

Some perks are more valuable, from a financial perspective, than others, but even little perks (like free coffee for Starbuck's workers) can go a long way to help with worker satisfaction.

How to Evaluate a Job Offer

There are a variety of factors that you will need to analyze in order to decide whether you should accept the job you have been offered. The company culture, future opportunities, flexibility, and the job responsibilities are all as important as your potential paycheck.

The following is a list of factors to consider when evaluating a job offer:

- Job responsibilities (you want to do this job)
- Management (you are comfortable with the boss and coworkers)
- Salary
- Benefits
- Work environment (flexibility, hours)
- Opportunities for advancement

Another way to evaluate a job offer is to look at the average benefits that most companies offer workers (from the Bureau of Labor Statistics) and to compare them to what you are being offered:

- Average number of paid holidays: 8 days
- Vacation after one year of service: 8.8 days
- Vacation after three years of service: 10.7 days
- Vacation after five years of service: 13.4 days
- The average percentage of health insurance premiums paid by employer: individual, 82 percent; family, 70 percent
- The percentage of employers offering life insurance: 50 percent

Sometimes though, there are intangible benefits that are more important than all the factors you are analyzing. For someone with

TOOLS YOU NEED

▶ The Bureau of Labor Statistics has a useful tool you can use when evaluating a job offer. You can find out how many employees offer paid vacation days, sick leave, child care assistance, a pension plan, disability insurance, and medical care benefits. Simply check the benefits you want to know about to get percentages of workers who are covered. It's available at http://data.bls.gov/cgi-bin/surveymost?eb.

▶ More and more employers are offering flexible benefit plans. When they are available, the employer will contribute a certain amount of money toward your benefits. You can then choose which benefits you want based upon your and your family's needs. You may be able to choose between several health insurance plans, opt for dental or life insurance coverage, and other benefit options.

young children, having a boss who is flexible when the kids are sick can be worth more than any salary you could earn.

Similarly, Mary Beth, one client I worked with, wanted to find a job where she could work around her graduate school schedule. She was able to find an employer who basically let her set her own schedule. This enabled her to work and go to school, which was worth a lot to her.

Samuel, a computer programmer, is able to work from home when the weather is too bad for an easy commute. His employer provided him with two computer systems—one in the office and another portable system, so he can work from anywhere.

Sometimes, especially when balancing work and life options, the flexibility offered by an employer is worth more than money. Employers are more cognizant of the value of being flexible than they were in the past. Having someone who is willing to do their job from wherever they might be is a plus.

The number of companies that offer **flextime**, where employees can set their own schedule, is rising. Some companies are even offering flexible scheduling as a way to actively recruit candidates to work for their firm, especially moms who are returning to the work force.

Always consider opportunities for advancement. Especially when you are starting out in an entry-level position, growth is an important factor to bear in mind when deciding on a job offer. If your plans for the future are to advance, you will need to make sure that there is a career path available to you.

When interviewing or mulling over a job offer, it's perfectly acceptable to ask about opportunities for growth. In fact, it's important to know what your career path will be so you can decide if the next job is one you want to have.

Anna, a visitor to the Discussion Forum on my About.com site, was worried about turning down a job as a store manager. However, she knew that if she took the job, she would most likely get promoted at some point and would have to move, because that's how the company worked. She didn't want to leave her hometown, so she declined the position in favor of a local employer.

Jack e-mailed me because he was pondering a job offer that would require him to move to a different state for a year's training program. After the training was completed, he would be able to select several locations where he would prefer to work. However, management made the final decision on placement. Jack decided that he wanted to work for this company and the compensation and benefits were well worth having to relocate.

On the other hand, you may want a job where you aren't expected to move up the career ladder. Dick, for example, retired after many years as a space planner for a major retailer. He was semiretired and worked for me on a part-time on-call basis when I worked for a greeting-card company. He didn't want additional responsibilities or a promotion; after thirty years of moving up the career ladder, Dick only wanted this job to keep busy.

What's important then is to decide what you want and to consider whether this job offer is going to get you where you want to go, from a career perspective. Some questions you might want to ask is whether there a clear path from this job to the next and the one after that and if that career path is clearly defined and articulated by the organization.

In conjunction with advancement, evaluate salary prospects. It's important that your salary progresses along with your career. When asking about advancement opportunities, also ask what performance evaluations and salary reviews are conducted after you are hired.

ELSEWHERE ON THE WEB

▶ **What do you know about negotiating salaries? More importantly, what don't you know about salary negotiations? This quiz from Salary-Negotiations.com will help you figure out how what you earn can impact more than just your paycheck. For example, it can affect your performance on the job and your future earnings power. Check it out at** www.salarynegotiations .com/salaryquiz.html.

It's important to know what you can expect to make in the future, as well as what you are going to earn today. If there is a performance review and a chance for a salary increase, in ninety days, for example, that might offset a starting salary that is somewhat less than you expected. So, ask about performance and salary reviews. You will need to know about timing—how often they are conducted and what typical salary increases may be.

Ask for the job offer in writing. This is the best way to make sure that there are no questions regarding the offer. That way you will understand, clearly, what you are being offered and will be able to address any issues with the hiring manager.

Even if you have already discussed a compensation package verbally, getting the offer in writing will confirm the agreement.

This is important, because if it isn't in writing you have no recourse if there's a problem. Kenneth, a visitor to my About.com site, accepted a contract job that, he was told, would become permanent in three months. After the three months had passed he inquired as to when he would officially be on the payroll. He was informed that the contract job was actually a three-month trial position and there was no guarantee that he'd be hired. That was a very unpleasant surprise that could have been avoided if the job offer had been in writing. The job offer letter should include:

- Job title
- Salary
- Benefits
- Starting date
- Vacation, sick time, holidays
- Any contingencies like passing a background check or drug screening

The details for each of these listed items should be spelled out in the job offer letter so it is clear, to both you and the employer, what you have agreed upon. You may be expected to sign an agreement acknowledging your acceptance of the offer once the terms are agreed upon.

Negotiating Compensation

Once you've taken the time to research salaries, benefits, and perks and you've come up with a ballpark (at least) amount of what you should be getting paid, what's the best way to get it?

There are a variety of strategies you can use, depending on what has happened during the interview process. Start by trying not to be the first one who brings up compensation. If you're asked what your salary requirements are, say that they are flexible based upon the job and the entire compensation package, including benefits.

Another option is to mention to the hiring manager that you want to know more about the job prior to discussing salary. Alternately, give the employer a range based upon the salary research you've conducted.

Remember that you don't have to respond to the offer immediately. A simple "I need a few days to consider the offer" may get you an increase in the original offer. When you're not sure about the position, turning it down can get you a better offer too. I once turned down a job I knew I didn't want at any salary. I received several follow-up phone calls increasing the salary offered. The employer thought I was negotiating, but that wasn't the case. I just didn't want the job.

Be careful about turning down a job unless you are absolutely sure that you don't want it. If you do need it or want it, there's a risk that the employer may accept your "no" and you will have lost the job offer.

The job offer may not be negotiable. According to a Career-Builder (www.careerbuilder.com) survey, 30 percent of hiring managers said the first offer was final, while 60 percent will extend a second offer, and 10 percent will extend another offer twice or more if they really want to hire the candidate. So, there's no guarantee that turning down the job will get you a better offer.

This means that the offer you get may not be negotiable. In fact, many companies have a set salary structure in place and won't waiver from it. If that's the case, you may be able to negotiate benefits—or you may not. Again, it depends on company policy.

When the compensation package isn't negotiable, it actually makes your decision easier. You can take the offer or leave it.

Finally, if you know you don't want the job, politely decline. There is no need to specify why you don't want it (don't say the job is awful or the pay stinks!). Thank the employer politely for the offer and move on to the next opportunity. You don't have to give a reason for turning down the offer; you can simply say "No, thank you." without specifying a particular reason for turning down the job.

Resign with Class

How you resign is important. When you're ready to resign from your job, it's important to do so, when you can, in a way that doesn't harm your relationship with your current employer. If you handle your resignation correctly, you'll be able maintain a positive relationship with your company.

This is important because you will need your former employer to give you a reference. You will also want to use your past coworkers as network contacts, and you never know when someone from your past can help you in the future.

TOOLS YOU NEED

▶ What's most important is that you are comfortable with the job offer. You're the one who will be working for the company and you need to decide whether the salary, the benefits, and the perks, as well at the job itself, are what you want. Once you have thoroughly researched everything you need to know to make an educated decision, you will be able to make a decision on whether the job is right for you.

The following tips will help your resignation run smoothly:

- **Give notice:** If you have an employment contract, follow the terms; otherwise two weeks' notice is appropriate.
- **Tell your supervisor first:** The first person you should notify is your supervisor, then you can let your coworkers know that you are leaving.
- **Write a resignation letter:** Even if you have verbally resigned, put it in writing.
- **Be positive:** There's no point in being negative even if you hated the job.
- **Request a reference:** Ask your manager if he or she will write a reference letter for you.

The following is a sample resignation letter you can use:

> *Dear Mr./Ms. Last Name:*
>
> *I would like to inform you that I am resigning from my position as Merchandiser Supervisor for GAD company effective January 1.*
>
> *I appreciate the opportunities for professional and personal development that you have provided me with during the past three years. I have enjoyed working for the company and sincerely appreciate the support provided to me during my tenure here. Thank you for all you have done for me and for my career.*
>
> *If I can be of any assistance during this transition, please let me know. I would be glad to help, however I can.*
>
> *Yours truly,*
> *Signature*

ELSEWHERE ON THE WEB

▶ Salary.com (www.salary.com) is the Web site you need to visit when you want detailed salary information. There are salary reports for just about every job in every industry, as well as detailed information on salary, benefits, salary negotiations, calculators, including a benefits calculator, and salary quizzes you can take to find out what you should be earning or where you could progress in your career.

As you can see, the letter is simple and self-explanatory. There's no reason to include lengthy explanations as to why you are leaving or any details about where you are going. You have no obligation to provide any information other than the basic fact that you are leaving.

Check your benefits. It's also important to find out what benefits you are entitled to upon leaving. Do you have vacation time you haven't used that you will be paid for? What happens with your pension plan or 401(k)? Can you continue health insurance coverage if you're not starting your new job right away? Ask to meet with your Human Resources Department so you can get answers to these and any other questions you might have.

This can be important, because you don't want to be without health insurance coverage. If there is going to be a lapse in coverage, ask about COBRA (Consolidated Omnibus Budget Reconciliation Act). COBRA provides some workers who leave a job with the right to temporary continuation, under specific circumstances, of health coverage at group rates. That way you won't have a gap in coverage.

Once you have accepted the offer, plan your departure from your current job and your transition into your new one. Offer to provide whatever assistance you can as you leave, and ask your new employer what you can do to prepare to start your new job.

If you can, take some time off between jobs so you have a chance to relax a little and enjoy what you've accomplished during your job search. You've earned it!

Get Linked

Here's more advice and information on evaluating job offers and negotiating compensation from my **ABOUT**.com *site. These will point you toward more online resources that will help you decide if the job you have been offered is the one that's right for you.*

EMPLOYEE BENEFITS

Here you will find employee benefit information, including worker's compensation, health insurance, life insurance, disability insurance, and related resources.

 http://about.com/jobsearch/benefits

SALARY NEGOTIATIONS

This resource offers strategies for successfully negotiating salary, including how to evaluate salary offers, how to analyze benefits, and how to get paid what you're worth.

 http://about.com/jobsearch/salarynegotiation

WAGE AND SALARY INFORMATION

This directory of wage and salary resources for job seekers includes minimum wage, overtime, and compliance resources.

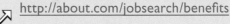 http://about.com/jobsearch/salaryinfo

Chapter 14

Job Search Communications

Perfect Correspondence

Why is it so important that all your job search correspondence is perfect? Well, if yours isn't perfect, someone else's will be. That person's resume will move ahead of yours in the "to interview" pile because they took the time and effort to make sure there wasn't a single error in their resume or in their cover letter.

That said, it isn't just your resume and cover letter that needs to be perfect. One candidate had an exemplary resume and cover letter; she also interviewed really well. She was on the list to get called for a second interview when the hiring manager received her thank-you letter. That follow-up letter had several errors. This gave pause to the hiring manager and caused her to reconsider which candidates would make it to the second round. The candidate who made the mistakes didn't get called for a second interview.

Can I stretch the truth a little on my resume? It would definitely help my chances for employment.

▶ I often get asked the same question. Visitors to my About.com site read about executives who stretched the truth (or lied) on their resumes and wonder why they can't too. Unfortunately, the truth does come back to haunt you. Dawn Rosenberg McKay's (About.com's Career Planning Guide) article on lying on resumes is a must-read for anyone interested in the topic: http://about.com/career planning/resumelies.

Unfortunately, we usually don't get a second chance when job searching. The candidates who take the time, up front, to make sure that everything is perfect are typically the ones who get the jobs.

The following tips will help you ensure that all your job search correspondence is perfect:

- Consult a dictionary and thesaurus when writing.
- Proofread for grammar, punctuation, and spelling, then proofread again.
- Ask someone to proofread for you.
- Keep your letters short and to the point.
- Write resumes and cover letters that are clearly focused on the jobs for which you are applying.
- Make sure there is plenty of white space on the page and all your documents are easy to read.

It's important that all your correspondence is pleasing to the eye and easy to read. Nobody wants to attempt to read a font that's so tiny that you have to squint to decipher it. On the other hand, hiring managers don't want to read a cover letter that's three pages long because the font was so large or because the person wrote too much.

There are ways to ensure that your e-mail and instant-messaging communications are professional. Even though there are lots of images and gadgets you can use, you're better off avoiding them.

To communicate professionally online, follow these guidelines:

- Use a simple font that is large enough to easily read.
- Don't use all capital letters (it's considered shouting).
- Don't use emoticons (smiley faces) in e-mail or instant messages.

- Avoid using acronyms like TTYL (talk to you later) or BRB (be right back).
- Keep your e-mail messages and instant messages brief and to the point.
- Be sure to complete the subject line of your message.
- Don't forget to add a signature that includes your full contact information in your e-mail messages.
- Proofread your e-mail messages as carefully as your paper correspondence.

It's important to keep your correspondence concise and to the point. You need to catch the reader's interest within the first few sentences. Those sentences need to engage the reader and convey your message. It can be tough to be brief, but if you don't make a compelling case for your candidacy within the first paragraph, especially in e-mail, you're not going to have any hopes of connecting with the reader. And that first paragraph should only be, at most, three or four sentences.

Here is a reason why brevity is important. When readers have lots of information to get through, they want to be able to skim the material and pick up the highlights of what they are reading. They don't want to read the "great American novel." They want to read a quick article, at most, or a brief advertisement of your qualifications. So, consider how you can sell yourself using the least amount of words.

Act fast when job searching. Applying and responding in a timely manner is important too. I've never understood why some people wait to respond to an inquiry from a prospective employer (or from anyone, for that matter). It can cost you the job.

One candidate for employment e-mailed me because she wasn't sure whether she should apply to a job that she had read

WHAT'S HOT

▶ My article on writing job letters is in the What's Hot section of my About.com site. It's got advice on general letter writing, as well as advice on writing cover letters, reference letters, resignation letters, and thank-you letters. There's also advice on how to request reference letters. For my top letter-writing tips, visit http://about.com/jobsearch/lettertips.

▶ *Grammatically Correct: The Writer's Essential Guide to Punctuation, Spelling, Style, Usage and Grammar* by Anne Stilman is an excellent resource for job seekers who need assistance with their writing. It has sections on spelling, problem words, and punctuation that you can use to make sure all your correspondence is error free. Review it before you start your correspondence to ensure that you make a good impression with each and every letter you send.

about in a newsletter. She said she had tried to find more information on the company but couldn't. I'm not sure what happened, but I found the company's Web site on Google in a few seconds. During the time she had spent writing to me and looking for information, the employer had interviewed several candidates and was about to make a job offer.

Waiting too long to apply cost the candidate what may have been an excellent job opportunity. If you're not sure about a job, apply anyway if you're qualified. You can always withdraw your application, but if you're too late you're not going to get considered for the position.

Apply for jobs and follow up to inquiries from recruiters or hiring managers within twenty-four hours, or sooner if possible. You want to be sure that you come across as interested and responsive. Responding in a timely manner speaks to the type of employee you'll be, as well as the type of candidate for employment that you are. I'd start having second thoughts if someone took more than a couple of days to get back to me after a call to schedule an interview.

Also make sure you're reachable. Provide an e-mail address and a phone number (typically a cell phone) where the hiring manager or recruiter can reach you. They don't have the time to play telephone tag, and they want to schedule interviews in an expedient fashion. Check for messages frequently so you can respond immediately.

Why and How to Follow Up

Following up after you submit a resume and cover letter can be tricky. There is one school of thought that says you should follow up every resume you send with a phone call within a week. There's another that says you need to follow the employer's instructions. If the job posting says don't call, don't. If the help-wanted ad says the company will contact the candidates they want to interview, wait.

I agree with the experts who recommend following the instructions. There isn't much that annoys a hiring manager more than someone who doesn't follow the rules. The other problem (besides being annoying) with attempting to call is that with the increase in hiring online, there often isn't a phone number for the person responsible for hiring.

What you can do instead, though, is e-mail the contact person if you have a contact at the company, or write to the e-mail address where you sent the resume to confirm that your resume was received. Also ask if there is any additional information you can provide.

Here's a sample letter you can use to follow up on your application:

> *Dear Hiring Manager,*
>
> *I submitted a resume earlier this month for the marketing assistant position advertised on ABC Web site. I would appreciate you confirming receipt of my resume and I would like to reiterate my interest in the position.*
>
> *I am very interested in working at DEF Company. My skills and experience would be a perfect match for this opportunity.*
>
> *I would be glad to resend my application materials or to provide any further information you might need regarding my candidacy. I can be reached at email@email.com or at (111) 111-1111.*
>
> *I look forward to hearing from you. Thank you very much for your consideration.*
>
> *Sincerely,*
> *Signature*

Note that, in addition to following up on his application, the writer has reiterated his interest in the job and offered additional

TOOLS YOU NEED

▶ An online portfolio can be a useful tool for communicating your qualifications and revealing your credentials to prospective employers. It allows you to package your resume, artwork, certifications, articles, photos, images, and everything else that you want to share in a form that's easily accessible on the Web. More information on employment portfolios is available at http://about.com/jobsearch/portfolio.

information to the employer. Both are good ways to reinforce that he would be a good candidate for the job.

Use your contacts. If you have contacts at the company where you are seeking employment use them now, if you haven't already. Ask your contact person if he or she can check with the Human Resources Department on the status of your resume. Also ask if your contact can put in a good word for you with the hiring manager. This is a good time to use your connections to help get your resume reviewed. It may make the difference between getting an interview and not being called.

You will also want to use your company contacts once you have been called for an interview. Keep in mind that you can find contacts at networking sites, like LinkedIn, if you don't have personal connections. Use your connections to help with your company research, to get interviewing advice, and to get a recommendation for employment.

Employers are typically thrilled when they get a personal recommendation for a candidate for employment. A reference, especially from a current employee, can help validate their decision on a choice of candidate and can even help sway a decision in your direction if the employer isn't sure who to hire.

The last time I referred someone for a job, I got very nice thank-you letters from both the candidate and the hiring manager. They were both thrilled that I helped make a match that developed into a hire. I, of course, was happy that my help was appreciated.

Thank-You Letters

It's important to say thank you to your interviewer(s) as soon as possible after the interview. You can either say thank you by typing and mailing a letter, by sending a hand-written thank-you note, or by sending an e-mail message. It is fine to send an e-mail thank-you

TOOLS YOU NEED

▶ It's always a good idea to check your grammar and punctuation as you write. Purdue University has a great online resource you can use to check grammar, punctuation, and spelling. Check it out at http://owl.english. purdue.edu/handouts/ grammar, and be sure to use it to double-check all your job search correspondence— before you send it!

note, especially if the company is making decisions on second interviews sooner rather than later.

The fact that you are saying thank you is more important than which method you use to you say it. I've read estimates that suggest that only 10 to 25 percent of candidates send thank-you notes after an interview. When you are one of those people who do say thank you, there's no better way to help you stand out from the crowd.

By sending a thank-you letter you will cover several bases. You will let the employer know you appreciated them taking the time to interview you. You will also let the interviewer know that you are definitely interested in the job. In addition, you can also use this opportunity to highlight why you're a strong candidate.

So, sending a thank-you note is appropriate for several reasons. You will make a good impression on the interviewer and you will be reiterating your interest in the job. You can also use your thank-you note to share information you might have forgotten to mention in the interview or as a way to clarify facts that you didn't properly explain.

When you're not sure what to write, review some samples, then edit the sample to fit your situation. There are samples available on my About.com site at http://about.com/jobsearch/thankyousamples. Don't just copy a letter though. You will need to personalize it so it fits the job you are applying for and the skills and experiences that you are offering the employer.

Here are some tips for sending thank-you letters:

- **Collect business cards:** Ask for business cards when interviewing or networking. That way you'll have all the information you need to send a thank-you note.
- **Buy cards:** I keep a box of thank-you notes in my office desk. That way I can send a quick thank-you note at any time.

ELSEWHERE ON THE WEB

▶ Do you know what you should or shouldn't be doing when you job search or communicate online? When in doubt visit NetManners.com (www.netmanners.com) to make sure you're following the appropriate netiquette (Network Etiquette E-mail Etiquette and Proper Technology Use) protocol when communicating online. Manners do matter when you're job searching online, so be sure that yours are perfect!

- **Write fast:** Send your thank-you notes as soon as you can after the interview.
- **Thank everyone:** Take the time to thank everyone who helps you.
- **Proof your thank-you letters:** As with your other job search correspondence, make sure your letters are perfect.

If you interview with a group, send a thank-you note to everyone you met while interviewing. Similarly, if you have a second interview, send a second thank-you note. Especially after a second interview, take the time to write a personal message to the people who interviewed you. You want to connect with them, and you also want to convince them to you hire you.

Also take the time to thank employees you might have met while you were visiting the company, even though they may not have direct input into hiring you. As I've said, everyone likes to feel appreciated, regardless of their role in the company and their responsibility, or not, for hiring.

When I worked as an administrative assistant to a vice president of sales and marketing, I was responsible for arranging an interview for a prospective district manager. Paul was coming from out of town, so I scheduled airline flights, a hotel room, and a full day of interviews. None of that seemed like much work, but the day after Paul left, I received a beautiful bouquet of flowers as a thank-you gift for arranging the interview.

Of course, I was duly impressed and so was my boss. Paul's thoughtfulness moved him a notch or two up on the candidate list. He ended up getting a job offer, for more reasons than just the flowers. If he hadn't been a good candidate, it wouldn't have mattered as much, but taking the time to say thank you made us think even more highly of a very good candidate.

Timing is important. Don't wait. Your thank-you letters should be sent within twenty-four hours of your interview. That way, the people who are considering who to hire should receive it before, or while, they are making a hiring decision. It can be a way to cement the fact that you're a strong candidate in the decision-makers' minds.

Once you have found a job, it's also important to thank everyone who has helped with your job search. Don't forget to send a thank-you note, e-mail or otherwise, to all those who have supported your job search endeavors.

If your job search is lengthy, and it can be, it's also appropriate to send a thank-you note while you're job searching. Sending a quick note thanking your contacts for their help, so far, can also be a way to remind them that you're still seeking employment and may need some additional assistance. Most people are really busy and tend to forget that someone needs help, unless they're reminded. So, a hello, along with a gentle reminder, can get you some additional assistance, including referrals and jobs leads.

Do thank everyone who has helped you with this endeavor. I know that adds to the work that you need to do, but it is important not only to thank the people who have helped you, but also to solidify their position in your network for when you need them the next time around.

The following is a list of some of the people you should remember to thank:

- ○ Career counselors
- ○ Interviewers
- ○ Hiring managers
- ○ Recruiters
- ○ Networking contacts
- ○ Anyone else who has helped with your search

WHAT'S HOT

▶ "A Second Look at First Impressions" is one of the most popular articles on my About.com site. It discusses how everything you do—from how you treat each member of the interview team to what you say or don't say during the interview—is noted and is as important as how you present yourself on paper. You can read it at http://about.com/jobsearch/firstimpressions.

Remember, it only takes a few minutes to say thank you. The time you take will be time well spent. People notice those who take the time to let them know they are appreciated. They also are more willing to help again in the future when someone takes the time to thank them.

What Not to Do When Job Searching

I am continually amazed at how many people do the wrong thing when job searching. Sometimes it's deliberate—job seekers think that they can do it their way, instead of the right way, and the employer will notice. The employer will definitely notice, but not in the way the applicant wants.

On my About.com site, I've mentioned over and over again how important I believe it is for job seekers to follow the rules when job searching. Explaining why doesn't always help though. I receive more resumes via e-mail than I can count. Sometimes there's a message asking for help finding a job or asking me to edit the resume. In other cases, there's just a resume attached to an e-mail message with nothing to indicate why the person sent it.

Sometimes I ask why the person sent the resume to me, because I have information on my site that clearly says that as much as I would like to provide individual assistance, I don't have the resources to do so. I haven't received a good response yet. Some people think that I can help, even when, unfortunately, I'm not able to. Others simply blast their resume to anyone who might read it. Neither action is a good one.

I have a friend who is a human resources manager. She calls herself "the dragon lady" because she's tough. She doesn't have much tolerance for errors and she expects the people she interviews, the people she hires, and the people who work for her company to excel at what they do. Her expectations are high, and if you're

WHAT'S HOT

▶ The About.com Job Searching Forum is a great place to visit to get your correspondence reviewed and to get advice on what to say and how to say it. You can post your resume and letters in the Resume and Cover Letters folder to get suggestions on what to include and how to format your application materials. If you're not sure what to write, there's help available for that too. Check out the Forum at http://about.com/jobsearch/forum.

one of those people with typos on your resume or inappropriate interview attire, you're most likely not going to get the job.

Her company is very successful. It's full of high-caliber employees who do excel. The reason for this, I believe, is because they were held to a higher standard from their first contact with the company. She expected the best and she hired the best.

What's even more interesting is that her employees enjoy working at the company, they love their jobs, and they are proud to be part of the organization. That's the type of job we all should have, and that's one reason why it's important to do the best you can while job searching.

When you take the time to ensure that your resumes, cover letters, and other communications are perfect, you will be doing yourself a favor, as well as your potential employers.

Taking the time to thoroughly prepare for a job search, including preparing for interviewing, will help you make a compelling case for your candidacy. That's going to help you get the job you want. It will also help you get the job fast, because the fewer questions and concerns the company has about you, the quicker they will be able to get to the point of making a job offer.

Follow the rules! I think there are a couple of issues when it comes to following the rules. Many people, and I can be guilty of this too, simply don't read the directions thoroughly and don't pay attention. This one is easy to fix. I make a conscious effort now to read every single step of the instructions. Then I read it again. That way, I'm pretty sure that I'll get it right.

Other job seekers, as I mentioned, think that they will do better job searching their own way. They think that the rules don't matter and if they ignore them, they'll get ahead. Unfortunately, I don't think that's the case. The candidates who are the least likely

ELSEWHERE ON THE WEB

▶ CareerLab has a list of the Twenty-Eight Most Common Mistakes made by job seekers. There is information on typical typos, paragraphs that should never be written, and stories about mistakes like forgetting to put the letter in the envelope. Some are funny, unless they have happened to you, of course. Review it carefully so you don't make one of these embarrassing mistakes. Check it out at www.careerlab.com/letters/intro06.htm.

to follow the instructions are the ones who are most likely to knock themselves out of contention for the job.

There are a variety of things you shouldn't do when job searching. Not following the rules is only one of the mistakes job seekers tend to make. There are others, too, and some of them are easy to avoid. Most importantly, if you take the time to do it right, you'll have a much better chance of success. The following are some of the tips I've collected over the years on how not to job search:

- **Don't follow the instructions.** Not following the directions in the job posting is the quickest way to get your resume into the reject pile.
- **Apply for jobs you're not qualified for.** Applying for jobs that you're not qualified for is a waste of your time and the employer's time. There are too many other candidates who are qualified for every job opening.
- **Limit your job search.** Sending out a resume or two a week or making a phone call every now and then isn't going to cut it. The more resumes you send, the better your chances of getting an interview.
- **Contradict yourself.** Make sure your interview responses match your resume.
- **Undervalue your worth.** If you don't think you can do the job, your prospective employer isn't going to think so either. Be sure to realize that you're going to be a valuable employee for your next employer.
- **Make a mistake.** Typos, of course, are a problem, but under-dressing or overdressing for an interview can knock you out of contention too.

- **Let the employer know you're desperate.** Even if you really, really need this job, don't let the employer know. You'll lose your negotiating power if you show your desperation.

Privacy Issues

There are a multitude of privacy issues that can arise when job searching. Confidential information can be used for identity theft, to access your bank account, or to steal your credit card number. There are too many unscrupulous companies that will charge uninformed or unaware job seekers for helping them apply for jobs, for kits to start a home business, or for guaranteed job placement. If it sounds too good to be true, it is. Just search Google for "work at home" and skim through some of the over 4 billion results to get an idea of what's out there. Just a few of the listings I read include:

- **PC data entry:**
  $30,000/month
- **Work at home typist:**
  $1,000 to $7,000 per month
- **Internet marketing:**
  $15,000 per month

Again, if sounds too good to be true . . . . There is no way, I guarantee it, that you will make that kind of money doing data entry, typing, or marketing something online. Don't give your money to anyone for anything related to a job search unless you are absolutely sure what you are paying for (a resume-writing service, for example) and who you are paying.

Don't give your personal information to any of these sites either. Once you sign up, you'll get more invitations to participate in more scams, and you'll probably get extra spam e-mail as well.

ASK YOUR GUIDE

I realized after I e-mailed a cover letter that it had a mistake. Should I send another (edited) copy?

▶ It's really easy to send an e-mail before you have had a chance to proof it thoroughly. Sometimes that Send button seems to click itself! I wouldn't bring the mistake to the hiring manager's attention though, because he or she might not even notice it. If you tell the employer about it, you'll only highlight your mistake.

There are a variety of scams that are used to take advantage of job seekers:

- Identity theft
- Fraud (asking for payments for processing hiring paperwork)
- Work-at-home scams
- Pay for application kit scams
- Pay for job placement scams

The other problem is that there really isn't an effective way for anyone to police the Internet. The job sites try to remove illegal ads and listings that are scams from their databases, but it's often hard to manage them, mainly because of the sheer volume of listings.

Anyone can put up a Web site in short time. It's easy to buy a URL, a Web-hosting package, and a canned Web site that you can put online without having to know HTML or any other Web design skills. There is no way for you, or most of us, to know whether the company is legitimate or is out to make some quick money from unwary job seekers. That's why it's important, especially when looking for work-at-home jobs, to investigate every company that lists jobs you are interested in applying for.

In order to protect yourself while job searching, don't give out confidential information without being 100 percent sure of whom you are giving it to, including the following:

- Social Security number
- Bank account number
- Credit card number
- Date of birth
- Driver's license number
- PayPal account number

ELSEWHERE ON THE WEB

▶ Job-Hunt.org has an excellent section on job search privacy (www.job-hunt.org/privacy.shtml). There's information on the risks involved in searching for jobs online and how your privacy can be jeopardized. In addition, there's safety tips, as well as information on how you can safeguard your privacy while securely job searching on the Web.

Employers need your Social Security number and date of birth when they offer you a job, not before. There is no reason that any prospective employer will need confidential information like your bank account or credit card numbers.

Be very cautious about giving out any confidential information. In fact, a good rule of thumb is not to give out anything confidential until after you have met with the company in person and know that the firm is legitimate.

Privacy is a concern for other reasons, too. Another important privacy concern arises when a job seeker is employed. The last thing that you want is to have your employer find your resume on Monster or any other job site. You also don't want your boss reading your personal blog when you've made unflattering comments about him or the company. That's a good way to get unemployed in a hurry.

Use the following tips to make sure your confidentiality is protected when job searching:

- Use your personal e-mail address (not your work one) when job searching.
- Put your home and cell phone numbers (not your office number) on your resume.
- Use your home computer for job searching.
- Post your resume on job sites where you can block your employer from finding it.
- Make your resume confidential, so it's only available to companies you apply to.

Interviewing can be an issue too. You don't want to do anything that will be a red flag to your current employer. There's no point in taking a chance of having issues at work if you can avoid it.

ELSEWHERE ON THE WEB

▶ Monster's article "A Smart Job Search Is a Safe Job Search" has advice you can use when dealing with prospective employers. It reviews the information you shouldn't provide to anyone, employer or otherwise. There are articles on how to avoid scams and information on how to report a questionable job posting. Check it out at http://help.monster .com/besafe.

Tips for interviewing while employed include:

- Be careful when interviewing. Don't show up to work in a suit when the company dress code is casual.
- Try to schedule interviews early or late in the day.
- Use vacation and personal time for interviewing.

Discretion is really important. Be very careful who you tell that you are job searching. Unless you absolutely trust the person, don't divulge the fact that you are looking for another job to anyone at work. It's too easy for someone to slip, and then you could be in trouble. Certainly, networking is important, but not if it leads to your boss discovering that you're seeking a job before you're ready for her to know.

Get Linked

Check out the following resources from my 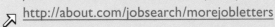 *site for more advice on how to communicate effectively while job searching:*

JOB LETTERS

This resource covers job search correspondence that is relevant for a variety of employment-related situations, including samples that you can review and edit to fit your personal circumstances.

 http://about.com/jobsearch/morejobletters

HOW NOT TO FIND A JOB

This article, instead of telling you what you should do, discusses what you shouldn't do when job searching.

 http://about.com/jobsearch/whatnottodo

THANK-YOU LETTERS

Here's everything you need to know about employment-related thank-you letters, including who to thank, when to say thank you, and what to write in your thank-you letter correspondence.

http://about.com/jobsearch/thankyouletters

About.

Chapter 15

Job Search Tips and Strategies

Best Job Search Strategies

What strategies are best when job searching? This advice might surprise you, but one of the best strategies that I've found that works to ensure job search success is to do a really good job—in fact, the best job you can do, at the job you have.

Why does it matter? It matters because the more valuable an employee you are to your current employer, the more you will be worth to a future employer. In addition, employees who are considered hard working and are respected by their supervisor and their coworkers enhance their chances of career success.

The importance of always doing a good job was a lesson that I learned the hard way. I was a kid working at my first job and it wasn't an easy one. I worked from 8:30 A.M. until 6:30 P.M. (with an hour for lunch and a couple of breaks) five or six days a week at our local supermarket. It was a long day, especially during the

▶ Job searching, in conjunction with career development, has become more of a lifelong endeavor than a one-time event. The average person changes jobs ten to fifteen times during his or her career, which means a good amount of time is spent changing employment. Networking, along with staying on top of the job market, has become an integral part of everyday work life, rather than something you do once or twice during your career.

summer when it seemed like everyone, except me, was at the beach or the park.

One beautiful summer day, I didn't feel well and asked my mom to pick me up from work. When I felt better, a few hours later, I thought maybe a trip to the beach was in order. My dad had a better idea and told me that if I was well enough to go to the beach, I was well enough to go to work. He drove me back to my job.

That was one of my first lessons about work, and it was an important one. My boss (even though he didn't know the entire story) appreciated my dedication and my willingness to come back to work. Between that and the fact that I was willing to learn more and do more and was available to work during every break I had from college got me a better job in the store the next summer.

The best employees make the best candidates for employment. This is a prime reason why referrals are one of the top ways companies find candidates. When people make referrals for employment, they usually refer someone who they know will do an excellent job. Employees who work hard and excel at their jobs will most likely do the same thing when applying for jobs and will continue to do so when they are hired.

At every company where I've worked, the people who have succeeded from a career perspective, are employees who have done the best job they could regardless of the responsibilities listed in their job description. They have been willing to do more, to do things differently, when appropriate, and have been willing to go above and beyond the job requirements.

Most of all, the people I've known who are successful in one way or another (remember, success isn't necessarily tied to the amount of your paycheck) are people who find joy in their work, people who have fun doing their job, and people who want to do their best and who want to work.

I had a conversation with a contractor who has been installing heating systems for almost fifty years. His nickname is Hawk, and he told me that over the years, the best employees he's had are those who have listened and learned and who have wanted to do the job right. He said some of the others didn't last long working with him, because if his workers were too tired to do the job right, he was too tired to pay them!

The workers who didn't do a good job didn't get a good recommendation when they left, I'm sure. That's another reason why it's important to do your best, even if you are planning on leaving your job. You will want the best recommendations you can get so your career can progress accordingly.

Impressions matter. Another important factor that contributes to success is the impression you make. That doesn't just mean how you interview. It means how you treat everyone involved in the process. Everyone you come in contact with should be treated politely, with dignity, and with respect.

To be successful you also need to be conscientious. You need to follow up with hiring managers and networking contacts in a timely manner. All your job search material (resume, cover letters, follow-up letters, and references) should be submitted according to the employer's specifications and should be error-free and professional.

Responsibility is also important. Don't leave your current employer in the lurch and quit without notice. Your new employer won't expect you to do that and may even think less of you if you are willing to forgo the standard practice of giving notice.

Honesty is important, too. Some people might debate that. There's a discussion in my About.com Forum (http://about.com/jobsearch/forum) about whether lying on your resume hurts or helps your career. Some people think that it's okay to lie. They believe that's the only way to get ahead. Nobody can convince me

ELSEWHERE ON THE WEB

▶ "How to Make an Employer Fall in Love with You" should be read by every job seeker. Susan Heathfield, About.com's Guide to Human Resources, explains how to impress a potential employer and how to make your resume or job application stand out from the pack. It will also help you save your own time, and your potential employer's time. Check it out at http://about.com/humanresources/applicantdos.

that there is ever a reason not to tell the truth when job searching. It might help you get a job today, but, in the long run, lying is not going to help your career.

Consider what happens to top executives who have been caught lying on their resume. They are out of a job and their career, in most cases, is irreparably damaged. It's not worth taking a chance on that happening to you. Every time someone important is caught in a lie it's on the news. When it's a regular person who is caught, they might not make the news, but they will still lose their job.

That saying about what goes around comes around works for careers as well as for life. If you take the time to give a reference when someone needs one, they'll remember that you helped and will reciprocate. When you send a job listing to someone who is looking or recommend someone for a job, you'll make out when you need assistance.

In order to job search successfully, it's important to plan out your job search and to keep track of what you're going to do and when you're going to do it. It's also important to strategize—to consider what type of job you want and how you are going to find it.

There are strategies you can formulate to make sure that you are conducting your job search as expeditiously as possible. A little advance planning can ensure that your job search is streamlined—and successful.

The following are strategies you can implement to ensure job search success:

- **Work at your job search:** Spend time, energy, and effort seeking employment.
- **Perfect your resume and cover letters:** Triple-check all your job search correspondence to ensure it's perfect.

ELSEWHERE ON THE WEB

▶ When you need to stay on top of the latest news about your company, industry, or career field, Google News Alerts are a good way to get the news as it happens. You can sign up at www .google.com/alerts. If you create an account you will be able to manage your alerts from the Web to change the frequency, add new search terms, and to designate what alert results you would like to receive.

- **Be prepared:** Get everything you need ready, like references and interview attire, so you don't have to scramble at the last minute.
- **Use your network:** Ask everyone you know to help with your job search.
- **Check for new job listings daily:** Spend time every day looking for jobs to apply to and get your application in right away.
- **Get help:** If you're not successful on your own, get someone to help you with your job search.
- **Stay positive:** Sometimes this is hard to do, but the more positive and focused you are, the more successful you'll be.
- **Take a break:** I know I told you to work at this, but taking a break is good too. Taking some time for yourself is rejuvenating and will help you recharge.
- **Don't give up:** Job searching isn't easy and can take a while, but you will find a new job.
- **Don't settle:** It's also important not to settle for the first job that comes along if it's not the right job. Otherwise, you'll be starting this process all over again sooner rather than later.

It can be hard some days not to get disillusioned. Even if you're doing all the right things, you may not get the job offer you expected. You may not even get the interviews that you had hoped for either. When that's the case, please don't give up.

Take some time to regroup, take a few days off from job searching (everyone is entitled to a vacation!), do something you enjoy, and then start again. Sometimes walking away from something is the best way to clear your head, to see things in a different light, and to refocus your energy to get back on track.

ASK YOUR GUIDE

I don't have much experience. How can I get my career started?

▶ A lot of visitors to my About.com site worry about not having enough experience. Remember, none of us had any experience when we started our careers. The best thing to do is to build your skills (intern, volunteer, take a class), be flexible, and always be willing to learn (and try) something new.

▶ "Local Job Search Tips" frequently makes it to the top of the "What's Hot" list on my About.com site. It's got simple instructions for how you can refine your job search to find local job listings, along with examples and directions on how to find a local job. Check it out at http://about.com/jobsearch/localjobs.

Tips to Expedite Your Job Search

Sometimes we can job search at our leisure. If you are employed in a job that's okay and you don't absolutely have to leave, it makes sense to take your time when looking for a new job opening. You can spend some time each day looking for jobs to apply to and to network, but you don't have to be in a hurry.

Even when you are gainfully employed and don't urgently need a new job, take some time, even if it's only an hour or two here and there, to make sure all the materials you need to job search are in order. Spending a brief amount of time on a regular basis is much easier than spending hours rushing to pull together everything you need when you're in a crunch situation.

When you've just been fired or laid off from your job you don't have the luxury of time. You will need to find a job fast. There are some things you can do to make sure you're ready, just in case you need to start a job search when you don't expect to. There are also ways to expedite your job search to get on the fast track to finding a new job.

Before you start your job search, make sure that you have filed for unemployment if you are eligible, and check on the benefits you're entitled to receive from your last job. It's easier to tie up any loose ends so you can make a clean break from your last job and start your job search with a clean slate, without distractions.

How to expedite your job search:

- **Write a resume.** It's always wise to have a current version of your resume, because you never know when you might need it.
- **Get references.** Always have a current list of references you can use.

- **Be prepared.** Everyone who is contemplating a job search should have an e-mail address, phone number, and computer available to use for job searching.
- **Dedicate time.** Plan to spend a significant amount of time job searching. The more time you spend, the better results you will have.
- **Network, network, network.** Many jobs are never advertised. It's the people you know who can help you access the jobs you won't find listed.
- **Be flexible.** When you have to find a job, be flexible as to the type of job you'll take. Have an open mind about what you are willing to do, at least for the interim.
- **Stay connected.** Check your e-mail and your phone messages frequently.

There are also ways to expedite the hiring process. Even though most candidates are hired on the employer's timetable, there are ways you can help the process run smoother and move faster.

First of all, be available. Have an e-mail address and a phone number on your resume where the company can contact you during the day. Your cell phone number is your best bet. That way you can check messages and return calls during a break from work or during your lunch hour. Return the call as soon as you can. The quicker you respond, the faster you will be able to get an interview scheduled. Don't make the call from your office. You don't need anyone overhearing your conversation.

Let employers know that you are available at their convenience. Do the same thing when there's a second interview. The more flexible you are, and the more willing you are to adjust your schedule to the interviewers, the faster the hiring process will move.

I like my job and I haven't updated my resume or looked at jobs in a long time. Does it matter?

▶ You never know when you might need to look for a job, so it's always a good idea to be prepared. Your company could go out of business or restructure and you might lose your job. It always makes good sense to have a current resume and to have an idea of the types of jobs you might want to apply for, just in case the need arises.

When the employer asks for references, have a list ready to give to the hiring manager. Having a list ready to provide allows the company to start checking your references immediately.

Ask interviewers if there is any other information you can provide to help them make a decision. If a background check is required, complete and return the form giving the employer permission to check right away.

Have all your paperwork in order. If you get a job offer, you will be required to complete a lot of paperwork. Have everything you need, like your Social Security card, ready to provide to the employer.

If you're really in a crunch, there is a way to try to push the employer into making a decision sooner than the company had planned. Sometimes if there is a really strong candidate, the employer won't want to lose that person to another company.

When you're juggling job offers you can let the company know that you need an idea about when you will hear. If you really want a job offer in a hurry, you could tell the company you want to work for that you have another offer and ask when you might expect to hear a decision. Do add that you prefer this job to the other one.

All of these timesavers might only save a little time here and there, but they can add up to make a difference of days, or even weeks, and can help you get a job offer in the fastest amount of time possible.

When you've lost your job, it's important not to panic. When you don't expect to be out of work it can be difficult not to stress over when your next paycheck is coming. You may need to broaden your job search to consider jobs that you wouldn't have thought about under other circumstances. Take some time to look at a variety of job options and consider what you could be doing, in addition to what you really would like to be doing. Flexibility is important when you need to find a new job fast.

Broadening your horizons can work to your benefit as well. At one point in my career, I was downsized and very worried about making ends meet. I took a temporary position that paid less than half of what my prior position paid. I needed a job, the job sounded interesting, and I figured I could scrimp by on the salary.

In the long run, it was one of the best career moves I ever made. The job ended up being perfect, the benefits were terrific, the salary increased, and I couldn't have made a better decision. Even though there was a risk involved in taking a temporary, lower-paying job, it ended up being a good career move.

Taking risks reminds me of a discussion I had on the phone with a client. She was debating two potential jobs and was really concerned about which one would look better on her resume. In my opinion, how the job looked on her resume should have been the last thing she should have been worrying about. You can spin job responsibilities a lot of different ways to make them sound good on a resume. It's much hard to spin the job you are actually doing into something different if you don't like it.

I tried to impress on her that it was more important to worry about which job was the "right" job, not only for herself and her career, but because each job involved a move to a different city, for her family. The last thing you want to do, I told her, is to take a job just because it would look good on your resume. In fact, you won't need to worry about your resume for some time, hopefully, if you accept the job that's the best fit.

I believe that the best career move, and the best decision-making you can do when weighing job offers, is to consider which position most closely matches your skills, abilities, and qualifications, and what you are seeking in a job and in a company.

TOOLS YOU NEED

▶ When you want to stay on top of what's happening in the world of careers and employment, reading relevant Web logs will help you stay current. Blogs related to job searches are a good way to stay informed about what's happening in the job market and what's new and newsworthy in the careers' arena. Here's a list of job blogs: http://about.com/jobsearch/jobblogs.

Tips from Career Professionals

I asked a variety of career professionals if they would share their best tips and advice on job searching . There's a lot of good advice you can use when job searching and if you heed it, it will help you achieve the career-planning and job search success we all want to have in our lives.

Some of the advice is traditional, and other professionals have some different ideas that you might not have considered. All are worth reviewing to see if you can use them in your job search.

Career Options

Make sure the career you choose inspires you. Learn enough about it so your choice is based on facts and not assumptions. While you may not love your job every day, overall, you should be able to say that you love what you've chosen to do with your life. And, if you ever find that you aren't getting from your career as much as you are giving to it, or if your life changes so that your career is no longer compatible with it, then it's time to start exploring other options.

—*Dawn Rosenberg McKay,*
About.com Career Planning Guide

Your career is made up of choices. You choose what you want to do, where you will do it, and what type of education will get you there. Some of your choices empower you and others hold you back. Either way, you have power over what you choose in your career.

—*Deborah Brown-Volkman,*
President, Surpass Your Dreams, Inc.

Job Search Planning

Plan for your job search well in advance of when you may actually need a new job. That means keeping skills current and building and maintaining professional and personal connections. By doing this, you are either super-marketable at a job you keep or extremely well prepared in the event that circumstances change and you need to make a transition. The difference between success and failure might be only a few hours per month and it can be the best investment you ever make.

—*Janet Scarborough, Ph.D.,*
Bridgeway Career Development

Networking

Finding a job is all about people. It's not about looking for advertised positions, sending a resume, and waiting for a response. Ask any successful job-seeker. They'll tell you they found out about open positions and eventually got hired through their personal network, including referrals from friends, leads from people inside the company, or by contacting people they thought could help.

—*Frank Traditi, Career Strategist, Author*

It is best to use as many tools as possible when job searching. This is the time to use your personal and professional network and continually work to keep expanding it as you meet new people. Contacting alumni from your college who are currently doing work of interest to you can be very helpful. Finding out more about different careers through informational interviews, job shadowing, internships, and volunteer work can open up new ideas and expand your horizons.

—*Penny Loretto, Assistant Director/Internship Coordinator,*
Career Services, Skidmore College

After you know the type of work you want to do, make two lists: one a prospect list of twenty-five companies where your research suggests you might be happily employed; the other a networking list of twenty-five to seventy-five people who might go out of

ELSEWHERE ON THE WEB

▶ **Monster's Careers at 50+** (http://careersat50.monster. com) has a wealth of information for middle-aged job seekers. There's advice on how to find employers who are age neutral, on how to phase into retirement, and how to return to the work force after retirement. There is also an Age Issues Forum where you can ask questions and get advice specifically targeted to job seekers for whom age is an issue.

their way a little to help you—family, friends, affable acquaintances, church members, affinity group members, former classmates, alumni, vendors, hair stylists, neighbors—anyone at all. E-mail your prospect list to your networking list, saying you'll be calling to see if they know anyone at any of your preferred companies, organizations, or government agencies who can help you get hired. If you connect, try to get your networking contact to arrange an appointment for you, or at least to open the door.

—Joyce Lain Kennedy, Career Expert and Author

Interviews

The purpose of an interview is not to get the job. It is to discover whether your talents, abilities, interests, and direction are a good fit for the job, the company, and the company's mission. The interview is also your opportunity to present yourself professionally so that if all else is a good match, you are selected for the job. So, be yourself during an interview. Canned answers sound like exactly that—canned. Let your personality, interests, and abilities shine through at the meetings. After all, you wouldn't want, and the company wouldn't want, a stranger to show up for work the first day on the new job.

—Susan Heathfield, About.com Guide to Human Resources

Using Your Strengths

If you're an introvert, identify and embrace your natural strengths and use them in your job search. Don't try to be something you're not—i.e., an extrovert or someone who tries to use quite extroverted job search strategies, such as cold calling. For starters, if you do go the route of trying to be something you're not, you almost certainly won't follow through with any of the associated job search strategies. More importantly, though, if you identify and run with your natural strengths as an introvert, you will a) actually follow through with the associated job search strategies, and b) almost certainly have more success when it comes to both uncovering job leads and actually landing the job.

—*Peter Vogt, Co-editor, Campus Career Counselor*

Being Persistent

I would suggest that if people don't get their "dream jobs" not to give up. Many people have been able to get the careers they want after their third, fourth, fifth, etc., attempt.

—*Marcia J. Eagleson, Career Counselor, Adjunct Faculty,*
Western New England College

Tips from Job Search Experts

Job search experts from around the country (and the Internet) took the time to share their words of wisdom on how best to job search. Here's a selection of the best tips from experts in the field.

Networking

Ask your friends. I've been amazed at how many jobs I've seen friends get just from asking around. Seems like a no-brainer, but so many people forget to let people know they're looking.

—*Matt Law, Director, Community, About.com*

Always try to send your resume in through a referral. It doesn't have to be someone you know well; it just has to be a live person who passes it along to another live hiring manager. This not only increases your chances of having your resume paid attention to, but it also increases the likelihood that you'll get feedback. Even if you don't get an interview, you'll typically at least get a response as to why you weren't considered a good fit.

—*Kay Luo, Online Marketing Manager, SimplyHired*

ELSEWHERE ON THE WEB

▶ CareerJournal.com has a series of articles on job search strategies. The articles include topics like following up to get a job after you have been rejected and how to get back into the work force after a hiatus, as well as advice on how to tailor your job search and other articles with strategies for successful job searching. You can read them at www .careerjournal.com/job hunting/strategies.

On Being Flexible

Follow those hunches, take risks, work and play hard, be flexible, and make plans—but also bend with life's flow.

—*Michael Landes, Author,*
The Back Door Guide to Short-Term Job Adventures

Using the Internet to Job Search

Networking itself is not a revolutionary concept, but how people are networking and connecting to great opportunities is changing with next-generation job sites that combine job search and networking. People can now find jobs using powerful search tools on the Web and get jobs based on the strengths of existing relationships.

—*Jason Goldberg, CEO, Jobster*

The Internet can give your job search an amazing reach. It is the perfect tool for finding possible job leads, researching employers and careers, networking, and even finding support groups. But remember that it is only one part of your search, and you must continue to network and search off-line as well.

—*Margaret Riley Dikel, Author, The Riley Guide Web site*

The Value of Internships

The opportunity often exists to work for the company you interned with after graduation. That is, if you were a good employee. While accepting a position with your intern company can make your job search infinitely easier, it also limits your scope of opportunities to just one company. If the company is everything you ever wanted, if they provide you with opportunities for growth and advancement, go for it.

—*Brian Krueger, President, CollegeGrad.com*

The Importance of Skills

There is no job security, only skill security. Pay attention to the skills that are in demand—*and* that you would enjoy developing—and work constantly on developing those skills through training, volunteering for projects, working with mentors, etc. The more you focus on keeping your skills updated, the more likely it is that *when* (not if) you lose your job, you'll be able to find something more quickly.

—*Michele Martin, The Widing Group*

On Life

Finally, one of the most important tips I'll share with you isn't from anyone connected to jobs and careers. It's from singer/songwriter Bob Franke, who wrote in his song "Thanksgiving Eve," "What can you do with your days but work and hope: let your dreams bind your work to your play." (Copyright © 1982 Robert J. Franke. Used by permission of the author.)

When you have a job that you love, it really doesn't feel much like work, and that's what we should all be looking for—a job that we enjoy and that's a good fit with our aspirations for our career, and, most importantly, our life.

TOOLS YOU NEED

▶ An important tool you can use to help with your job search is a Career Action Plan. About.com's Career Planning Guide, Dawn Rosenberg McKay, has a worksheet you can print out at http://about.com/career planning/careeractionplan. There are also instructions on how to complete the plan, as well as advice on how to use it to create short-term and long-term career goals. In addition, there's information on how to get around barriers that can hinder you in achieving your goals.

Get Linked

*Here's more job search tips and advice from my **ABOUT**.com site. There are suggestions on every component of job searching.*

JOB SEARCH TIPS

This section of my About.com site has job search tips, resources, and tools to help you find that perfect job.

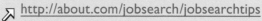
http://about.com/jobsearch/jobsearchtips

JOB INTERVIEW TIPS

Here you'll find advice and tips on effective interviewing for employment, interview questions and answers, and post-interview thank-you letters.

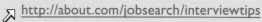
http://about.com/jobsearch/interviewtips

TEN TIME-SAVING JOB SEARCH TIPS

These ten tips will help expedite your job search. Follow this advice to get started on a job search or to jump-start one that is already in progress.

http://about.com/jobsearch/timesave

Appendix A

Glossary

applicant tracking system

An applicant tracking system is an integrated system that streamlines the recruiting and application process for employers.

association

An association is an organization whose members have similar credentials or interests.

background check

A background check is a verification of your past education and employment history. It may also include checking criminal history, medical history, and military records.

behavioral interview

Behavioral interviewing is based on the premise that your behavior in the past predicts your success in the future. The interviewer will ask specific questions about your experiences as they relate to the skills the employer is seeking.

blog

A blog (Web log) is an online journal that is available to the public. A career-related blog may be written by a company, by a job or career site, or by a job seeker looking for work.

The Bureau of Labor Statistics

The Bureau of Labor Statistics (BLS) is the division of the U.S. Department of Labor that provides occupational and career information, employment statistics, and wage, earnings, and benefits data.

career counselor

A career counselor is a certified professional who assists people with career and life issues.

career networking

Career networking involves using the people you know and people they know to help with a job search.

CareerOneStop Center

CareerOneStop Centers are sponsored by the Department of Labor. Clients can get career advice and job hunt assistance. There are also special programs available for job seekers with disabilities, veterans, and displaced workers.

career personality test

Career personality tests analyze the type of personality that you have in order to connect your personality to related career options.

COBRA (Consolidated Omnibus Budget Reconciliation Act)

COBRA provides some workers (and their families) who leave a job with the right to temporary continuation, under specific circumstances, of health insurance coverage at group rates.

company Web site

A company Web site is published by an organization in order to provide information on its products, services, mission, and career opportunities.

cover letter

A cover letter is sent with your resume when applying for a job. The purpose of writing cover letters is to interpret the facts on your resume and to pitch your experience and skills to prospective employers.

curriculum vitae

A curriculum vitae (CV) is similar to but more extensive than a resume. It includes a summary of your educational and academic background, your teaching and research experience, and publications, presentations, awards, honors, and professional affiliations.

discussion forum

A job search discussion forum is an online bulletin board where you can post questions and comments about job searching.

employee benefits

Employee benefits are nonwage compensation provided to workers, including life insurance, health insurance, sick leave, vacation, and holidays.

Employment Eligibility Verification Form (I-9)

An Employment Eligibility Form must be completed for all new hires. Employees must provide documents to prove that they are legally entitled to work in the United States.

flextime

Flextime is the ability to set your own schedule. This can include scheduling your own workdays and starting and ending times.

group interview

A group interview takes place when a candidate is interviewed by more than one interviewer at the same time. Alternately, it can mean that a group of candidates are interviewed at the same time by a hiring manager.

informational interview

An informational interview is a meeting with someone working in a job that interests you, which is conducted to gain information from an insider perspective.

internship

An internship is a preprofessional work experience that provides students, recent graduates, and career changers with a chance to find out more about a certain career.

interview thank-you letter

An interview thank-you letter is sent to the people who interview you. It lets the employer know that you appreciate being considered for the job. It also reiterates your interest in the position and can be used to provide additional information on your qualifications.

job application

A job application is a form (either paper or online) that candidates for employment complete to be considered for a job.

job bank

A job bank is a Web site that lists job openings.

job club

A job club is a formal or informal group of job seekers. The purpose of a job club is to assist with a job hunt and to give and get job search support and advice.

job search agent

A job search agent enables job seekers to set up searches on job sites so that they are automatically notified by e-mail of new jobs as they are posted.

job search engines

Job search engines search the Internet for job listings. The results include listings from the major job boards, top newspapers, as well as from associations and company Web sites.

job shadowing

Job shadowing involves spending time with a career mentor to explore career options and to see how the skills you have learned in school relate to work.

keyword

A keyword is a word that is relevant to the job you are searching. When you search for a job by keyword, all the positions that contain the term you entered will be listed.

niche job site

A niche site lists jobs in a specific occupation or geographic region.

reference

A reference is a person who can attest to your credentials, your skills, and your attributes as they relate to employment.

resume

A resume is a compilation of your work experience, achievements, education, and accomplishments.

salary calculator

A salary calculator is an online tool you can use to determine how much your job offer is worth and how far your paycheck will go in a specific location based on the cost of living in that area.

salary negotiations

Salary negotiations involve discussing a job offer with a prospective employee to negotiate a salary and benefits package that meets your needs.

seasonal job

A seasonal job is one that is available for a certain part of the year—for example, a summer job, ski job, or tax season job.

screening interview

A screening interview is conducted to determine if the applicant has the qualifications needed to do the job for which the company is hiring.

transferable skills

Transferable skills are the abilities you have that can be used in a variety of different jobs.

U.S. Equal Employment Commission

The Equal Employment Commission regulates employment and handles claims from workers who have been discriminated against during the hiring process or on the job.

Appendix B
Other Sites

About.com Job Searching Technical

When you are seeking technical employment, Steven Niznik's site is an essential job search resource. He provides advice on writing technical resumes and letters, on finding technical jobs, and on the top tech employers.

http://jobsearchtech.about.com

About.com Salary Center

Visit the About.com Salary Center to find out how much you should earn, what it will cost you to relocate, and how to evaluate job offers.

http://about.salary.com

America's Job Bank

America's Job Bank from the U.S. Department of Labor provides a means for job seekers to connect to state employment service sites, search for jobs, and post a resume. Job seekers can also find local CareerOneStop Centers for personal assistance.

www.ajb.org

CareerBuilder

CareerBuilder is affiliated with local newspapers nationwide. It is an excellent source of job listings for job seekers who want to work in a specific location.

www.careerbuilder.com

Cool Works

When you are looking for a summer or seasonal job, start by using Cool Works. There are thousands of summer and seasonal job listings, plus a free weekly e-mail newsletter.

www.coolworks.com

Craig's List

Craig's List doesn't have a lot of bells and whistles, but it works. Click on the city where you want to find a job to review the list of job openings, categorized by type of position.

www.craigslist.org

Indeed.com

Indeed searches the job Web sites for you, including job banks, newspapers, and association and company career sites. There are advanced search options available so you can focus your search to provide job listings that match the criteria you select.

www.indeed.com

LinkedIn

Networking is a critical component of job searching, and networking Web sites like LinkedIn can help you find contacts who can help with your job search. The site can also put you in touch with decision-makers at companies of interest.

www.linkedin.com

Monster/MonsterTRAK

Monster is perpetually on the list of top job sites, with job listings ranging from hourly local jobs to professional positions at locations throughout the United States and abroad. MonsterTRAK is the college version of Monster with job and internship listings specifically for college students and graduates.

www.monster.com

SimplyHired

SimplyHired is a job search engine that searches job banks, newspapers, classified ads, and company Web sites. In addition to a variety of search options, job seekers can find contacts at LinkedIn and can research salary information.

www.simplyhired.com

The Riley Guide

The Riley Guide lists many online sites and services that will help with your job search.

www.rileyguide.com

Yahoo! HotJobs

In addition to providing job listings, Yahoo! Hot-Jobs is a good resource for integrated job searching. Users can check e-mail, review new job listings, check their calendar, and keep job search notes.

http://hotjobs.yahoo.com

Appendix C
Further Readings

The Back Door Guide to Short-Term Job Adventures by Michael Landes

This is one of my favorite books. If you are interested in a summer job, an internship, a career change, or even just a break from your normal routine, you need to read this book. In addition to advice on how to find a short-term position, there's information on many opportunities in a very wide variety of career fields.

The Elements of Resume Style by Scott Bennett

This little book is packed full of information on how to create powerful resumes. It explains the resume-writing rules you need to follow and provides tips and suggestions on writing compelling resumes.

Grammatically Correct: The Writer's Essential Guide to Punctuation, Spelling, Style, Usage and Grammar by Anne Stilman

This book is an excellent resource for job seekers who need assistance with their writing. It has sections on spelling, problem words, and punctuation that you can use to make sure all your correspondence is error free.

Job Interviews for Dummies by Joyce Lain Kennedy

Career expert Joyce Lain Kennedy consistently provides good advice to job seekers. This book provides job interview tips for all levels of job seekers, along with advice on how to prepare and practice for an interview.

Job Interview Tips for People with Not-So-Hot Backgrounds by Caryl and Ron Krannich

When you have been fired or laid off or don't have good references, you may need special assistance in preparing for interviews. This book lets you know what can be red flags for an employer and provides advice on how to handle problems.

How to Prepare Your Curriculum Vitae by Acy Jackson and Kathleen Geckeis

Here's help for job seekers who need to prepare a curriculum vitae. Whether you are applying for an academic position or applying for graduate or professional school, this book covers everything you need to do to create a professional curriculum vitae.

Knock 'em Dead 2006 by Martin Yate

This book combines job search and interview techniques with career management planning. There are also answers to interview questions and advice on how to negotiate job offers.

The Guide to Internet Job Searching by Margaret Riley Dikel and Frances E. Roehm

When you're job searching online, this book, co-published with the Public Library Association, will provide you with the information you need to conduct an in-depth job search.

The Secrets of Executive Search: Professional Strategies for Managing Your Personal Job Search by Robert M. Melançon

Even though the title of the book references executive search, the content is relevant for anyone who is job searching. It helps readers navigate the job search process and gain insight from the author's experiences in executive search.

The Virtual Handshake by David Teten and Scott Allen

When you need to make contacts online, this book will help you use online tools, like networking Web sites, e-mail, discussion forums, and blogs to enhance your career.

What Color Is Your Parachute by Richard Nelson Bolles

Anyone who is considering a job or career change should read this book. It provides advice on discovering what it is that you really want to do, then helps you transition into that new job or career.

INDEX